T0320124

Welfare, Environment and Changing US–Chinese Relations

ISPI
(ISTITUTO PER GLI STUDI DI POLITICA INTERNAZIONALE)

Founded in 1933 by Alberto Pirelli, ISPI is one of Italy's oldest and most prestigious Institutes specialising in activities of an international nature. It was created as a private association and became a non-profit organisation in 1972, operating under the supervision of the Ministry for Foreign Affairs.

ISPI's principal fields of interest are international politics and economics, in addition to analysing international relations and strategic problems. The Institute's goals are to promote the study and analysis of international issues, to provide a forum for debates including representatives of the political, academic and business worlds, and to prepare individual experts for work in international environments.

ISPI is at the same time a research centre, an information centre, and a training centre. ISPI is also a documentation centre open to the public and publishes a quarterly review, as well as books and working papers related to the research projects.

This book is the result of a project organised by ISPI. ISPI's research activities are framed into sections corresponding to political and economic regions of the world. Asia occupies a peculiarly important place in this framework. This research has been preceded and will be followed by other projects, monitoring the developments of an area that we deem strategically crucial for our understanding of international relations. Each of ISPI's projects is the responsibility of a co-ordinator and it involves a network of contributors located in Italy and abroad, assisted by a group of young research fellows at the Institute. Maria Weber is Senior Research Fellow for Asia.

Welfare, Environment and Changing US–Chinese Relations

21st Century Challenges in China

Edited by

Maria Weber

Associate Professor of International Relations and Comparative Politics, Bocconi University, Milan, Italy

In association with

ISPI
ISTITUTO PER GLI STUDI DI POLITICA INTERNAZIONALE

Edward Elgar
Cheltenham, UK • Northampton, MA, USA

© Maria Weber 2004

All rights reserved. No part of this publication may be reproduced, stored in a retrieval system, or transmitted in any form or by any means, electronic, mechanical or photocopying, recording, or otherwise without the prior permission of the publisher.

Published by
Edward Elgar Publishing Limited
Glensanda House
Montpellier Parade
Cheltenham
Glos GL50 1UA
UK

Edward Elgar Publishing, Inc.
136 West Street
Suite 202
Northampton
Massachusetts 01060
USA

A catalogue record for this book
is available from the British Library

ISBN 1 84376 827 5

Printed and bound in Great Britain by MPG Books Ltd, Bodmin, Cornwall

Contents

Tables

Figures

Abbreviations

ABC	Agricultural Bank of China
ACCA21	Administration Centre for China's Agenda
ACFTU	All China Federation of Trade Unions
ADB	Asian Development Bank
AIG	American International Group
AMC	Asset Management Company
APEC	Asia–Pacific Economic Cooperation
ASEAN	Association of Southeast Asian Nations
ASEM	Asia–Europe Meeting
BOC	Bank of China
BWC	Biological Weapons Treaty
CASS	Chinese Academy of Social Sciences
CBC	Construction Bank of China
CC	Central Committee
CCER	China Centre for Economic Research
CCP	Chinese Communist Party
CIRC	China Insurance Regulatory Commission
CIS	Commonwealth of Independent States
CITIC	China International Trust and Investment Corporation
CJV	Contractual Joint Venture
CMS	Cooperative Medical System
CNOOC	China National Offshore Oil Company
COD	Chemical Oxygen Demand
COE	Collectively-Owned Enterprise
CSCAP	Committee of Security and Cooperation in the Asia–Pacific
CSIS	Centre for Strategic and International Studies
CTBT	Comprehensive Test Ban Treaty
CWC	Chemical Weapons Convention
DB	Defined Benefits
DC	Defined Contributions
EDAC	Economic Development Advisory Conference
EIA	Energy Information Administration
EJV	Equity Joint Venture
EPS	Epidemic Prevention Service
ERS	Economic Responsibility System
ESMAP	Energy Sector Management Assistance Programme

ETIM	East Turkestan Islamic Movement
EU	European Union
FASC	Food and Agricultural Statistics Centre
FDI	Foreign Direct Investment
FTA	Free Trade Area
GAE	Gross Allocation Effect
GATS	General Agreement on Trade in Services
GATT	General Agreement on Tariffs and Trade
GDP	Gross Domestic Product
GIC	Government of Singapore Investment Corporation
GIS	Government Insurance Scheme
GMD	Guomindang (Taiwanese Nationalist Party)
HDR	Human Development Report
HRW	Human Rights Watch
IAEA	International Atomic Energy Agency
ICBC	Industrial and Commercial Bank of China
ICBM	Intercontinental Ballistic Missiles
ICT	Information and Communication Technology
IISS	Institute for International and Strategic Studies
IMF	International Monetary Fund
INPRS	International Network of Pensions Regulators and Supervisors
IPCG	Intergovernmental Panel on Climate Change
IPO	Initial Public Offering
IT	Information Technology
KEDO	Korean Peninsula Energy Development Organization
LIS	Labour Insurance Scheme
MOCA	Ministry of Civil Affairs
MOF	Ministry of Finance
MOFCOM	Ministry of Commerce
MOH	Ministry of Health
MOL	Ministry of Labour
MOLSS	Ministry of Labour and Social Security
MSA	Medical Savings Account
MTCR	Missile Technology Control Regime
NACO	National Agriculture Census Office
NHC	National Health Congress
NIE	Newly Industrialised Economy
NMD	National Missile Defence
NPC	National People's Congress
NPL	Non-performing Loan
NPT	Non-Proliferation Treaty
NRDC	National Resources Defence Council
NSSF	National Social Security Fund

OECD	Organisation for Economic Cooperation and Development
PBoC	People's Bank of China
PICC	People's Insurance Company of China
PLA	People's Liberation Army
PPP	Purchasing Power Parity
PRC	People's Republic of China
R&D	Research and Development
RCA	Revealed Comparative Advantage
RMB	Renminbi
SARS	Severe Acute Respiratory Syndrome
SC	State Council
SCRE	State Commission for Reform of the Economy
SDPC	State Development Planning Commission
SDRC	State Development and Reform Commission
SEPA	State Environmental Protection Administration
SEZ	Special Economic Zone
SIA	Social Insurance Agency
SITC	Standard Industrial Trade Classification
SOE	State-owned Enterprise
SPM	Suspended Particulate Matter
TB	Tubercolosis
TFP	Total Factor Productivity
TMD	Theatre Missile Defence
TPSSM	Transitional Product-specific Safeguard Mechanism
TSP	Total Suspended Particles
TVEs	Township and Village Enterprises
UHS	Urban Household Survey
USA	United States of America
USTR	United States Trade Representative
WHO	World Health Organisation
WTO	World Trade Organisation

Contributors

Giacomo Boati graduated in Political Economics at Bocconi University. He is currently undertaking a Masters in International Relations at the School of Advanced International Studies, The Johns Hopkins University. He was formerly a researcher at the Institute for International Political Studies (ISPI). His research interests include economic development and the issues related to Chinese economic development.

Andrea Boltho was educated in Italy and at the Universities of London (LSE), Paris and Oxford. From 1966 to 1977 he worked at the OECD's Economics Department. Since 1977 he has been a fellow of Magdalen College, University of Oxford. Among his works are: *Japan – An Economic Survey* (1975) and *The European Economy: Growth and Crisis* (1982). He has recently edited a volume comparing the Italian and Japanese economies.

Nicoletta Marigo holds an MSc in Economics with reference to the Asia Pacific Region from SOAS (University of London). A former lecturer in Chinese Political Economy at the University of Lecce (Italy) and Research fellow at ISPI, she is a Research Associate in Energy Policy at the Institute of Energy and Environment Economics and Policy (IEFE) at Bocconi University, Italy. She is currently completing a PhD in Environmental Science and Technology at Imperial College (London). Her research interests include: innovation systems and policy in response to environmental problems in developing countries.

Vasco Molini is PhD candidate in Development Economics at the University of Florence. He contributed to the project 'Regional Disparities in Human Development' by United Nations University–WIDER in Helsinki. In 2003 he published 'The determinants of East Asian trade, a gravity equation approach' in the *Journal of Asian Economics*. His research interests include spatial inequality in Asian transition economies and economic development in East Asia.

Anna Stenbeck graduated in Economics from Bocconi University, Milan, and is currently pursuing postgraduate studies in Comparative Politics at the London School of Economics and Political Science. She has held internships at the Italian Trade Commission in Hong Kong and in the East Asia office at

ISPI. Her research interests include international trade and comparative public policy.

Benedetta Trivellato is currently studying for a PhD at the University of Milan Bicocca and is a Researcher in the East Asia Department at ISPI (Institute for International Political Studies), Milan. She holds an MSc in Economics for Development from St Antony's College, University of Oxford, and a first degree in Economics from Bocconi University, Milan, Italy. Her research interests include South East Asian development issues, international trade and the WTO, and the role of ICTs in promoting development.

Maria Weber is Associate Professor of International Relations and Comparative Politics at Bocconi University in Milan and Senior Research Fellow on Asia at ISPI. She is the author of many publications on China and East Asia. Her book *Vele verso la Cina* ('Sails toward China', Edizioni Olivares, 1996) won the Booz Allen Hamilton–Financial Times Awards 1996. Her latest books are *After the Asian Crises*, published by Macmillan in 2000, *Reforming Economic Systems in Asia*, published by Edward Elgar in 2001, and *Il miracolo cinese* ('The Chinese Miracle') published by Il Mulino in 2003 (second edition).

Editor's Introduction

Maria Weber

The People's Republic of China (PRC) recorded a GDP growth rate higher than 8 per cent in the 20 years prior to 2004, contributing to the country's becoming the world's fifth largest economy. According to the World Bank, it could surpass America by 2020 (World Bank, 1997). The truly surprising aspect of this growth is that the country managed to move at a high pace over a very long time span (more than two decades) and in spite of its very large population of 1 billion 294 million inhabitants.

The open-door policies promoted as of 1979 allowed China to record significant results. Quality of life was noticeably influenced: while 270 million Chinese lived below the poverty threshold in 1978, this figure has fallen to 60 million in 2004 and life expectancy rose from 64 in 1975 to 71.4 in 2000. The quick economic growth that changed the look of China in the past 20 years was due to multiple factors, first and foremost to the open-door policies promoted to attract foreign investment and increase business flows, as well as to a practical and gradual approach to reforms, which allowed for testing different policies in specific areas at first and then on a national scale, once their efficacy was ascertained. The structural change of the economy was also important (as a cause, as well as a consequence, of economic development) and resulted in a reduced contribution of agriculture to the GDP in favour of the industrial and service sectors.

The Chinese miracle is the result of an export-oriented development model, partly borrowed from other Asian countries and by now known as 'free-market socialism'. Free-market socialism is a hybrid ideology, justified by Beijing with the consideration that some economic instruments, labelled as capitalist for a long time, are actually neutral and may be used to promote economic growth. Socialism and the free market are not in contradiction, because the market does not necessarily lead to capitalism and even capitalist economies include some forms of economic planning. The concept of 'free-market socialism' was officially included in the constitutional charter in March 1993, when the People's National Congress (NPC) amended the Constitution by including the concept of free–market socialist economy instead of the planned-economy one.

The economic reforms that developed into free-market socialism started in 1979, when the Chinese government tried to promote the expansion of international economic relations through the gradual opening of the country to foreign investments, known as the 'open-door policy' – as literally translated from the Chinese *kaifang zhengce* (Howell, 1993). The open-door policy was implemented through a set of sub-policies in the fields of foreign trade and foreign direct investments, including the testing of a free-market economy in the so-called Special Economic Zones (SEZs), carefully selected in the southern regions of the country close to Hong Kong, in particular in the provinces of Guangdong (Shenzhen, close to Hong Kong; Zhuhai, facing Macau; and Shantou) and of Fujian (Xiamen, facing the isle of Taiwan). In 1984, in the wake of the positive outcome of this attempt, the isle of Hainan was added to the first four. In the same year, the central authorities decided to open 14 more coastal cities to foreign trade and investments (from Dalian, in Liaoning, in the north of the country, to Behai, in Guangxi, in the south-west).

CHINA'S INTEGRATION WITHIN THE GLOBAL ECONOMY

The open-door policy attracted a large flow of foreign direct investments (FDIs). A significant share of the world's foreign investments were performed in China from 1978 to 1999, worth on average $40 billion annually. It should be noted, however, that at least two-thirds of the foreign investment flow came from the Chinese community in South-East Asia, whose high investment skills made it one of the largest investors in the country of origin and a major promoter of business activities. There are about 50 million Chinese overseas, known as the diaspora, who fled in waves from China during the 20th century and now live scattered throughout various countries in South-East Asia. Thanks to the power of traditional family networks and to a shared cultural and language background, the Chinese overseas were the first and main investors in China after the launching of the open-door policy. The powerful corporations, established on a family basis and managed according to paternalistic and autocratic principles, invested massively in the provinces of origin of the families, where they built industrial conglomerates and operated all kinds of trade. According to some researchers, approximately 80 per cent of the foreign direct investments made in China in the last 20 years were directly or indirectly managed by Chinese families overseas (Lassere and Schutte, 1999, pp. 102–10).

In many cases, western investors also preferred to entrust their business to Chinese companies in Hong Kong or Taiwan, rather than take upon themselves the risk involved by a direct investment. However, while in the 1980s FDIs mostly came from industrially advanced Asian economies, such as Japan and South Korea, FDIs from the west increased in the 1990s, especially from the

United States and the European Union, with Germany, the UK, France, and the Netherlands accounting for the largest share.

Multinational companies continued to perform massive investments in China during 2002, attracted by quick industrial development and competitive labour costs. Inbound FDIs increased by 12.6 per cent, totalling a record of $52.7 billion, equal to 4.2 per cent of China's GDP and to one-tenth of the world's flows. Hong Kong is still the main source of FDIs, with more than one-third of inbound flows. In evaluating the FDI flow in China, it should be noted that a significant share of FDIs from Hong Kong (by far the main investor) actually comes from other countries, including China itself, but pass through companies established in Hong Kong to enjoy tax reductions, as well as the better contract protection ensured by the Basic Law. In 2003 too, while lower than expected, the utilized FDIs grew by 1.4 per cent and the contracted ones by 39 per cent. China today is the primary destination of foreign direct investments: more than half of the world's 500 top companies have offices in the Pearl River Delta.

Table 1   Foreign Direct Investments ($ bn)

	1997	1998	1999	2000	2001	2002	2003
Net flows	45.2	45.4	40.3	40.7	46.8	52.7	53.5

Source: Ministry of Commerce (MOFCOM).

Foreign direct investments in China in the 1990s changed in form and type: in particular, they turned from investments into minority joint ventures aimed solely at technological transfers in the 1980s to majority joint ventures, mostly aimed at processing for export, attracted by the availability of low-cost labour and government incentives, including the possibility to import duty-free equipment and capital goods and tax exemptions, the so-called 'tax holidays', in the 1990s. FDIs increased in the few years prior to 2004 in the service sector, in technological and innovative manufacturing industries, and in chemical industries, while FDIs in transport equipment manufacturing and energy supply decreased.

The open-door policy also promoted a sharp increase in business flows. In the first twenty years of implementation of the open-door policy, China's participation in world trade rose from 0.8 per cent in 1978 to 4.7 per cent in 2002. China's exports have grown quickly during the past twenty years, with a proportionally stronger increase in manufactured goods exports. In 2001, China's foreign trade exceeded $500 bn, and exports to its main trade partners – the USA, the EU, Japan, and South Korea – grew at a high pace, in spite of a slowing global economy. In 2002 China significantly promoted world trade, exceeding \$620 bn and accounting for 4.7 per cent of the total trade flows. In the same year, China enjoyed a boom in exports, which increased by 22.3 per cent to a total of \$325.6 bn, as well as of imports, which rose by 21.2 per cent. The most dynamic sectors included machinery and electrical–electronic products; more traditional exports like clothing and footwear, on the other hand, recorded an increase around 10 per cent.

The volume of business transactions in 2003 was about \$851.2 bn. Exports from China recorded a 34.6 per cent growth compared to 2002, while imports recorded a 39.9 per cent growth. The surplus of China's trade balance for 2003 amounted to \$25.54 billion. The breakdown of exports clearly reflects the development recorded by China's industry: the goods that contributed to the strong growth in the 1980s and early 1990s (clothing, toys, and other low-tech products) have increasingly been replaced with technological goods from the information technology (IT), electronic, and telecommunication sectors (Zhang Yongjin, 2003).

IS CHINA'S DEVELOPMENT SUSTAINABLE IN THE LONG TERM?

China's economic expansion has been remarkable since the beginning of reforms in the late 1970s. From 1978 to 2000, annual GDP growth was close to 10 per cent, with per capita incomes multiplied by a factor of about five. Few countries in the world have ever experienced similar success (Boltho, 2004). Nor, according to many observers, is this miracle over. Medium to longer-run projections suggest that growth could still average some 7 per cent per annum through the next two decades – a rate that would imply a further quadrupling of the country's output. Should such projections materialise, China would clearly become a dominant player in the global economy. Boltho's chapter in this volume (Chapter 1) reminds us that the only other example of a similar development is provided by the rise of the United States a century ago. Indeed, China may perform even better in the 40 years following the start of economic reforms than America did in the 40 years prior to World War I. If the output is measured at purchasing power parity (PPP), China's share of the world's GDP could rise by some 15 percentage points between 1978 and 2020, compared with 10 per cent recorded by the United States between 1870 and 1913. As a consequence, China might even become the world's largest economy, at least in PPP terms. The increase in China's impact on world trade may not be as dramatic, but by 2020 the country could still be the world's second largest exporter and importer. Such projections raise two important questions, one of a domestic and one of an international nature. Would it indeed be possible for China to expand at such rates for a further 20 years, given the many and well-known economic problems the country faces?

In the event of such growth, what would be the likely impact on the rest of the world, and on Asia, of a continuing and very rapid industrial expansion by a highly competitive and (presumably) increasingly efficient producer?

An outstanding challenge to sustainable development in China comes from the growing inequalities between different regions of the country and between the urban and rural populations. Chinese provinces, in fact, have benefited in various ways from the economic growth, and more developed coastal regions, with a higher GDP, contrast with inland western ones, still characterized by poor vitality and limited development (see Molini, Chapter 3). Recent research has demonstrated that high inequality is attributable to a large rural–urban income gap and to growing macroregional (East–West–Centre) or coast–inland disparity. The widening gap between rural and urban areas is a direct consequence of the urban-biased policies implemented before the reform period, but only from the 1980s did that gap become a reason for concern and assume a macroregional dimension. Since the end of the 1980s, per capita production and consumption started to diverge massively across different provinces in China, as well as between rural and urban areas within the provinces. At the end of the 1990s, the initially rich urban areas of coastal provinces were on average better off, while the interior provinces had become relatively poorer.

Molini's analysis shows a limited but constantly increasing gap between the Western and Central regions. Such gap is clearer if we split the macroregions into rural and urban areas, and increased particularly in the rural areas, which accounted for about 70 per cent of the population of both macroregions: in 1990, Western rural average consumption was 95 per cent of average Central consumption, while it fell to 83 per cent by 2000. In 1990, in the urban areas, average Western consumption was higher than average Central consumption, but the situation reversed in 2000. Central and local government policies made this imbalance worse, rather than correcting it. Nonetheless, in 2000 there were positive signs of a changing attitude towards inland areas. To encourage the development of the Western provinces, the government launched the 'Great Western Development Strategy' or 'Go West Strategy', a campaign for public investment in infrastructures (in particular transport and energy), and the creation of special economic zones similar to SEZs. The aim of this policy, after China's accession to the WTO, is to foster the competitiveness of Western regions and create opportunities for foreign investors.

A further challenge to sustainable development in China is posed by the increasing constraints set by the exploitation and the dramatic deterioration of natural resources (see Marigo, Chapter 2). A combination of structural changes in the economic structure, pressures deriving from population growth and heavy dependence on coal burning to meet the increasing energy demand have contributed to shaping the present state of China's environment. Air pollution as well as the scarcity and poor quality of water are the two most serious environmental concerns in the country. China's concentrations of both particulate matter and SO_2 are among the highest in the world and barely a third of the 340 monitored Chinese cities meets national air quality standards, which are below the ones recommended by the World Health Organisation. As a consequence respiratory diseases are one of the leading causes of death in China.

The lack of clean fresh water presents an equally serious threat with more than 70 per cent of the water monitored in the seven main Chinese river basins being unsuitable for direct human contact (SEPA, 2002).

In the light of the medium- to longer-run projections suggesting that high growth rates could still be maintained through the next two decades, Marigo raises some important issues pertaining to the quality and the sustainability of China's future economic development. She addresses the questions of whether pollution should be the unavoidable price for China's further growth and whether the adoption of less polluting technologies could be an affordable development strategy. By revising the recent available literature, Marigo's chapter argues that environmental improvements are possible and feasible in China even at current levels of income. A cleaner development path is a complex and challenging process but could be achieved by enforcing a strong environmental regulatory regime and by building the capabilities needed to select, absorb and develop technologies that lie outside the conventional pollution-intensive path.

AN EMERGENT KEY INTERNATIONAL PLAYER

Weber's chapter (Chapter 4) shows that China's diplomatic rise has been one of the most significant events in the international arena. Such a rise was seen with increasing concern by the US State Department, which has been pushing for a policy of containment towards China since 1980. Those who support the 'containment approach' believe that China's economic growth and re-emerging nationalism will drive the country to take a hegemonic role within the region, hence the need for an international effort to contain it. However, the growing importance of China's international trade and the vast potential of its domestic market exert a pull on the United States. President Clinton's visit to China in July 1998 was a clear sign of the significance that the US administration and business community ascribe to the country. Following this visit, Washington recognised the need to involve Beijing in the solution to Asia's problems. Soon after the elections, however, President Bush reversed his predecessor's foreign policy by defining China as the US main strategic competitor, an attitude which was further reinforced by the Bush Administration's decision to sell weapons to Taiwan, thereby marking a further pro-Taiwan policy.

However, the tragedy of September 11 turned US–China relations inside out. Immediately after the terrorist attack against the United States, the Chinese government expressed its strong disapproval of international terrorism and its support for the American people. During the course of 2002, meetings between Bush and China's President Jiang Zemin focused on cooperation in the fight against terrorism, with an explicit will to expand logistic and intelligence cooperation. On the occasion of the US President's visit to China, Jiang officially designated his successor, Vice-President Hu Jintao, who subsequently became President after the XVI Congress of the Communist Party. Despite President Bush's recognition of China's significant regional role within the wider global economy, tensions between the two countries have not subsided, particularly as far as Taiwan is concerned. However, following China's and Taiwan's accession to the WTO, convergence between the two economies is increasing to a point where many believe that the establishment of a free trade area may be feasible, thereby marking a first step towards a peaceful solution of the Taiwan issue.

DOMESTIC CHALLENGES: SOE REFORM AND UNEMPLOYMENT

Several issues are still open and should be solved by the new political leadership that emerged from the Sixteenth Congress of the Chinese Communist Party (CCP) (November 2002), in order for China to continue, in the next few years, on the way to economic development. The Sixteenth Congress marked the shift of power from the old ruling class to the so-called fourth generation (following the generations of Mao Zedong, Deng Xiaoping, and Jiang Zemin). In his report, President Jiang Zemin repeated that, within the first two decades of the 21st century, the CCP will bring wealth throughout China and specified the four objectives for the accomplishment of this welfare society:

1. to achieve a fourfold increase of the current GDP by 2020, fully implementing the free-market socialism model and expanding the opening of the current economic system;
2. to improve the socialist democracy, and to respect and effectively ensure the people's political, economic, and cultural rights and interests;
3. to improve standards in ideology, morality, science, culture, and health in the whole country and establish a comprehensive public education system, a new technical-scientific and cultural system, and a medical healthcare system covering the population at large;
4. to strengthen the sustainable development capability, with special focus on environmental balance; to ensure an effective use of resources and promote a balanced development between mankind and nature.

Open issues include the completion of the State-owned Enterprise (SOEs) reform. In the last 20 years, the role of non-state enterprises has increased steadily at the expenses of SOEs, which dominated the industrial sector during the planned economy years. China's non-state sector, which comprises all production units not owned or not directly controlled by the state (such as collectively-owned enterprises, private businesses and joint ventures), has been the engine of the country's rapid economic growth in the past two decades. In 1999 it was generating about 70 per cent of China's industrial output, while the share of state-owned enterprises shrank from 65 per cent in 1985 to 28 per cent in 1999. Since 1995, the Chinese government has been looking for a solution for state-owned enterprises, burdened by increasing debt, obsolete equipment, poor quality of management, and excess workforce.

The definition of a strategy for SOEs was clear in its main lines: reorganise the whole sector, disregard small companies and focus on medium-large ones, turn about 1000 of the larger ones into true conglomerates; sell, shut down, or perform mergers or acquisitions for most small and medium enterprises. The reform project started from the consideration that only 500 SOEs significantly contributed to the state's income, and only 50 of them suffered serious losses. Their reorganization was initially scheduled for completion by 1998. All the other SOEs had to be either half-privatised, turning their employees into shareholders, or declared bankrupt. Small-sized state-owned companies had to be acquired by larger ones or assigned to private owners. According to these plans, the government decided to launch a pilot reform: to test a new large-scale enterprise model, with all the characteristics of capitalist companies. Five hundred and twelve medium and large SOEs were selected for this trial, accounting alone for 43.7 per cent of the total sales of the state industry and 65.8 per cent of its profits. The same trial was repeated on a local scale, with 2500 medium and small companies, including half joint-stock companies and limited liability companies, using the 'Company Law' of 1994 (Weber, 2001). The SOEs' reform process, however, caused growing unemployment to become an issue which the Chinese government had to address.

China's labour market dynamics seem to pose one of the main challenges to the social stability of the nation in the near future. Boati's contribution to this volume (Chapter 5) reminds us that it is generally agreed that the official calculation of the urban unemployment rate in China needs to be reviewed, and various Chinese scholars and government departments are considering new ways of doing this. The literature is full of attempts to estimate and evaluate the real urban unemployment rate. Such attempts, however, seem to have limited significance: the evaluations start from unsound Chinese data and the results vary considerably. The main point quoted by scholars in evaluating unemployment data is that registered urban unemployment does not consist of many categories of the *de facto* unemployed. There is a variety of definitions for people who are out of work in China. In fact, the definition of registered urban unemployed person (*shiye*) taken from the *China Statistical Yearbook* is quite restrictive, not including laid-off workers (*xiagang*), i.e. workers from SOEs who have been dismissed but maintain a link with the enterprise that decided to eliminate their job. The number of laid-off people is higher than the number of the unemployed and, if these are added to the number of the officially unemployed in the unemployment calculation, the ratio is doubled, reaching 8.4 per cent, according to data from the *China Statistical Yearbook*.

Boati's overview of Chinese unemployment highlights a labour market in transition from a SOE-centred social welfare unit to an independent system with a comprehensive social safety net. The country, following the reforms of the public sector, still has to reabsorb millions of redundant SOE workers. IMF estimates indicate a substantial worsening in the unemployment condition due to the reform of SOEs and to the large amount of new entrants in the labour market. The future impact of worsening unemployment conditions on social stability will largely depend on the ability of the working class to join together into a single entity. Our analysis, however, shows a lack of capability on the part of the unemployed to form a united class with effective bargaining power. Boati is confident that, due to this incapacity, the Chinese government will be able to maintain social stability in the country, even if the conditions of the unemployed continue to deteriorate.

SOCIAL WELFARE REFORM

The other reform linked to the SOEs' reform concerns the social welfare system, including pensions and healthcare (see Weber and Stenbeck, Chapters 6 and 7). It should be noted that state pensions only covered state employees and included a monthly allowance, a subsidy to buy wheat, a subsidy to buy other staples, and a subsidy for funeral expenses. The reform project, still under discussion, emphasizes the creation of a pension system fit for a market economy and the fact that the state, companies, and individuals should share all responsibility for pension fund collection. With this aim, the government provided incentives for the population to subscribe to the packages offered by several private insurance companies, including foreign ones, offering both life and health insurance and supplemental pension schemes.

The social welfare reform is undoubtedly one of the greatest challenges that China will have to face in the next few years. An organic and systematic reform involves a number of major issues. Firstly, the ageing of the population creates the need for a complete reorganization of the pension system. Secondly, the national healthcare system also requires urgent reform as it is increasingly perceived as incapable of handling the needs of an ageing population and, for the time being, discriminates unfairly against people in rural areas. Many problems affect healthcare in China. The greatest, unequal access to social security schemes, virtually deprives poorer population groups resident in farming areas of any kind of support. China's healthcare system developed in parallel with the rest of the economic system: in Mao's era (1949–76) collectivism ruled, in Deng's era (1979–97) early reforms were implemented, and in the post-Deng era (1997–2003) widespread privatisation took place. Under Mao, the government focused healthcare policies on rural areas. The system organised around collective farming, free of charge, and funded by 'communal welfare funds'.

During the 1980s, following the start of economic reforms, China's healthcare resources were redirected towards the building of hospitals in urban areas while rural investment declined. During those years, the service gap between rich and poor areas widened continuously and medical prevention was neglected. Following the collapse of collective farming, most rural residents no longer enjoyed free access to medical care. Moreover, urban health insurance did not cover the unemployed, workers that migrated from the countryside (approximately 20 per cent of the Beijing population and even more in Shenzhen). In Deng's time, due to the scarcity of funds, the government vacillated between the wish to restore the collective models and the pursuit of new social security systems. Hospitals were largely forced to finance themselves by focusing on profitable services. In 1997, the government approved drastic reforms, with the introduction of medical insurance for employees in all sectors. In 2000, in view of China's accession to the WTO, the new legislation also allowed Sino–foreign joint ventures (equity and cooperative, but not contractual), to be set up in medical institutions.

The constant increase in healthcare expenses, growing in real terms at an 11 per cent average rate since 1986, has forced the government to reduce the scope of the state insurance schemes and gradually introduce private expenditure and insurance systems. The measures were necessary to curb expenses, but provided a negative incentive for poorer citizens to use healthcare facilities. With the elimination of rural cooperative medical systems, and the increasing shift of healthcare costs onto the individual as the planned economy retracted, more and more Chinese can no longer afford necessary medical care. China is now facing the urgent task of restructuring and coordinating both its healthcare provisions and its financing. The choice of a generally market-based approach, due to efficiency and affordability concerns, should be coupled with a (hitherto lacking) strengthening of government regulation, coordination and enforcement. Perhaps the SARS (Severe Acute Respiratory Syndrome) outbreak would not have been so devastating if China's healthcare authorities had carefully monitored it since its inception.[1]

BANKING REFORM

Another important reform, launched in the 1990s by the Chinese government but still not implemented, concerns the banking system, burdened by non-performing loans and affected by inefficiency and poor regulations. A review of banking reform does not fall within the scope of this book and therefore only its main steps will be mentioned here. The banking reform is closely related to the state enterprises' reform: major banks, in fact, are publicly owned and most of their loans are directed towards the SOEs. From 1978 to 1997 non-performing loans increased from RMB 190 billion to RMB 7.5 trillion, and doubled as a percentage of the GDP (from 53 per cent in 1978 to 100 per cent in 1997). The loan system expanded mostly as a consequence of the disruption in the state enterprise sector, whose debts at the end of 1995 exceeded 500 per cent of its turnover (Lardy, 1998).

As of the mid-1990s, the banking system underwent a wide reorganization. In 1993, with the reform of the commercial banks, the role of the People's Bank of China (PBoC) was redefined; development banks, performing funding activities according to political guidelines, and several commercial banks, operating according to market principles, were established. The structure of the banking system, ten years after the launching of the reform, may be summarized as follows: besides the four large state-owned banks – Industrial and Commercial Bank (ICBC), Agricultural Bank (ABC), Bank of China (BOC) and Construction Bank (CBC) – there are three development banks (State Development Bank, Agricultural Development Bank and Export–Import Bank of China), two subsidiary banks (CITIC Industrial Bank and China Investment Bank), and two specialized banks (Yantai Hopusing Savings Bank and Bengbu Housing Savings Bank). Within the banking system, state-owned banks dominate financial assets, even if their power is declining: in 1993 they controlled 78 per cent of financial assets, compared with 60 per cent in 2004; commercial banks control 7 per cent, rural and urban cooperatives 14 per cent, and other banking institutions 10 per cent (Weber, 2001).

In order to relieve banks from non-performing loans, in 1999 the Treasury established four financial companies, known as Asset Management Companies (AMCs), one for each commercial bank: Cinda (CBC), Huarong (ICBC), Orient (BOC), and Great Wall (ABC). Each bank received RMB 10 billion as a current capital fund to cover its expenses. There was a dual purpose behind this move: on one hand, to restore the balance of banks and allow them to focus on more profitable operations; on the other, to ensure a more effective financial management of companies running at a loss (Dornbush and Giavazzi, 1999). AMCs operate with three aims: to collect, classify, and settle bad loans, to create swap arrangements to settle debts, and to enter into financial agreements to manage the reorganization of SOEs. The establishment of the AMCs, however, does not seem to have significantly enhanced the financial health of the four state-owned banks. In November 2003 vice–finance minister Lou Jiwei confirmed that one of them would soon be selected for capital injection, thereby fuelling analysts' opinion that the big four, which make 61 per cent of the country's loans and hold 67 per cent of deposits, may be technically insolvent. Their NPLs are estimated by the government itself to be RMB 2.4 trillion, equal to 23 per cent of total loans ('Don't bank on a bail-out', *The Economist*, 6 December 2003). At the end of December 2003, the government did indeed inject $45 bn (one tenth of its foreign exchange reserves) into two of the country's largest banks, dividing the funds between the Bank of China and the China Construction Bank.

ACCESSION TO THE WTO AND THE INSURANCE MARKET

After 15 years of negotiations with the members of the WTO,[2] on 11 December 2001 China was officially admitted as a member of the trade body (Holbig and Ash, 2002). As part of the Protocol of Accession to the WTO, China had to list its opening commitments under the General Agreement on Trade in Services (GATS). The GATS, which came into force in January 1995, provides a legal framework for addressing 'market access' and 'national treatment'[3] limitations affecting trade and investment in services. It includes specific commitments by WTO members to restrict their use of those limitations and provides a forum for further negotiations to open service markets around the world. These commitments are contained in national service schedules, and are listed for each of the four modes through which trade in services can be performed according to WTO rules. These four modes are defined by the GATS as follows:

1. as with trade in goods, 'cross–border delivery' occurs when a service crosses a national border;
2. 'consumption abroad' takes place when the consumer travels to the territory of the supplier to purchase the service;
3. 'commercial presence' involves foreign direct investment (FDI) by a foreign service provider, for instance through the establishment of a branch or a subsidiary[4] in a country's territory;
4. 'movement of individuals' occurs when independent service providers or the employees of a multinational company temporarily move to another country.

In the case of China's Schedule of Commitments, modes 1 and 2 are either fully open or unbound (i.e. not subject to specific restrictions) for most sectors. As to mode 4, entry is only guaranteed for managers, executives and specialists, as well as for salespersons on exploratory business visits. No commitments are made for other categories of natural persons, such as unskilled personnel. However, a number of restrictive measures were admitted in several service sectors with respect to mode 3. As far as the form of establishment is concerned, for instance, there is often a requirement to form a joint venture, which may be either an equity joint venture (EJV) or a contractual joint venture (CJV).[5] Foreign ownership in EJVs is frequently restricted to specified levels, and branches may only be established in specific sectors. Moreover, business activities are only allowed in specific cities or in special economic areas. As for the business scope, transactions are only allowed with a subset of consumers, and are restricted in some other ways (Mattoo, 2002; Drysdale and Song, 2000).

With respect to the opening of the newborn Chinese insurance market to foreigners, Trivellato's chapter (Chapter 8) reminds us that insurance services play a significant role in a modern economy, protecting enterprises against a variety of risks, and providing individuals with security in key areas such as healthcare and pensions. China's accession to the WTO provides a wider range of opportunities to foreign investors to access the domestic insurance market, including the life segment, which is believed to have a substantial growth potential following the reform of the Chinese welfare system. However, prospective investors should pay attention to two elements in particular: the details of the evolving regulatory framework and the changing characteristics of the domestic market structure. Most of the past restrictions have been lifted, and many more will be phased out over the next few years. However, the need to protect a still-developing insurance industry implies that the Chinese authorities have been introducing (and will probably continue to do so) a number of regulatory measures which may pose an unexpected burden to prospective investors. Such investors should therefore continue to monitor these regulatory developments, and to cooperate with the Chinese authorities to reduce their impact where possible. On the other hand, China's accession to the WTO will not only affect the trade and investment regime, but the entire legal system too. Key principles such as normative uniformity, transparency, equal treatment, and jurisdictional control over the acts of the public administration will need to be included in the Chinese legal system (Cavalieri, 2003). Over the longer term, this trend is likely to have a positive impact on the uncertainty of the legal environment, which appears to be of major concern to several foreign insurance companies.

NOTES

1. The first cases of SARS were recorded in the Guangdong province in November 2002. In February 2003 the epidemic moved to Hong Kong and in early March it broke out in Beijing.

But only on 20 April did President Hu Jintao and the neo-premier Wen Jiabao launch a campaign to start disclosing the truth about the disease. The Minister of Health, Zhang Wenkang, and the Mayor of Beijing, Meng Xuenong, were demoted and Ms Wu Yi, the former minister of foreign trade (1993–97), was appointed Minister of Health. To curb the epidemic, Wu Yi decided to stop the celebrations for 1 May, discourage travelling, close all public places in Beijing, quarantine over 12 700 people, and implement controls and roadblocks on the routes out of the city.

2. The WTO, established in 1995, is the successor to the General Agreement on Tariffs and Trade (GATT), founded in 1947. Although China had been one of the founding members of the GATT, in 1950 the nationalist government based in Taiwan decided to withdraw from the agreement.

3. 'National treatment' is defined as a treatment which is no less favourable than that granted to domestic suppliers.

4. A wholly-owned subsidiary (like a joint venture) is a local institution incorporated under the host country's law and is a legal entity separated from its parent company; the parent company is thus not liable for the debts of the subsidiary in the host country. A branch is a legal extension of the parent company, which is liable for the branch's debt.

5. As specified in the Report of the WTO Working Party on the accession of China (2001):

   The terms of the contract, concluded in accordance with China's laws, regulations and other measures, establishing a 'contractual joint venture' govern matters such as the manner of operation and management of the joint venture as well as the investment or other contributions of the joint venture parties. Equity participation by all parties to the contractual joint venture is not required but is determined pursuant to the joint venture contract.

BIBLIOGRAPHY

Boltho, A. (2004), 'China – Can Rapid Economic Growth Continue?', *Singapore Economic Review*, **29** (2), October.

Cavalieri, R. (2003), *L'adesione della Cina alla WTO. Implicazioni giuridiche*, Quaderni Università di Lecce, ARGO Editrice.

Cheng, Bifan (2002) *Interaction between Political and Economic Factors in Relations across the Taiwan Strait*, paper presented at Monash Asia Institute's Prato Security Conference, 17–18 May.

Chow, Gregory C. (2002), *China's Economic Transformation*, Malden, Mass.: Blackwell Publishers.

Dornbusch, R. and Giavazzi, F. (1999), 'Heading off China's Financial Crisis', in *Strengthening the Banking System in China: Issue and Experience*, BIS policy papers, Banks of International Settlements, Basel.

Drysdale, P. and Song, Ligang (eds) (2000), *China's Entry to the WTO: Strategic Issues and Quantitative Assessments*, London: Routledge.

Economy, E. (2003), 'Changing Course on China', *Current History*, September, 243–49.

Economy, E. and Oksenberg, M. (eds) (1999), *China Joins the World: Progress and Prospects*, New York: Council of Foreign Relations.

Hale, D. and Hughes Hale, L. (2003), 'China Takes Off', *Foreign Affairs*, **82** (6), 36–53.

Holbig, H. and Ash, R. (eds) (2002), *China's Accession to the World Trade Organization*, London and New York: RoutledgeCurzon.

Howell, J. (1993), *China Opens Its Doors, The Politics of Economic Transition*, Hemel Hempstead: Boulder, Colo: Harvester Wheatsheaf; Lynne Rienner.

Lardy, N.R. (1998), *The Unfinished Chinese Revolution*, Washington: Brookings Institutions.

Lasserre, P. and Schutte, H. (1999), *Strategies for Asia Pacific: Beyond the Crisis*, London: Macmillan.

Mattoo, A. (2002), *China's Accession to the World Trade Organization – The Services Dimension*, Policy Research Working Paper No. 2932, The World Bank, December.

Medeiros, E.S. and Fravel, M.T. (2003), 'China's New Diplomacy', *Foreign Affairs*, **82** (6), November–December, 22–35.

National Bureau of Statistics (2002), *China Statistical Yearbook*, Beijing: China Statistical Publishing House.

Ross, L. (1998), *Environmental Policy in China*, Bloomington: Indiana University Press.

Sinton, J.E. and Fridley, D.G. (2000) 'What Goes Up: Recent Trends in China's Energy Consumption', *Energy Policy*, **28** (10), 671–87.

State Environmental Protection Administration (SEPA) (2002), *The Tenth National Five-Year Plan for Environmental Protection (Abstract)*, http://www.zhb.gov.cn/english/plan/Tenth.htm.

Weber, M. (ed.) (2000), *After the Asian Crises. Perspectives on Global Politics and Economics*, London: Macmillan.

Weber, M. (ed.) (2001), *Reforming Economic Systems in Asia*, Cheltenham, UK: Edward Elgar.

Weber, M. (2002), 'China's 21st Century Challenge: a Balance of Power between Japan and US', *The European Union Review*, **7** (1).

World Bank (1997), *China 2020. Development Challenges in the New Century*, Washington: The World Bank.

World Trade Organization (2001), *Working Party Report on the Accession of China, WT/ACC/CHN/49*, available at http://docsonline.wto.org/DDFDocuments/t/WT/ACC/CHN49.doc.

Zhang, Yongjin (2003), *China's Emerging Global Business. Political Economy and Institutional Investigations*, New York: Palgrave.

PART I

OUTSTANDING CHALLENGES

1. Can Rapid Economic Growth Continue?*

Andrea Boltho**

1. INTRODUCTION

China's economic expansion since reforms began in the late 1970s has been remarkable. Over the period 1978–2000, GDP may have grown at an annual rate of close to 10 per cent, with per capita incomes having been multiplied by a factor of about five. Few countries in the world have ever experienced similar success. Nor, according to many observers, is this 'miracle' over. Medium to longer-run projections suggest that through the next two decades growth could still average some 7 per cent per annum, a rate that would imply a further quadrupling of the country's output. Indeed, this was the objective put forward by the Communist Party's Sixteenth National Congress in November last year (*Beijing Review*, 26 December 2002).

Should such projections materialize, China would clearly become a dominant player in the global economy. The only other example of a similar development is provided by the rise of the United States a century ago. Indeed, China may achieve even more in the 40 years following the start of economic reforms than was achieved by America in the 40 years to World War I (Table 1.1). If output is measured at purchasing power parity (PPP), China's share of world GDP could rise by some 15 percentage points between 1978 and 2020, as against the 10 percentage points recorded by the United States between 1870 and 1913.[1] And as a consequence, China might even become the world's largest economy, at least in PPP terms. The increase in China's weight in world trade may not be as dramatic, but the country could still, by 2020, be the world's second largest exporter and importer.[2]

Such projections raise two important questions, one of a domestic and one of an international nature:

1. Would it indeed be feasible for China to expand at such rates for a further 20 years, given the many and well-known economic problems the country faces?

3

Table 1.1   The Emergence of the United States and of China (percentages)

	United States (1870–1913)		China (1978–2020)	
Share in world output (volume)	1870	8.9	1978	4.9
(at purchasing power parity)	1890	–	2000	12.3
	1913	19.1	2020	19.8[a]
Change		10.2		14.9[a]
Share in world exports (value)	1870	7.9	1978	0.8
(at current dollars)	1890	–	2000	3.9
	1913	12.9	2020	6.8[b]
Change		5.0		6.0[b]

Notes:
a. Assuming annual growth rates of 3.5 and 6.0 per cent for world and Chinese output respectively (see end note 1 to text).
b. Assuming annual growth rates of 7.0 and 10.0 per cent for world and Chinese exports respectively.

Source: Maddison (2001) and author's projections.

2. In the event of such growth materialising, what would be the likely impact on the rest of the world, and on Asia, of continuing and very rapid industrial expansion by a highly competitive and (presumably) increasingly efficient producer?

The following considers these two issues in turn, before setting out some summary conclusions. It should be noted at the outset that the focus is exclusively economic. The many political issues that China's continuing development will inevitably raise (for example, the process of internal democratization, the future status of Taiwan, relations with the United States, Japan and Russia, and so on) will not be considered. Such issues are, no doubt, of great importance and the way in which they will evolve could have significant effects on economic trends, but space constraints and considerations of comparative advantage dictate the need for a relatively narrow coverage.

2.   CAN CHINA CONTINUE TO GROW RAPIDLY?

The years from 1978 to the present (2004) have seen China grow at a very rapid pace, far outstripping what had been achieved in the first quarter-century of Communist rule. It is true that doubts have often been expressed about the accuracy of Chinese national accounts statistics. Some of these doubts extend over the whole reform period, others concentrate on the outcomes for the late

1990s. The literature is voluminous and no full consensus has yet been reached.[3] While it is likely that growth in the years 1998–2000 was overestimated, and it is possible that some upward bias has crept into the figures for the 1980s and 1990s as a whole, few would doubt that what China has achieved since reforms began has been impressive.

Can such rapid growth continue for another two decades (or even more)? Two rather simple arguments, based on comparative evidence, suggest that it can. First, international experience shows that economic 'miracles' of the kind registered by China have not been unique and have, at times, lasted for several decades. Table 1.2 presents some data which, inevitably perhaps, are entirely drawn from East Asia (economic miracles in other parts of the world have turned out, sadly, to have been either much shorter in duration and/or much less impressive in size).

Table 1.2   *Episodes of Rapid Economic Growth in the Longer-Run (average annual percentage changes in CDP)*

	1950s–60s	1960s–70s	1980s–90s
Japan	9.6[a]		
Korea		8.0	7.5
Taiwan		10.2	7.1
Singapore		9.3	7.5
China			9.6[b]

Notes:
a. 1953–73.
b. 1978–2000 (official data).

Source: IMF, International Financial Statistics Yearbook; OECD, National Accounts of OECD Countries; Republic of China, National Accounts.

While Japan did slow down substantially after the mid-1970s, Korea, Singapore and Taiwan have, so far, been able to grow at a sustained pace for at least 40 years. And one might expect China to be able to do so even more successfully for a further obvious reason. As shown in Figure 1.1, income per capita (measured in PPPs) is only a tiny fraction of that of the United States (12 per cent in 2001; measured in current dollars, that fraction is a mere 2.5 per cent). In other words, the scope for further catch-up is still enormous. Were per capita GDP to grow by 5 per cent per annum over the next 20 years, while US income expanded by 2 per cent, China would still not have reached 25 per cent of America's level by 2020 (as compared, for instance, to Korea's 50 per cent today).

Having a potential for catch-up does not, however, ensure that such a potential will necessarily be fulfilled, as the failure of so many poor countries

Figure 1.1   GDP per Capita (in Purchasing Power Parities; US = 100)

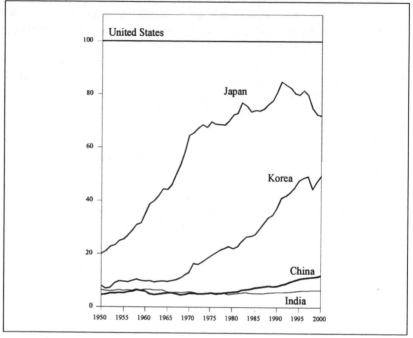

Source: Maddison (2001) and sources quoted in Table 1.2.

amply shows. Resources need to be mobilized and put to work efficiently. That China has resources would seem undoubted. There is vast scope for shifting underemployed labour from agriculture, which still accounts for nearly 50 per cent of total employment today, and capital formation can count on a domestic saving ratio which, in the second half of the 1990s, was equal to as much as 40 per cent of GDP or more. It would obviously be unwise to extrapolate this into the future, but East-Asian evidence has shown that high saving ratios in the area have lasted many decades.

Greater doubts surround the issue of efficiency or, in other words, whether a high growth of total factor productivity (TFP) can be achieved and sustained. Some earlier research suggested that this growth had been low, or even non-existent, in the 1980s and 1990s (for instance, evidence quoted in H.Wu (1997) but for a different view see Hu and Khan (1996)), or was likely to be low in future (Borensztein and Ostry, 1996). More recent estimates show, however, that TFP may, after all, have grown at a sustained pace in the 1990s (Y.Wu, 2000; Chow, 2002; Li, 2003). This need not continue, of course, yet several trends suggest that TFP may well advance rapidly in coming years as well (Caruso, 2002). First, WTO membership will put pressure on most industries to improve productivity; second, the private sector is expected to go on increasing its share in the economy at the expense of (inefficient) state-owned enterprises (SOEs); third, there is still a huge technology gap between China and the West; fourth, the appetite of foreign firms to invest in China remains unabated, and it is foreign firms that are most likely to stimulate technological progress; fifth, the banking system is under strong pressure to diversify its loans towards private firms and a better allocation of credit should raise efficiency. This list could, no doubt, be extended.

Successful development could still be derailed, of course, since it also requires, *inter alia*, a certain degree of social stability and, most importantly, appropriate micro– and macroeconomic policies that protect property rights and encourage risk taking. China's record over the past two decades suggests that these conditions have been broadly fulfilled and, barring some disastrous (and highly unlikely) lurch back to forms of central planning, should be maintained over the foreseeable future.

A number of uncertainties could, however, cloud a picture that otherwise looks relatively favourable. There are at least three potential risks that, it has often been argued, might endanger future growth prospects by either leading to inappropriate policies, and/or by generating social unrest (something the authorities are clearly in fear of):

1. The danger posed by a rapid rise in public debt, given the perceived needs to rescue a virtually bankrupt banking system and to supply proper welfare provisions to, at least, the urban population.
2. The problem of potential unemployment, which arises from continuing pressure to leave the land and from the inevitable, and possibly rapid, shedding of labour in the inefficient state sector.
3. The risk that the country may be increasingly divided, as rising inequalities between its different regions strengthen centrifugal forces.

2.1. Public Finance

On the face of it, China's public finances hardly appear out of control today, despite the significant efforts that have been made to pump-prime the economy in recent years.[4] The budget deficit in 2002 was only equal to some 3.5 per cent of GDP, while public debt stood at less than 20 per cent of GDP. Extrapolating the present deficit level into the future, and making some rough assumptions about interest rates, growth rates and inflation yields, via the well-known debt sustainability equation, a still very affordable public debt level equivalent to perhaps 45 per cent of GDP by 2010.[5]

The fears that have been expressed concentrate on the government's potential future liabilities. It has been argued, for instance, that given the very large weight of non–performing loans carried by the state-owned banking system (a result of politically-induced excessive lending to SOEs), the size of public debt is vastly underestimated. A full allowance for such bad loans could boost this debt to levels closer to 60–70 per cent of GDP (*The Economist*, 18 January 2003). And much more alarmist projections, incorporating also the potential costs of a fully-fledged social welfare system for the urban population, would boost future public debt levels to above 100 per cent of GDP. Should such estimates be close to reality, a fiscal crisis looms ahead which, it is argued, would require painful retrenching if it were not to lead to, first, sharp interest rate increases and, later, financial instability and inflation. In either case, growth could well be jeopardized.

Yet, many of these fears would seem to be exaggerated. For one thing, the recent pump-priming efforts, sparked off in part by the Asian economic crisis of the late 1990s, need not continue; for another, government revenues are rather low by international standards today (OECD, 2002), thus providing scope for them to be boosted in future.[6] More importantly, neither the problems of nonperforming loans, nor those of social welfare, have been left to fester. Policies are in place to deal with the first issue, and sensible reforms are planned to deal with the second (ibid.). These policies may not be quite sufficient as yet (*The Economist*, 6 December 2003), and additional public debt may well be created, but on nothing like the scale of some of the figures quoted above. Finally, experience from other countries with high domestic savings shows that even very large public debt levels, well in excess of 100 per cent of GDP (such as those of Italy in the early 1990s, or those of Japan at present), can be relatively easily financed without putting upward pressure on long-term interest rates, let alone threatening financial instability.

2.2. Employment

Greater difficulties, however, could arise on the labour market front. Employment creation since reforms began has been impressive (with, perhaps, 330 million jobs generated between 1978 and 2001). While the 1980s had still seen employment growth in both agriculture and in SOEs, in the second half of the 1990s, in particular, there was no net job creation in the rural economy and there was significant job shedding in the very uncompetitive industrial firms still in state hands (Table 1.3). Despite this, overall employment rose by some 50 million thanks to the creation of nearly 90 million jobs in the urban private, or semi-private economy.

This effort clearly needs to continue. The state-owned sector will have to retrench further, not least because of the competitive pressures that WTO entry will unleash. Its present roll call, at some 76 million workers, is down from a peak level of 112 million in the mid-1990s, but would still seem plethoric. A

Table 1.3   Recent Chinese Employment Trends (millions)

	1995	2001	Change
Total employment	681	730	50
Rural sector	490	491	1
Urban sector	190	239	49
of which:			
State-owned enterprises	113	76	−36
Private sector	77	163	86
Memorandum item:			
Manufacturing	98	81	−17

Source: China Statistical Yearbook (2002).

conservative estimate would put the likely number of redundancies over the next 20 years at 30 to 50 million. To this must be added the likely, and potentially huge, inflow to urban areas from workers in the countryside. WTO membership will add to this inflow since it will put increasing competitive pressures on Chinese agriculture. Estimates vary, from an OECD figure of perhaps 70 million by 2010 (OECD, 2002), to a report (surveying expert opinion) of some 200 million by 2020 (*Financial Times*, 10 December 2002). And, finally, demography is likely to boost the working age population by possibly a further 120 million in the next 20 years (Hussain, 2002). Jobs, in other words, might have to be found in the private, or semi-private, urban sector for possibly as many as 300 to 350 million extra workers.

Achieving this will be a tall order. A repetition of the relatively successful experience of 1995–2001, could generate some 200 million more jobs by 2020 (output growth may be somewhat slower over the forecast horizon than it was in the second half of the 1990s, but the economy is likely to gradually shift its demand towards labour-intensive services). This might well not be enough, however, to preserve full employment (and social peace). Two possible ways of curbing a rise in unemployment spring to mind (other than a decline in participation rates, which might well occur).[7] One would be to slow down the closing of SOEs, the other would be to continue the present restrictions on rural–urban migration. In the first case, however, the banking sector would find itself forced to extend yet further credits to firms that are virtually bankrupt. This would, in turn, exacerbate an already serious bad loans situation and would have inevitably unfavourable consequences for public finance. In the second case, under-employment on the land would continue, or indeed rise, and this might lead to further increases in regional inequality which, it has been argued, could threaten the unity of the country.

2.3. Regional Problems

The view is often put forward that China, because of its history, is subject to strong centrifugal forces. Growing income differentials between, in particular, the coastal and the inland provinces strengthen this fear, as does the possibly diminishing grip of the party over the country. Not that long ago it was, for instance, argued in a paper written by two Chinese political scientists (and widely circulated in Beijing), that:

> If a 'political strongman' dies, it is possible that a situation like post-Tito Yugoslavia will emerge. In years, at the soonest a few, at the latest between 10 and 20, the country will move from economic collapse to political break-up, ending with its disintegration. (*The Economist*, 25 September 1993, p. 86)

So far at least this has hardly happened since the incentives for break-up would, in fact, seem to be very limited. Poorer regions would have little to gain from any form of secession, while richer ones have, so far at least, avoided much of the spatial redistribution burden that a more egalitarian federal system might have imposed. It is true that regional inequality, after narrowing in the first 15 years of reform (Jian et al., 1996), has since then widened (Zhang et al., 2001). Measures of Gini coefficients of income inequality for provincial GDP per capita show a clear, and worrying, trend towards growing differentials from the early 1990s onwards (Figure 1.2).

Yet, there are at least two reasons for why this need not lead to major social conflict. First, the whole concept of regional income differentials is open to question. While selected groups of the population (for example, socioeconomic categories or decile groups in a household distribution) usually share some common income characteristics, this is much less so for regional groupings which will include both rich and poor in proportions not that dissimilar from the national average. Thus, regional distribution results tend to show much less inequality than other measures of income distribution.

Second, while China's regional divergences are large, they are not that unusual by international standards, as suggested by Table 1.4 which presents some data on other continental-sized economies. Care must be taken when making such international comparisons, partly because of differing data quality, but partly also because the Gini coefficient, in particular, is sensitive to the number of regions chosen (tending to increase when the number of regions rises). As the figures stand, they clearly show that the mature economies of the OECD area are spatially much more equal than is China, a result, no doubt, of a long history of growing internal factor mobility and successful economic integration. But by the standards of some other developing (or transforming) economies, China's position is not so exceptional. In both Brazil and India, let alone in Russia,[8] regional differentials are also pronounced. And interestingly, when one looks at

Figure 1.2   *Regional Income Inequality (Gini coefficients for provincial per capita GDP)*

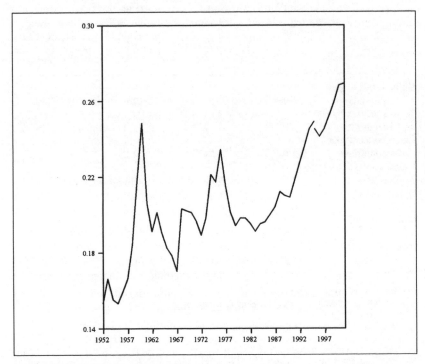

Source: Zhang et al. (2001) and author's estimates.

household (as opposed to regional) income distribution, China is no more unequal than the United States and significantly more equal than either Russia or Brazil. Arguably, the latter indicator is more relevant to the potential for social tensions than are indicators of regional disparities.

Nor is the increase that China has recorded in its regional Gini coefficient over the last two decades unique. Table 1.5 presents some of the scanty evidence on changes through time for those continental-sized economies for which data could be found.[9] Here again, Western Europe and the United States exhibit strong regional convergence in the post-World War II period, but the same is clearly less in evidence in India, where economic reform over the last 30 years has also been accompanied by widening regional differentials. Interestingly, the same may also have been true of the United States in the 19th century. The available data, which are for personal income rather than for GDP,[10] suggest not only that differentials were quite pronounced in the mid- to late-19th century, but also that they increased in America's early development period between 1840 and 1880.

Table 1.4   Selected Indicators of Regional Income Differentials

	Gini coefficient for regional GDP	Standard deviation of logs of per capita GDP	Ratio of per capita GDP in richest to poorest reg.	Memorandum item: Gini coefficient for personal income distribution
China (2001)				
31 provinces	26.9	0.57	12.9	40.3 (1998)
West. Europe (2000)				
16 countries[a]	6.2	0.19	2.0	–
Enlarged EU (2000)				
24 countries[a]	12.6	0.44	4.2	–
United States (1999)				
48 states	7.7	0.17	2.1	40.8 (1997)
Brazil (1998)				
27 regions	26.9	0.47	9.7	60.7 (1998)
India (1998/99)				
23 states[b]	21.6	0.43	5.2	37.8 (1997)[c]
Russia (1999)				
79 regions	31.2	0.37	21.9	48.7 (1998)

Notes:
a. In purchasing power parities (excluding Luxembourg).
b. Net state product.
c. Based on expenditure rather than income data.

Sources: China Statistical Yearbook (2002); National Accounts of OECD Countries (1989–2000); Survey of Current Business (August 2001); Brasil em números (2001); Statistical Pocket Book of India (2001); Rossiskii statisticheskei eghegodnik (2001); World Bank (2002).

Table 1.5   Changes in Regional Income Differentials (Gini coefficients)

China (provincial GDP)	1978	0.20	2001	0.27
Western Europe (national GDP in PPPs)	1950	0.20	2000	0.06
United States (gross state product)	1963	0.09	1999	0.08
(state personal income, 29 states)	1840	0.15	1880	0.17
(state personal income, 45 states)	1880	0.25	1919–21	0.19
India (net state product)	1970–71	0.14	1998–99	0.22

Sources: Easterlin (1960); Kuznets and Swaine Thomas (1957); Maddison (2001); Zhang et al. (2001); and sources cited in Table 1.4.

This is not to say that China's regional income gaps can be ignored, the more so as there seems to be little real policy effort designed to tackle this issue at present. Yet, in a rapid growth environment differentials may well stabilize or even diminish over time. As forcefully argued by the OECD, increased integration of both capital[11] and labour markets should work in that direction as will the (limited) policies designed to improve the infrastructure of the inland parts of the country (OECD, 2002). Interestingly, the absence of pronounced regional differences in industrial production structures, suggests that, so far at least, poor integration has prevented the exploitation of regional comparative advantages (ibid). This is a further area in which a potential would seem to exist for the reduction of spatial disparities. It is true, of course, that, as theories of cumulative causation (or the 'New economic geography' approach) suggest, even integration may fail to diminish regional productivity gaps (and this is indirectly suggested by the persistence of such gaps in, for instance, Italy or Germany), yet the bulk of the evidence would still seem to point in the direction of eventual regional convergence (Barro and Sala-i-Martin, 1991).

If a tentative conclusion can be drawn from all this, it is that further rapid Chinese economic growth is possible, despite the many problems the country faces. Indeed, rapid growth would by itself solve several of these problems. The public finance situation would obviously benefit from growing incomes and so would employment levels. And even if regional differentials remained large, absolute living standards would presumably rise fairly rapidly throughout most of the country (as they have done in the past), thereby lowering potential tensions. Hence the understandable emphasis put by the authorities on the pursuit of further economic success. With it, many of the problems that have been highlighted could be defused. Without it, they might all reinforce each other and degenerate into crisis.

3.   IMPLICATIONS FOR THE REST OF THE WORLD

The previous section has argued that further and rapid Chinese growth is possible. Many in the West might view such developments with disquiet.[12] Uninformed public opinion often sees China as a gigantic sweatshop, swamping world markets with cheap exports. The 60 per cent increase in the country's weight in the world economy over the coming 20 years suggested by Table 1.1 could, in such views, spell the end of most industrial production in the OECD area. Economists, on the other hand, tend to take a different (and more balanced) position. For them, such developments can only be seen as favourable, and this not only for China, but also for the rest of the world. For one thing, most of China's increased production will go to satisfy rapidly rising domestic demand. For another, to the extent that it spilled over into increased exports, these will be broadly matched by increased imports, since ever increasing current account surpluses are an obvious impossibility. More importantly, it must be remembered that international trade is not a zero sum game and that the rapid expansion of a major producer should lead to a reallocation of resources across the globe along comparative advantage lines and to increased competition in the world economy. Both these developments, by improving static and dynamic efficiency respectively, will generate benefits all round. Admittedly, however, as international trade theory reminds us, these overall benefits will not be evenly distributed and some industries and/or factors of production will suffer inevitable losses.

3.1. The Industrialised Countries

The potential for such adverse effects would seem to be relatively small for the industrialized countries of the OECD area. It is true, of course, that the increasing weight of China will lead to further industrial hollowing out in Japan, North America and Western Europe, as has already happened over the last two decades. Two consequences, in particular, could be feared (along the lines suggested by Wood, 1994): labour-intensive manufacturing jobs would be lost as a consequence of increased import penetration, and this could increase unemployment if labour markets were not sufficiently flexible, and/or income distribution could become less equal, as Chinese competition put downward pressure on earnings at the lower end of the wage distribution. Both these outcomes are possible and, indeed, likely. Yet, the empirical evidence on the effects of trade with the third world on both unemployment and income distribution suggests that the impact so far has been relatively small.

Taking income distribution first, while a sharp widening in wage differentials has clearly occurred in the United States over the last two decades, and, if to a lesser extent, can also be seen in some European countries, virtually all the research in this area has come to the conclusion that international trade, and *a fortiori*, therefore, China, have played only a relatively small role in this (see, for instance, Cline, 1997 or Fishlow and Parker, 1999). Technological progress seems to have been a much more powerful force in increasing earnings inequality.

Turning to the effects of trade on unemployment, it must be remembered that in many cases China's very rapidly growing exports of labour-intensive commodities have displaced not only domestic OECD production, but also, and to a much greater extent, sales from other developing countries. Table 1.6 provides some evidence on a few selected products in which China has made major gains in market shares over the last two decades. It will be seen that, at least for the particular products shown, many of China's gains have come at the expense of the NIEs.[13] The net impact on the OECD area, in other words, has been much smaller. This, of course, could change in future, as China upgrades its export structure. Indeed, looking at two other, somewhat less labour-intensive products in which China has also made very substantial gains on world markets (household electrical equipment and cycles and motorcycles), one sees no corresponding losses by the NIEs.[14] Clearly, pressures on jobs in the industrialized countries will continue.

Table 1.6 Asian Export Performance in Selected Labour-intensive Sectors (percentage Shares in World Exports)

		China	NIES[a]	ASEAN[b]	South Asia[c]
Clothing and apparel					
(SITC 84)	1980	4.2	15.7	3.3	1.9
	2000	18.1	4.9	6.6	6.0
	Change	13.9	−10.8	3.3	4.1
Toys and sporting					
goods (SITC 894)	1980	1.2	17.8	0.6	0.7
	2000	21.5	6.2	3.0	0.7
	Change	20.3	−11.6	2.4	0
Travel goods					
(SITC 83)	1980	3.1	32.7	2.9	0.6
	2000	24.0	4.1	5.6	2.4
	Change	20.9	−28.5	2.8	1.8
Footwear					
(SITC 85)	1980	1.6	20.2	1.1	0.5
	2000	22.9	2.4	6.0	1.2
	Change	21.3	−17.8	4.9	0.7

Notes:
a. Korea, Singapore and Taiwan (see endnote 13 to text).
b. Indonesia, Malaysia, Philippines and Thailand.
c. Bangladesh, India and Pakistan.

Source: UN International Trade Data Bank (various years).

Yet, against this, must be set the potential gains that could accrue to OECD countries from continuing Chinese growth. First, the economic structures of the two areas are today broadly complementary, with China still in need of capital- and technology-intensive goods, and likely to increasingly demand advanced internationally traded services, all of which will be job-creating in the OECD area. Such complementarity may not last for ever, but the experience of Japan shows how even the very successful upgrading of that country's industrial structure has not led to its trade with America or Europe drying up – on the contrary, other areas of mutual comparative advantage have emerged, and the same is likely to happen with China. Second, successful Chinese industrial exports should lead to terms of trade gains for the OECD, which, by adding to real income growth, should also boost spending and, thus, employment. Add to this the vast scope for continuing successful foreign direct investment flows, and it would be difficult to argue that a booming China could represent an economic threat to Western prosperity.

3.2.   Asia's Developing Countries

The prospects for the rest of Continental Asia may seem less rosy. While China should represent a clear opportunity for advanced countries, it could be seen as a threat for many developing ones which often (and particularly in Asia) compete in the same products as those that China exports. Indeed, this competition could be fierce, since 'World Bank estimates suggest that the elasticity of substitution between Chinese and other developing countries' manufactured exports is likely to be very high – possibly as high as 10' (Boltho et al., 1996, p. 278). The data shown in Table 1.6 would seem to indirectly corroborate this view. While China made massive strides on world markets for some of the more important labour-intensive commodities exported by developing economies, neither ASEAN, let alone South Asia (whose population is roughly similar to that of China), were able to achieve anything like equivalent market share gains in the period under review. In other words, it is not implausible to think that China's growth was in part achieved by the crowding-out of textile and leather good exports to the West by, say, India or Indonesia.

Table 1.7 looks at this issue in somewhat greater detail by presenting, for the year 2000, two different indicators of the potential overlap between China's 'revealed comparative advantage' in manufacturing products and that of a selection of other Asian countries. As it stands, the evidence for total exports is mixed.

The three NIEs shown in the table would appear to have an export structure whose correlation with that of China is now very limited (the correlation was much stronger in the 1980s, suggesting that Korea and Taiwan, in particular, have managed to successfully 'trade up' their commodity composition). The same would seem to be true for Malaysia. For Indonesia, the Philippines, Thailand and South Asia, on the other hand, the data do suggest that China is highly likely to have been, and still be, a major competitor. And this finding is broadly confirmed if, instead of looking at total manufacturing trade, attention is focused on China's exports of products intensive in unskilled labour (which still account for over 40 per cent of the country's sales abroad). Here too, China would seem to be in direct competition with ASEAN's poorer countries and with Bangladesh and Pakistan, though not with India.

Yet this overlap need not spell inevitable gloom for developing Asia. As was argued above, international trade does not involve zero sum games, as indirectly suggested by the very successful development experience of much of non-Chinese Asia over the last two decades, just when Chinese exports were growing so rapidly. For one thing, the competition provided by China is likely to generate growth stimuli in other countries, raising their efficiency. More importantly, growth of the Chinese domestic market has also created a massive demand for imports. While the greatest beneficiaries of this are likely to have

Table 1.7   Comparative Advantage Correlations between China and Selected Asian Countries, 2000

	Simple correlation coefficient		Weighted rank correlation coefficient[a]	
	for revealed comparative advantage[b] in manufacturing in:			
	Total manufacturing[c]	Unskilled labour intensive manufacturing[d]	Total manufacturing[c]	Unskilled labour intensive manufacturing[d]
	between China and:			
Korea	0.03	−0.04	−0.04	0.19
Singapore	−0.05	−0.08	−0.32	0.17
Taiwan	0.14	−0.03	0.10	0.22
Indonesia	0.23**	0.10	0.51**	0.59**
Malaysia	0.13	0.06	−0.05	0.20
Philippines	0.26**	0.59**	−0.09	0.81**
Thailand	0.41**	0.50**	0.40**	0.76**
Bangladesh	0.38**	0.38**	0.77**	0.86**
India	0.28**	0.16	0.04	0.06
Pakistan	0.35**	0.47**	0.64**	0.83**

Notes:
a. The coefficient (a modified version of the simple Spearman rank coefficient) weighs rank differences by the product's importance in the two countries' exports, and is equal to: $1 - [(6\Sigma d_i^2 w_i)/(n^2 - 1)]$, where d_i are the differences in rank, w_i the weights of each product group and n the number of observations (see, for instance, Hufbauer (1970)).
b. Indices of revealed comparative advantage measure the ratio between a country's share in world exports in a particular product and its share of total world exports.
c. For 149 SITC 3-digit categories.
d. For 47 SITC 3-digit categories classified as being intensive in unskilled labour in Cline (1997).
* Significant at the 5 per cent level.
** Significant at the 1 per cent level.

Sources: Author's calculations using UN International Trade Data Bank (various years).

been primary producers and the advanced industrialized countries, Asia's economies have also gained (and most notably so in 2002–3). Both these favourable features are likely to continue over the coming decades.

In addition, two possible future trends could also improve the outlook for China's neighbours. First come likely exchange rate developments. Economic theory suggests (and international evidence confirms) that rapidly growing countries eventually experience appreciating exchange rates. China has, so far, resisted this trend, and in the light of the fragility of its banks such resistance is understandable. Over the longer run, however, further opening of the economy and liberalization of the financial system will mean that today's capital controls are bound to become progressively less effective. And an appreciating exchange rate should erode some of China's competitiveness on world markets. Second, China may also become a large net importer of services. This has already happened over the last decade, which has seen China move from surplus to deficit in invisible trade, with service exports (in current dollars) being multiplied by five, but service imports being multiplied by as much as ten. Such trends will, almost certainly, continue. While some of this growth will benefit the OECD countries, a rapidly rising demand for tourist services, in particular, could provide a major boost to activity in neighbouring Asia as well.[15]

China's future growth, in other words, presents the rest of the world with both challenges, but also opportunities. The latter are clearly beneficial, the former can be so too, if they lead to appropriate economic responses. Looking at the past 20 years during which China entered the world economy, an admittedly impressionistic judgement would be that the benefits for other countries outstripped (and probably vastly outstripped) the costs. The same, surely, is likely to be the case in future.

4.   CONCLUSIONS

This chapter has, optimistically perhaps, argued that further and rapid Chinese economic growth is feasible. Whether it will actually materialize will, of course, crucially depend on the surrounding geo-political context. However, and in the absence of major conflict (or major world recessions), there are no compelling economic reasons to fear a sharp deceleration, let alone a prolonged period of crisis. The country, no doubt, faces some serious problems but, equally, the economic policies it has put in place, however imperfect they may be, face up to many of these. A further quadrupling of output over the coming 20 years, in other words, is possible and would vastly improve the living standards of what is still an overwhelmingly very poor population. On this ground alone, rapid Chinese growth should be welcomed. Yet, it should also be welcomed because of its likely effects on other countries.

China's entrance into the world economy was, in the Introduction, compared to that of the United States a century ago. At that time, United States expansion made Americans the richest people in the world. On this occasion, Chinese growth may transform China into the largest economy of the world (at least when measured in PPP terms). At that time, American export growth benefited the rest of the world by supplying new and cheaper products, while American import growth provided trade partners with a vast new market. It is true, however, that US exports of grain were seen as a threat in Europe and powerfully contributed to the return of protectionism in the late 19th century (*Financial Times*, 19 November 2003). At present, the surge in Chinese exports appears to threaten labour-intensive sectors in both developed and developing economies and could have similarly unfortunate consequences for free trade. Yet, quite apart from the welfare gains for the consumers of such labour-intensive products, Chinese import demand (and thirst for foreign investment) have also created, and will continue to create, huge new opportunities for the rest of the world. Policy makers in the West will hopefully realise the scope for such further gains and the folly of pursuing protectionist policies, since few prospective economic developments have the power to deliver more benefits than would a continuation of rapid growth in China.

NOTES

*   Reprinted by permission from the *Singapore Economic Review* (2004).
** The author would like to thank Chris Allsopp and Vanessa Rossi for many helpful inputs. He remains solely responsible for the final output.
1. Table 1.1 updates to 2000 Maddison's (2001) level estimate of GDP in PPP terms in 1999 (a level considered relatively high by some), and assumes that output (in PPPs) will grow at 6 per cent per annum, rather than the 7 per cent that is officially targeted. The difference attempts to allow, if very imperfectly, for the likely longer-run convergence between PPP and market exchange rate based measurements of output, a convergence that reflects the inevitable workings of the so-called 'Balassa–Samuelson effect'. Since the adjustment is *ad hoc*, the base line is controversial and the forecast uncertain, the 2020 results here shown are clearly very tentative.
2. In fact, already today, China is a major participant in international trade. In 2002, for instance, China was the world's fifth largest trading country, with exports similar to those of France and imports above those of Italy.
3. Investigations by Woo and Maddison (cited in H. Wu, 1997) have come to the conclusion that growth in the 1980s and in the first half of the 1990s may have been overestimated by perhaps 1 percentage point a year. More recent research has suggested that, in the light of data on energy consumption, late 1990s GDP growth rates were overestimated by a good deal more (Rawski, 2001). For the three years 1998–2000, for instance, Rawski argued that output, rather than increasing at the officially announced annual rate of 7.6 per cent, grew at much lower rates, possibly as low as 0.7 per cent per annum. It should be noted, however, that this extreme position has come under severe criticism, as has been partly recognized by the original author himself (Rawski, 2002). On the one hand, the data used to measure energy consumption contained a number of inaccuracies; on the other, consideration of buoyant import growth (a variable that lends itself to fewer potential statistical errors than does the calculation of GDP or even that of energy use) would seem to broadly corroborate the official data. A sensible adjustment may, perhaps, lop off at most some 3 percentage points per annum from the 1998–2000 official growth rate figures.
4. It has been estimated that public expenditure increases contributed as much as 1.5 to 2 percentage points to GDP growth in 1997–2002 (quoted in Rawski, 2002).
5. The debt sustainability equation:

$$\Delta D/Y = (r - y)D/Y - PB/Y \tag{1.1}$$

shows that the change in the ratio of public debt to GDP ($\Delta D/Y$) is equal to the difference between the real interest rate (r) and the economy's real growth rate (y) times the D/Y variable, minus the ratio of the primary balance to GDP (PB/Y), that is the public sector balance net of interest payments on public debt. Assuming that the (controlled) interest rate on public debt stays around 5 per cent while prices go on declining at 1 per cent per annum and real growth is of 7 per cent per annum, would result in a progressive decline of the debt/GDP ratio. If one assumes, however, a continuation of today's primary deficit (which is close to 3 percentage points of GDP), then debt would, nonetheless, rise through time, though far from explosively.

6. Thus, the OECD argues that '... there is significant scope within the current tax structure for [tax revenues] to increase further' (OECD, 2002, p. 53).
7. China's participation rate is very high by international standards, a legacy of the 'full employment' policy of the past.
8. The value of Russia's regional Gini coefficient may well be boosted by the very large number of regions taken into account.
9. The observation for Western Europe is not strictly comparable to that of the other countries shown, given that the area did not enjoy fixed exchange rates through the 50 years examined. Yet, over most of that period, exchange rates were fairly stable.
10. Personal income is likely to be somewhat more evenly distributed than GDP per capita, thus biasing downwards the values of the Gini coefficient for the United States relative to those shown in Tables 1.4 and 1.5 for other countries.
11. Not only are there restrictions on labour mobility between rural and urban areas, but also, and surprisingly perhaps: 'Capital mobility has been limited, due in part to the limited outlets for transferring savings among regions and to protectionist barriers to business establishment across regional jurisdictions' (OECD, 2002, p. 28).
12. One reason for this disquiet might be the fear of rising environmental pollution in China which could spill over to the rest of the world. This is, indeed, a potential danger, but one that can only be tackled by international agreements.
13. For many of these commodities, of course, Chinese successes owe their origin precisely to a shift of production by Hong Kong, Taiwanese and, if to a lesser extent, Korean firms away from home and to the Chinese mainland. The table, in fact, underestimates the decline in the NIEs' share since it does not show data for Hong Kong, a significant exporter in 1980, but no longer today. It is true that Hong Kong's official statistics still show sizeable exports for these products, but most of these are, by now, re-exports either originating from, or destined for, the Mainland.
14. Between 1980 and 2000, China's world market share of SITC 775 (household electrical equipment) rose by 12 percentage points (while the NIEs' share rose by a more moderate 4.5 percentage points). For SITC 785 and 786 (cycles and motorcycles), China's rise was equal to as much as 21 percentage points, with the NIEs also gaining nearly 4 percentage points. Growing Japanese direct investment may well have something to do with such trends. Fears for the car sector in the West may, on the other hand, seem premature, despite buoyant domestic production growth. China's RCA for cars was, in 2000, the lowest of all its manufacturing sectors. But it should not be forgotten that the same was broadly true for Japan in, say, 1955, when the country's car RCA ranked 72nd out of 82 sectors. By 1975, it had climbed into the top 20 sectors, and by 1995 it was ranked fifth.
15. Between 1990 and 2001, Chinese demand for foreign travel services (in dollar terms) has risen at an annual rate of as much as 35 per cent (WTO, 2002).

BIBLIOGRAPHY

Barro, R.J. and X. Sala-i-Martin (1991), *Convergence across States and Regions*, Brookings Papers on Economic Activity, No. 1, pp. 107–82.
Boltho, A. (2004), 'China – Can Rapid Economic Growth Continue?', *Singapore Economic Review*, **49** (2), October.
Boltho, A., U. Dadush and S. Otsubo (1996), 'China's Emergence: Prospects, Opportunities and Challenges', *Asian Economic Journal*, **10**, pp. 271–89.
Borensztein, E. and J.D. Ostry (1996), 'Accounting for China's Growth Performance', *American Economic Review*, **86**, pp. 224–8.
Caruso, M. (2002), 'Procyclical Productivity and Output Growth in China: An Econometric Analysis', *Open Economies Review*, **13**, pp. 251–74.
Chow, G. (2002), 'Accounting for Economic Growth in Taiwan and Mainland China: A Comparative Analysis', *Journal of Comparative Economics*, **30**, pp. 507–30.
Cline, W.R. (1997), *Trade and Income Distribution*, Institute for International Economics, Washington, DC.

Easterlin, R.A. (1960), 'Interregional Differences in Per Capita Income, Population, and Total Income, 1840–1950', In NBER, *Trends in the American Economy in the Nineteenth Century*, Princeton University Press, Princeton, NJ.

Fishlow, A. and K. Parker (eds) (1999), *Growing Apart: The Causes and Consequences of Global Wage Inequality,* Council on Foreign Relations Press, New York, NY.

Hu, Z. and M.S. Khan (1996), *Why is China Growing So Fast?*, IMF Working Papers, No. 96/75.

Hufbauer, G.C. (1970), 'The Impact of National Characteristics and Technology on the Commodity Composition of Trade in Manufactured Goods', in R. Vernon (ed.), *The Technology Factor in International Trade*, Columbia University Press, New York, NY.

Hussain, A. (2002), 'Demographic Transition in China and its Implications', *World Development*, **30**, pp. 1823–34.

Jian, T., J.D. Sachs and A.M.Warner (1996), 'Trends in Regional Inequality in China', *China Economic Review*, **7**, pp. 1–21.

Kuznets, S. and D. Swaine Thomas (eds) (1957), *Population Redistribution and Economic Growth – United States, 1870–1950*, Vol. I, The American Philosophical Society, Philadelphia, PA.

Li, K.-W. (2003), *China's Capital and Productivity Measurement Using Financial Resources*, Yale Economic Growth Center Discussion Paper, No. 851.

Maddison, A. (2001), *The World Economy: A Millennial Perspective*, OECD, Paris.

National Bureau of Statistics (NBS) (2002), *China Statistical Yearbook*, China Statistical Publishing House, Beijing.

OECD (2002), *China in the World Economy: The Domestic Policy Challenges*, OECD, Paris.

Rawski, T.G. (2001), 'What is Happening to China's GDP Statistics?', *China Economic Review*, **12**, pp. 347–54.

Rawski, T.G. (2002), *Measuring China's Recent GDP Growth: Where Do We Stand?*, mimeo.

Wood, A. (1994), *North–South Trade, Employment and Inequality: Changing Fortunes in a Skill-driven World*, Clarendon Press, Oxford.

World Bank (2002), *World Development Indicators, 2002*,Washington, DC.

WTO (2002), *International Trade Statistics*, Geneva.

Wu, H.X. (1997), *Measuring China's GDP*, East Asia Analytical Unit, Australian Department of Foreign Affairs and Trade, Briefing Paper No. 8.

Wu, Y. (2000), 'Is China's Economic Growth Sustainable? A Productivity Analysis', *China Economic Review*, **11**, pp. 278–96.

Zhang, Z., A. Liu and S. Yao (2001), 'Convergence of China's Regional Incomes, 1952–1997', *China Economic Review*, **12**, pp. 243–58.

2. Economic Growth and the 'Luxury' of a Clean Environment: Is a Short Cut Possible in China?

Nicoletta Marigo

1. INTRODUCTION

Since the 1980s, China's rapid economic growth has improved people's standard of living, but also depleted the natural resource base and created serious pollution problems. The consequences are sadly apparent in the health statistics of China's most polluted areas and in the increasing economic costs associated with environmental depletion and degradation.

There are no signs that China's economic miracle is over. Indeed, as it is argued in other parts of this book, projections suggest that growth could still average some 7 per cent per annum through the next two decades. This raises concern for the state of China's environment in the coming years and leaves two important questions open: is growing pollution the unavoidable price for China's further growth? Given the many pressing development needs, are environmental improvements affordable?

There is a widespread perception that environmentally friendly behaviour is too expensive, and environmental protection essentially becomes a luxury out of reach for developing nations. This chapter will argue that this is not necessarily the case and that environmental improvements are possible and feasible in China even at current levels of income. However a cleaner development path is bound to be a complex and challenging process.

By surveying the recent available literature, the first part of this chapter analyses the importance of economic, demographic and social factors in shaping the current state of the environment in China. A synthetic assessment of the most serious environmental problems is also provided. The second part of this chapter addresses the two questions put forth in this introduction and indicates a possible way forward. The key objective of this chapter is to raise awareness and encourage further dialogue on how China could better meet the challenge of economic development and environmental protection.

2.   THE IMPACT OF ECONOMIC GROWTH AND DEMOGRAPHIC INCREASE ON THE ENVIRONMENT

China's outstanding growth over the past two decades has been accompanied by a variety of changes that are challenging the environment in different ways. The shift from a planned and supply-driven economy towards a market-oriented and demand-driven one has had substantial implications for both industrial and agricultural production. At the same time economic reform has created a larger role for non-state and private businesses, increasing in this way the number and variety of operators in the national economy. Furthermore, the last twenty years have also witnessed an impressive population increase which, in conjunction with the demand for higher standards of living, has increased the per capita consumption and the pressure on natural resources. These developments have had a very complex impact on the environment leading in some cases to significant reductions in environmental pressures while in others to a dramatic deterioration of the environment and in the exploitation of natural resources.

Three factors have been particularly important in shaping the state of China's environment through the years: changes in the industrial production and ownership, population growth and increased mobility, and large scale energy consumption.[1]

2.1.   Changes in Industrial Production and Ownership

China's industrial growth has been extremely rapid in the last twenty five years, but also a primary source of environmental damage (SEPA, various years). When Deng Xiaoping started to implement economic reforms in 1978, he abandoned the development of heavy industry, with its serious pollutant in favour of an export oriented strategy that encouraged both the emergence of light industry and the involvement of new operators in the industrial scene. In the last twenty years, the role of non-state enterprises has increased steadily at the expenses of state-owned enterprises (SOEs) which dominated the industrial sector during the planned economy years. These changes in both industrial ownership and sectoral composition of output have been affecting the environment in several ways.

China's non-state sector, which comprises all production units not owned or not directly controlled by the state (such as collectively-owned enterprises, private businesses and joint ventures), has been the engine of the country's rapid economic growth in the past two decades. In 1999 it was generating nearly 80 per cent of China's industrial output (see Table 2.1) while the share of state-owned enterprises shrank from 65 per cent in 1985 to 28 per cent in 1999.

Table 2.1   China's Industrial Output by Ownership

Year	Total gross industrial output (100 million yuan)	SOE (% of total)	Non–state enterprises		
			Collective enterprises (% of total)	Individually owned (% of total)	Other types of enterprises* (% of total)
1985	9716	64.9	32.1	1.9	1.2
1990	23924	54.6	35.6	5.4	4.4
1991	26625	56.2	33.0	4.8	6.0
1992	34599	51.5	35.1	5.8	7.6
1993	48402	47.0	34.0	8.0	11.1
1994	70176	37.3	37.7	10.1	14.8
1995	91894	34.0	36.6	12.9	16.6
1996	99595	36.3	39.4	15.5	16.6
1997	113733	31.6	38.1	17.9	18.4
1998	119048	28.2	38.4	17.1	22.9
1999	126111	28.2	35.4	18.2	26.1

Notes: * 'Other Types of Enterprises' include foreign investment firms and Sino–foreign joint ventures.

Source: National Bureau of Statistics, 2000.

In general, SOEs are more pollution-intensive (i.e. they generate more pollution per unit of output) than other plants as a consequence of their lower operating efficiency (Wheeler et al., 2000). However a recent study by the World Bank found that town and village enterprises (TVEs) alone (among the non-state enterprises) increased their combined pollutant emissions by about 120 per cent between 1990 and 1995, while emissions from SOEs actually declined by 9 per cent (World Bank, 2001). If this can be explained by the decline in SOEs, industrial output share, it also reveals the difficulties in regulating the dynamic and fast growing non-state sector. Major industrial polluters and in particular those still retaining the status of SOEs are easier to regulate because they are stationary, relatively easy to identify and more amenable to pollution control than smaller polluters, such as the TVEs. These are characterised by dispersal through rural areas, small scale, low resources and energy efficiency and relatively obsolete industrial facilities (Xu et al., 2001). These aspects make the environmental control and improvement of TVEs a complex and challenging task for the county-level environmental protection bureaux, on which the environmental management responsibility of TVEs rests.

Since 1996 the government has taken action to shut down small operations in 15 sectors (such as chemical paper pulp–making, leather processing and dye production) that have been identified as the most polluting plants (Guo, 1998).

Despite more than 65 000 small factories having been shut down across the country by the end of 1997 for environmental reasons (Lei, 2002), it appears that this kind of measure might be socially disruptive and could not provide the basis for a long term approach.

Another important effect of the economic reform has been the modification of the sectoral composition of the industrial output in favour of light industries (such as electronics and household appliances) which tend to use fewer raw materials and to produce less pollution per unit of output. Although the industrial structure is still skewed towards relatively polluting upstream manufacturing units, the economic growth seems to favour less polluting industries (Wheeler, 2000; World Bank, 2001). This is proved by the fact that, during the 1989–99 period, industrial pollution loads[2] increased at a much lower rate than industrial output, and actually declined after 1995 (World Bank, 2001). This was the result of the changes in the sectoral output and its ownership but the environmental measures implemented by the government since the early nineties have also played an important role. Although much of the work necessary for significant reduction of industrial pollution intensity still remains, industrial restructuring is expected to expand the share of less polluting and high value-added manufacturing industries, with a consequent reduction of the overall environmental impact.

2.2. Population Growth and Mobility

Although there is a growing recognition of the important linkages between population and environment, our understanding of exactly how population size and growth rate, environmental change and development interact is still not well established (UN, 2001).

The relationship between China and its environment is marked by a limited amount of per capita natural resources and an uneven distribution of its population. In 2002 China's population reached 1.284 billion (ADB, 2003) despite its growth rate slowing down as a consequence of the nation-wide compulsory family planning programme. It is estimated that it will increase by another 260 million within the next three decades (Heilig, 1999). Today China's population comprises more than 20 per cent of the world total. Although China is the third largest country in the world in terms of size of its territory, it is relatively poor in natural resources and the ratio between resources and population is much lower than the world's average. In fact, the country has only 7 per cent of the world's arable land and fresh water, 3 per cent of the forests and only 2 per cent of the oil (Wong, 1999). In addition the population is unevenly distributed, with more than 90 per cent living in the south-east in little more than 30 per cent of the country's land area (Heilig, 1999).

More than twenty years of economic reforms seem to have further exacerbated this uneven distribution by relaxing the strictly controlled internal migration that, until 1978, prevented people from moving between regions and in particular from rural to urban areas. The eastern coastal areas, favoured by booming economic growth and characterised by an increasing demand for unskilled labour, are the ones that receive most migrants. They are becoming even more densely populated (Cook, 2000). Migration is one of the major driving forces behind China's increasing urban development. In 1990 only 27.4 per cent of the population was living in urban areas, in 2001 the percentage increased to 37.7 (ADB, 2003) and it is estimated that it will reach 55 per cent by 2025 (UN Population Division, 2003). Table 2.2 provides the general picture of the urban growth occurred in the last decade at various administrative levels.

Table 2.2   Urban Growth in China

	1991	1999
Number of cities, of which:	479	667
Super large (>2 million)	9	13
Very large (1–2 million)	22	24
Large (0.5–1 million)	30	49
Medium (0.2–0.5 million)	121	216
Small (<0.2 million) 297 365		
Number of 'administrative towns'*	10 000	17 341

Notes: * The term 'administrative town' indicates the urbanised part of the administrative unit known as a township.

Source: World Bank 2001.

As it is largely recognised in the literature (Jiang, 2000; Heilig, 1999; Kirkby, 1994), data on city growth are highly problematic in China due to inconsistencies in the Chinese classification systems for urban, rural and city populations. Despite this, there is little doubt, as illustrated by the table, that the bulk of urban growth occurred in medium- to small-size cities, most notably in townships which increased from about 10 000 in 1991 to more than 17 000 in 1999. This trend has important implications for the state of the urban environment. Medium- and small-size cities are in fact generally less equipped with financial and human resources to deal with rapid economic growth and its environmental consequences (World Bank, 2001). This represents a further challenge for both local and national authorities who are already struggling with a growing demand for resources and with increasing emissions from consumptive and productive activities by the urban population. Priority issues for urban areas are represented by: air pollution, wastewater treatment, solid waste management and urban encroachment on arable land.

Growing levels of urbanisation are increasingly eroding agricultural areas. It is estimated that, between 1987 and 1995, nearly 1 million hectares of cultivated land were taken by urban infrastructure development and expansion. This represents about 20 per cent of all cultivated land which were lost or converted during that period (World Bank, 2001). The agricultural land losses have been particularly relevant along Chinese coastal regions where the bulk of the population is concentrated and where urbanisation has been more widespread. Unfortunately the land around the cities is the best and the most productive. As urbanisation increases, maintenance of a sufficient extension of cultivated land will become considerably more difficult and will pose a serious threat to sustainable agriculture, thus affecting not only the existing population, but possibly many generations to come (Xu, 2000).

2.3. Energy Consumption

The huge demographic pressure together with the unprecedented economic growth experienced by the country during the last 25 years have transformed China into the second largest energy consumer in the world (EIA, 2003). Among the different energy sources, coal dominates both the consumption and the production patterns accounting for 66 per cent of the total energy consumption (see Figure 2.1) and 68 per cent of the total production respectively (NBS, 2003). Energy consumption, in particular coal but also the growing use of oil, is the main source of air pollution in China.

Figure 2.1   China's Energy Consumption (2002)

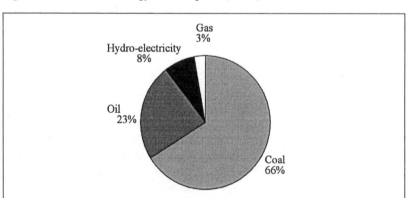

Source: National Bureau of Statistics, 2003.

It is well known that coal combustion produces several types of pollutant emissions, such as sulphur dioxide (SO_2), nitrogen oxides (NOx), particulates, along with carbon dioxide (CO_2), that adversely affect human health, the climate and the environment. Sulphur dioxide (SO_2) and particulate emissions are particularly severe in big cities where large amounts of fossil fuels are consumed for both industrial and domestic use. As a result, China's urban populations are exposed to a multitude of air pollutants, often at levels that are well above World Health Organisation (WHO) guidelines. Despite coal output in China having dropped precipitously since 1997,[3] it is still the most abundant energy source in China (China's resources are second only to Russia) and it is expected to continue to supply the bulk of China's energy demand for several decades to come.

Clearly, China is bound to increase its energy consumption in order to sustain its rapid economic growth. In this respect, the key question China is facing is not whether increased energy consumption is necessary but rather whether this increase could be met in an energy-efficient and environmentally sensitive way. The immediate challenge for the Chinese energy planners is to develop cleaner coal technologies, to broaden the energy source supply and to expand the renewable energy share in China's long-term economic and environmental interest.

3.   CHINA ENVIRONMENTAL PROBLEMS: AN ASSESSMENT

China's environmental problems derive from both *resource depletion* and *resource degradation*. Both processes are reasons for serious concern in China because they represent the quantitative and qualitative exhaustion of those natural resources that are an important source of revenue and of quality of life. The rest of this section will provide a brief overview of the two most serious environmental concerns in China: air and water pollution.

3.1.   Air Pollution

China has long recognised air pollution as one of the most critical environmental problems in the country (People's Daily Online, 2000; SEPA, various years). A report released in 1998 by the World Health Organisation pointed out that of the ten most polluted cities in the world, seven can be found in China.

The quality of the air can be affected by potentially harmful gases and particles that are emitted into the atmosphere on a global scale. The WHO distinguishes between six key air pollutants that can cause risks for human health: carbon monoxide (CO), lead, nitrogen dioxide (NO_2), suspended particulate matter (SPM) – including dust, fumes, mists and smoke – sulphur dioxide (SO_2) and ozone (O_3) (WHO, 1999). Measured by the frequency and degree of non-compliance with standards put forward by both the WHO and the Chinese State Environmental Protection Administration, total suspended particulates are China's most significant air pollutant, followed by sulphur dioxide (SO_2). Table 2.3 compares the concentrations of several air pollutants in different Chinese cities with other cities world-wide which have a similar population.

Table 2.3   Air Pollution in Main Chinese Cities versus World Cities

City	City population (thousands, 2000)	TSP* (1998, µg/m³)	SO_2 (1998, µg/m³)	NO_2 (1998, µg/m³)
Shanghai	12 887	246	53	73
Calcutta	12 918	375	49	34
Tokyo	26 444	49	18	68
Beijing	10 839	377	90	122
Delhi	11 695	415	24	41
Osaka	11 013	43	19	63
Chongqing	5 312	320	340	70
Toronto	4 651	36	17	43
Shenyang	4 828	374	99	73
Milan	4 251	77	31	248
Madrid	4 072	42	24	66
Taiyuan	2 415	568	211	55
Athens	3 116	178	34	64
Lanzhou	1 730	732	102	104
Stockholm	1 583	9	3	20

Notes: * TSP = Total Suspended Particulates.

Sources: Extracted from World Bank, 2002a.

The concentrations of both particulate matters and SO_2 in China are well above those of western cities. In some cases, like Taiyuan and Lanzhou, they exceeded the WHO guidelines until recently by nearly 10 times.

Table 2.4 provides instead an international comparison of national and per capita emissions of carbon dioxide (CO_2). Concentrations of CO_2, the most

Table 2.4   China's CO_2 Emissions in an International Comparison (2001)

Country	CO_2 emissions (million metric tons of carbon equivalent)	CO_2 emission as % of the world's total	CO_2 emission per capita (metric tons carbon equivalent)
USA	1 565.31	23.8	5.51
China	831.74	12.7	0.65
Russia	440.26	6.7	3.05
Japan	315.83	4.8	2.48
India	251.33	3.8	0.25

Source: Energy Information Administration, 2003.

prominent greenhouse gas (GHG) in the earth's atmosphere, have remarkably increased in the past century due mainly to fossil fuel burning (IPCC, 2001). This is rising concerns for an increase in the average temperature of the Earth (IPCC, 2001). As the table clearly shows, China is the world's second largest emitter of CO_2 contributing 12.7 per cent of the world's total. It is superseded only by the USA, which is responsible for 23.8 per cent of the total emissions.

Despite the seriousness of these international comparisons, since 1997 there has been a significant reversal in both local and global air pollution in China. SEPA notes that, although the overall pollution level remains very high, the trend of air quality worsening in China has somehow slowed down and the air quality of some cities is actually improving (SEPA, 2002). According to some analysts, reported emissions of both sulphur dioxide and particulates declined by over 20 per cent from their peaks in the mid-1990s (Logan, 2001; ESMAP, 2003), while carbon dioxide emissions have declined by 17 per cent since 1997, despite economic growth of 36 per cent over the same time period (see Figure 2.2).

Figure 2.2   China's GDP at Market Exchange Rates and CO_2 Emissions

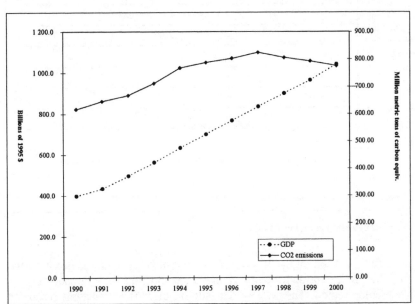

Source: EIA, 2003.

These reductions in air pollutants emissions reveal a break from previous trends and are unprecedented for any developing economy (NRDC, 2001). Most of the decline is due to a consistent drop in coal use resulting mainly from economic reforms and the closure of small, inefficient factories, power plants, and coal mines (Logan, 2001). Whether this trend can be maintained in the following years or even in the long term remains to be seen especially as other sources of air pollution are growing fast.

Since 1986, the number of motor vehicles on China's roads has increased by five times (compared to 28 per cent world-wide) reaching a total of 18 million in 2001, with 4.2 million cars (Zhao and Gallagher, 2003). Although China, with 12 vehicles per thousand people, is still at the beginning of its development as a mobile society, the current industrial development policies, together with income improvements, are pointing to high growth in personal vehicle ownership and associated environmental problems in the foreseeable future.

Figure 2.3   China's Vehicle Growth (1987–2002)

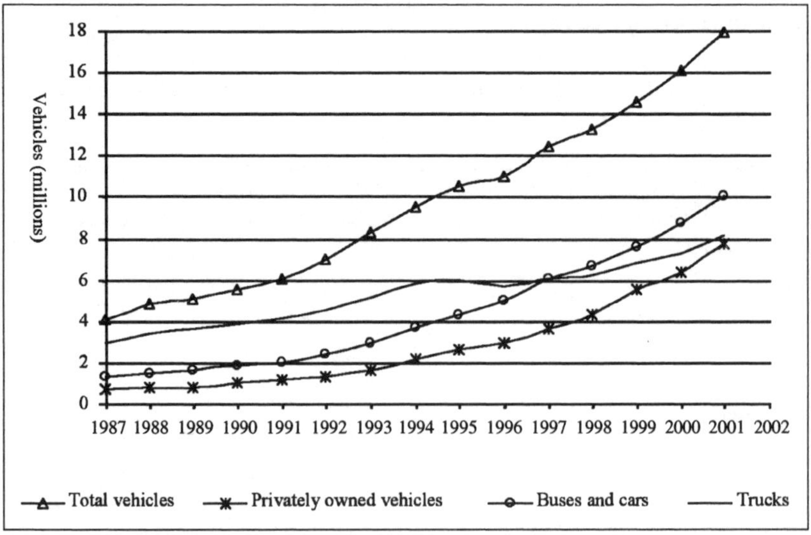

Source: Zhao and Gallagher (2003).

A further strain on China's efforts to control air pollution is given by the fact that the extent and type of air pollution in China vary dramatically by geographic region. This largely depends on the different natural resources endowments as well as on the degree of development reached by each region. Sulphur dioxide and particulate emissions are particularly high in the northern half of the country, where coal is extensively burned for both domestic and industrial uses.

3.2. Water Scarcity and Pollution

China's water is reason for serious concern for local and national authorities and it is mainly affected by two problems: shortage and pollution.

Table 2.5   China's Water Resources in an International Comparison, 1995 (cubic metres)

Country	Annual renewable resources	Water per capita
Canada	2901	98462
Brazil	6950	42957
Russian Federation	4498	30599
United States	2478	9413
China	2812	2292
Northern China	405	750
Southern China	2278	3440
India	2085	2228
World	41022	7176

Sources: World Bank, 1997.

China has a total of 2800 billion cubic metres of annually renewed fresh water and, as a country, it is sixth in terms of total water resources (see Table 2.5). However it is poor on a per capita basis with less than one third the world average (World Resources Institute, 1999). Water resources are also unevenly distributed: northern China is especially water-poor, with only one-fifth the per-capita water resources available in the South. Moreover, the rapid economic growth in the last decades has worsened the water shortage by increasing the demand for water. According to the World Bank, '... between 1980 and 1993, urban water consumption increased by 350 per cent and industrial water consumption doubled' (World Bank, 2001).

The constant and excessive extraction of groundwater has led to the dropping of the water-tables and land subsidence. The situation is so critical that it has forced the central government to establish two surface subsidence monitoring networks focusing on the Yangtze river delta and the North China plain, respectively (People's Daily Online, 2003). Ground subsidence is also creating significant economic losses. The People's Daily estimates that: 'Shanghai alone has suffered direct economic losses of 290 billion yuan (US$35.1 billion) in the last 40 years from destructive tidal waves, floods and other surface subsidence-related disasters' (People's Daily Online, 2003).

Only the seriousness of China's air pollution equals the poor quality of its water. Figure 2.4 shows water quality on the seven main Chinese rivers[4] in 2001. The State Environmental Protection Administration has defined five categories of freshwater quality standards. Grades I, II, and III permit direct human contact, while Grade IV is restricted to industrial use and Grade V is limited to irrigation; both Grades IV and V are deemed unsuitable for direct human contact. Each Grade sets a quality standard by specifying the maximum concentration of a certain number of pollutants. Exceeding the concentration standards for a given Grade disqualifies the measured water body from being designated as that Grade. The data (which are expressed in terms of the percentage of the water samples falling in the different Grades) illustrate the significant incidence of Grades IV and above. They confirm the poor quality of Chinese water. Although the percentage of samples falling in the first three Grades has increased through time (World Bank, 2001), the bulk of the samples (more than 70 per cent) are still concentrated in Grades IV and above.

Figure 2.4   Water Quality Trends in the Seven River Basins

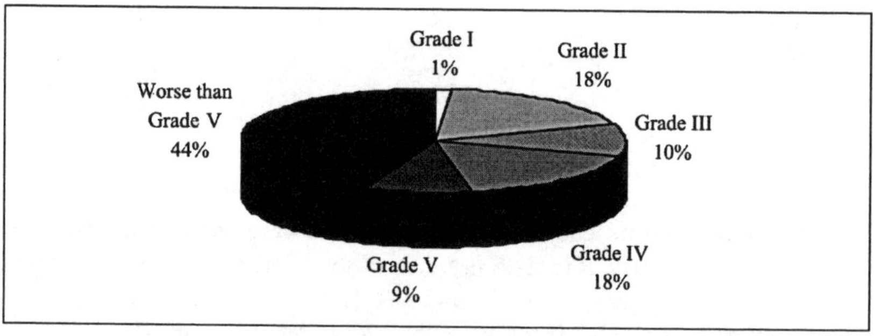

Source: SEPA, 2002.

As a developing nation, China lacks treatment plants and the infrastructure to properly treat sewage and purify drinking water. It is widely reported in the literature that only limited percentages of household and industrial wastewater receive any treatment before entering local irrigation ditches, ponds, lakes, and streams (Wu et al., 1999; Curry et al., 2003; Tsakok, 2003). The problem is particularly acute for medium- to small-size cities and for administrative towns that have witnessed an extraordinary growth in recent decades, but that are also less equipped with modern technology and human resources to face the mounting environmental problems. The difficulties experienced by city authorities in the management of water resources are illustrated by Table 2.6, which offers a picture of the evolution through time of wastewater flows and COD loads in China.[5]

The picture that emerges from the figures is clear: while wastewater from the industrial sector declined during the 1990s, that from municipal sources nearly doubled in the same span of time. Treatment of municipal polluted water lags far behind that of industrial wastewater, largely because of the inability of urban authorities to keep pace with growth and to coordinate economic development and environmental protection. Government officials

Table 2.6   Wastewater Flows and COD Loads in China

Wastewater source	Wastewater flows (million cubic meters)		Chemical Oxygen Demand (COD) (million tons)	
	1991	1992	1991	1999
Industrial	27 089	19 730	10.4	6.9
Municipal	10 020	20 377	4.0	7.0
National total	37 108	40 107	14.4	13.9

Sources: World Bank, 2001.

and enterprise managers often ignore environmental costs and benefits, as the yardstick of their achievements has been largely confined to the economic growth index. They are often reluctant to assess whether their growth strategy could be sustained and use the excuse of a 'developing economy' to escape the restraints of laws and regulations (Guo, 1998). Poor urban management of water is certainly one important factor in determining water quality but it is not the only one. Inappropriate use of chemical fertilisers and pesticides in rural areas, petroleum leaks and spills and other agricultural chemicals that are washed off from farm fields are also important elements of contamination.

4.   ARE ENVIRONMENTAL PROBLEMS THE PRICE CHINA MUST PAY FOR ITS FUTURE DEVELOPMENT?

The picture that has emerged in the previous pages leaves two important questions open:

1. Are pollution and the degradation of resources the price that China must continue to pay to ensure future generations' economic prosperity?
2. Given the many pressing needs that China is facing, how strongly should China respond to the environmental challenge? Does it make economic sense to tighten pollution control?

4.1.   Is Pollution the Unavoidable Price of Development?

The question of to what extent increases in economic activity affect the natural environment is a central one in economic development and environmental literature. A common approach consists in correlating a measure of environmental degradation against a measure of economic activity (normally the per-capita income). Studies that follow this approach (commonly known as environmental Kuznet curve literature) suggest that the relationship between environmental degradation and economic growth has an inverted U-shape where pollution from different sources initially increases with the level of per-capita income, reaches a maximum and then declines with further increases in per-capita income (Figure 2.5 illustrates the concept).[6]

Figure 2.5   The Environmental Kuznet Curve

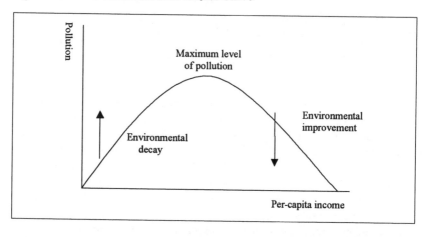

The empirical evidence emerging from this literature is not unequivocal and estimates of the per-capita income at which the different types of pollutants start to decline vary considerably between studies.[7] An important implication for developing countries is that they are nowhere near the income ranges associated with maximum pollution in the environmental Kuznet curve approach. If the findings of this approach are taken literally these countries are still too poor to be green, and an increase in their per-capita income will imply declining environmental quality for the foreseeable future. Fortunately emerging evidence demonstrates that this is not necessarily the case. A recent study by Dasgupta et al. (2002) provides some strong evidence that developing countries '... may be able to develop from low levels of per capita income with little or no degradation in environmental quality, and then at some point to experience improvements in both income and environmental quality' (Dasgupta, 2002). The study, whose evidence is mainly from China, does not reject the inverted U-shape curve but explains how the environmental Kuznet curve can become lower and flatter under the combined effect of economic liberalisation, improved information and more stringent pollution regulation. These findings are not isolated. China's recent reduction in air pollutant emissions could also be taken as an example. Although it may still be too early to say that the net sulphur dioxide emissions have peaked in China, it is important to notice that these reductions occurred at income levels far lower than the ones indicated in the environmental Kuznet curve literature for reduction in SO_2 concentrations.

What the above findings seem to suggest is that environmental improvements are possible in developing countries and that peak levels of environmental degradation can be reached at income levels lower than in countries that developed earlier. Hence, pollution is not necessarily the price that developing countries, and China in particular, should pay to develop further. A cleaner development path, as will be illustrated in more detail in the last section of this chapter, could be achieved by implementing not only a strong environmental regulatory regime but also, and most of all, by building the capabilities needed to select, absorb and develop technologies that lie outside the conventional pollution–intensive path (Perkins, 2003).

4.2. Is Environmental Improvement Desirable and Cost-effective?

Air and water pollution have a price which can be measured in terms of failed crops, ruined land, illnesses, and lost work time. According to a report published by the World Bank in 1997: '... the damages of excessive pollution – in the form of premature deaths, sickness, and damage to productive resources and urban infrastructure – are estimated to cost the Chinese about 8 per cent of GDP' (World Bank, 1997). As serious as they might seem, World Bank's estimates could well be an underestimate. Other findings suggest in fact that economic costs associated with ecological destruction and environmental pollution have reached as high as 14 per cent of the country's gross national product in recent years (Wu Changhu, 1999). Regardless of the exact figure, what really matters is that either estimate would effectively rule out recent economic growth which has remained above 7 per cent since 1995.

These costs are high, but even higher is the annual toll that China is paying in terms of physical damage. Table 2.7 offers a World Bank estimate of the number of deaths and diseases associated with air pollution among urban populations (World Bank, 1997). Using Chinese standards for air quality as a benchmark, they estimate the number of deaths that could be prevented if air pollution was reduced to those levels. According to their calculations, approximately 289 000 deaths (occurring both indoors and outdoors) could be prevented each year.

Wheeler et al. (2000) made a cost–benefit assessment of abatement costs for several air and water pollutants in five Chinese cities. They developed three scenarios which project pollution damage under varying assumptions about future policies. The three scenarios include: economic reform without pollution regulation being tightened and economic reform with tightened regulation where a 5 and a 10 per cent increase in air and water pollution levies are both tested. The study's assessment reaches two important conclusions:

1. Economic reform, and in particular reform-induced changes in sectoral composition, ownership and scale of production, should have a

Table 2.7   The Human Cost of Air Pollution in China

Problem	Number of cases averted annually
Urban air pollution	
Premature deaths	178 000
Respiratory hospital admissions	346 000
Asthma attacks	75 107 000
Chronic bronchitis	1 762 000
Restricted activity days	4 537 000
Indoor air pollution	
Premature deaths	111 000
Respiratory hospital admissions	220 000
Asthma attacks	47 755
Chronic bronchitis	1 121 000
Restricted activity days	2 885 000

Sources: World Bank, 1997.

considerable effect in reducing pollution intensity in China even without tightened pollution regulation. According to their findings for 2020, '... organic water pollution will stabilise in many areas and actually decline in some. Air pollution will continue growing in most areas, but at a much slower pace than industrial output' (Wheeler et al., 2000, p. 29).

2. Lack of action on regulation has an unnecessarily high cost in terms of serious respiratory damages and deaths from air pollution. Stricter regulation of air emissions in heavily-polluted areas is not only possible but very cost-effective. The study suggests that even a fifty-fold increase in the levy suggested by SEPA to cut down air pollution appears warranted from an economic perspective. Furthermore abatement of particulates from large non-state plants is so cheap that even an extremely conservative economic analysis confirms the benefits of very high abatement levels.

The Wheeler et al. study provides further evidence that pollution damage can be reduced even in developing countries, and in China in particular, and that tighter regulation of air emissions is a very cost-effective option for public health improvement. These findings are confirmed by Anderson who conducted a similar study on the effects of environmental policy on emissions in India (Anderson, 2002). The results of his simulation show that, if policies to encourage the emergence and use of clean technologies are introduced in India at the current level of income, the resulting positive externalities are likely to be appreciable and '... would well justify India introducing tax and regulatory incentives to support the development and use of the [clean] technologies' (Anderson, 2002, p. 30).

5. THE WAY AHEAD

What the previous section suggests is that not only are environmental improvements possible even at low levels of income, but also that the associated costs would not be prohibitive. However meeting the objectives of clean development in China, and in general in industrialising countries, is likely to be a challenging and complex process.

China is aware that the 'pollute first, clean-up later' approach is no longer possible and it is indeed taking greater corrective actions to change the emphasis from a quantitative development to a more qualitative one (ACCA21, 1995).[8] However, putting China on a sustainability path is certainly an opportunity to be grasped but also a great challenge. A major problem arises not from the lack of regulations that superintend environmental protection, but from their enforcement. Compliance with environmental regulations remains low (World Bank, 2001), mainly because economic development remains the country's top priority at all levels. Major problems arise from municipal and local authorities who are struggling to keep pace with rapid economic growth and who are generally reluctant to enforce environmental regulations which are perceived as adverse to economic growth indexes. Considerable challenges arise also from tight budget constraints and scarce diversification of the instruments applied to achieve environmental objectives.

Above all, achieving a cleaner path will ultimately require the ability to select, adapt and master clean technologies. This is a long-term process which requires ongoing policy support and guidance and goes beyond technology transfer for environmental protection. Imported technology in fact provides a crucial input into technological learning in China, as in many developing countries (Lall, 2002), but cannot be considered as a substitute for indigenous capability development.

Technology is often interpreted in the narrow sense of its hardware component. However, less polluting technologies can only be successfully absorbed and developed if 'soft' technological capabilities, such as training, institutions and infrastructures, are in place (Goldemberg, 1998). Furthermore, developing countries have needs for new technologies that are often different from those of already industrialised countries and measures to promote technological upgrading are bound to fail if they are not tailored to local circumstances. Recent studies (IPCC, 2000; Perkins, 2003) suggest that the development of technologies and capabilities for cleaner industrialisation in developing countries could be supported by two broad sets of policies, defined by Perkins as:

1. Functional interventions to create a macro-environment favourable to technological learning and innovation. These include, among others: the

provision of education and training systems; basic infrastructures and the creation of a conductive financial and legal environment that could make learning investments attractive.

2. Selective interventions needed to support clean development in sectors identified as playing a key role in a country's strategy.

China is already a favourable theatre for the indigenous development of clean technology capabilities. Rising energy demand and energy related emissions, together with increasing concerns for the dependence of oil supply from abroad are important drivers to promote less polluting energy solutions. The increasing percentage of students who enrol each year in tertiary education and attend technical courses is providing the country with substantial numbers of scientists and engineers (see Table 2.8), a crucial factor in mastering technological advancements for clean industrialisation.

Table 2.8   Investing in Domestic Technology Capability

	Gross tertiary enrolment ratio (%) (%)		Share of tertiary enrolment in science, maths and engineering (%), 1994–1997
	1980	1997	
Japan	30.5	47.7	23
United Kingdom	19.1	59.5	29
United States	55.5	72.6	17.2
Brazil	11.1	16.5	23
China	1.7	12.6	53
India	5.2	10.5*	25

Notes: * Refer to the most recent data available within two years of the year indicated.

Source: Figures for gross tertiary enrolment, World Bank, 2002b. Other data: UNDP, 2001.

Furthermore, China's ability to attract high inflows of foreign investment could be used as an instrument to develop less polluting technologies. Specific policies could in fact be designed to attract foreign investors with the ability to develop clean industrial production and processes.

6.   CONCLUSIONS

Since 1978 China has experienced a relatively sharp conflict between environment and development, where the emphasis has been more on the quantity rather than on the quality of development. This chapter has argued that adopting less polluting technologies is possible and a clean environment should not be considered a luxury, but a viable and cost-effective strategy.

However, increasing inputs into ecological and environmental protection in the short term, despite being a worthwhile policy goal, is likely to be a challenging process. Cleaner development could be achieved by implementing and enforcing a strong environmental regulatory regime but, most of all, by building the capabilities needed to select, absorb and develop technologies that lie outside the conventional pollution-intensive path. After all, the reasons why some developing countries have been more successful than others in developing diverse technological capabilities and in approaching innovation frontiers are various, but certainly national education systems, industrial relations, technical and scientific institutions, government policies and cultural traditions seem to play a crucial role.

NOTES

1. The World Bank's report *China, Air, Land and Water* (2001) provides a far-reaching and detailed account of the impact of China's economic growth on its environment. Also the OECD (2002) gives a good overview of the same issue.
2. Industrial pollution loads are defined as indexed emissions of China's three major pollutants: Chemical Oxygen Demand (COD), sulphur dioxide and soot.
3. The recent trends in China's energy consumption and coal output are not covered in this chapter. Sinton and Fridley (2000) provides an excellent update of the topic.
4. The seven rivers are: the Yangtze river, the Pearl river, the Huaihe river, the Haihe and Luanhe rivers, the Liaohe river and the Songhuajiang river.
5. The Chemical Oxygen Demand (COD) test is used to estimate the amount of organic matter in a sample and it is used as a measure of water quality.
6. The literature on the environmental Kuznet curve is abundant. Stern et al. (1996) and Stern (2003) provide a good review of the most significant contributions together with a critique of their theoretical approach and empirical findings. Other useful reviews and summaries are provided, among others, by de Bruyn and Heintz (2000) and Rothman and de Bruyn (1998).
7. Anderson (2002) provides a summary of the different estimates of the per-capita incomes at which the peaks occur. In 1985 purchasing power parity prices they are in the ranges:
   $ 3 000 to $ 13 400 for sulphur dioxide
   $ 3 300 to $ 16 000 for suspended particulate matter
   $ 5 500 to $ 21 800 for nitrogen oxide
   $ 2 700 to $ 8 500 for dissolved oxygen in rivers.
8. For example, as far as air quality is concerned, China is adopting new specifications for pollution emissions from cars modelled after the European standards of the 1990s.

BIBLIOGRAPHY

Administrative Centre for China's Agenda 21 (ACCA21) (1995), 'Progress on China's Agenda 21', *CA21 Update*, **1**, November 20, http://www.acca21.org.cn/update1. html.

Anderson, D. (2002), *Population, Environment and Development in India – Can the Achievement of Economic Prosperity in India be Reconciled with Environmental Concern?*, Wellcome Trust India Project, Working Paper 2, London: London School of Economics.

Asian Development Bank (ADB) (2003), *Key Indicators 2003*, Manila: ADB.

Cook, Ian G. (2000), 'Pressures of Development on China's Cities and Regions', in Terry Cannon (ed.), *China's Economic Growth*, UK: Macmillan Press Ltd, pp. 33–55.

Curry, L., A. Eastman, and A. Koon Bok Ming (2003), 'Financing cross–border solutions for water and wastewater infrastructure', *The Sinosphere Journal*, **6** (2), November, 15–23.

de Bruyn, S.M. and R.J. Heintz (2000), 'The environmental Kuznets curve hypothesis', in van den Bergh, J.C. (ed.), *Handbook of Environmental and Resource Economics*, Cheltenham: Edward Elgar, pp. 656–77.

Dasgupta, S., B. Laplante, H. Wang and D. Wheeler (2002), 'Confronting the environmental Kuznets curve', *Journal of Economic Perspectives*, **16** (1), 147–68.

Energy Information Administration (EIA) (2003), *International Total Primary Energy and Related Information. Primary Energy Consumption*, http://www.eia.doe.gov/emeu/international/total.html#IntlConsumption.

ESMAP (Energy Sector Management Assistance Programme) (2003), *China: Air Pollution and Acid Rain Control. The Case of Shijiazhuang City and the Changsha Triangle Area.* http://wbln0018.worldbank.org/esmap/site.nsf/files/ESMAP–China–31Oct03.pdf/$FILE /ESMAP–China–31Oct03.pdf.

Goldemberg, J. (1998), 'Leapfrog energy technologies', *Energy Policy*, **26** (10), 729–41.

Guo, Rongxing (1998), *Chinese Economic Sustainability – Situation, problems and constraints*, Occasional Paper No. 10, Centre for East Asian and Pacific Studies, University of Trier, Germany.

Heilig, G.K. (1999), *Can China Feed Itself? A System for Evaluation of Policy Options*, http://www.iiasa.ac.at/Research/LUC/ChinaFood/argu/trends/trend_10.htm.

IPCC (2000), *Methodological and Technological Issues in Technology Transfer*, Cambridge: Cambridge University Press for the Intergovernmental Panel on Climate Change.

IPCC (2001), *Climate Change 2001: The Scientific Basis*, New York: Cambridge University Press. Ch. 3. http://www.grida.no/climate/ipcc_tar/wg1/index.htm.

Jiang, Leiwen (2000), *Population and Sustainable Development in China*, Amsterdam: Thela Thesis.

Kirkby, R.J.R. (1994) 'Dilemmas of Urbanisation: Review and Prospects', in Denis Dwyer (ed.), *China the Next Decades*, Harlow, UK: Addison Wesley Longman Limited, pp. 128–55.

Lall, S. (2002), *Science and Technology Policies in Southeast Asia*, 'Proceedings of the Strata Consolidating Workshop', Brussels, 22–3 April, http://www.cordis.lu/improving/strata/workshop.htm.

Lei, Zhang (2002), *Ecologizing Industrialisation in Chinese Small Towns*, PhD Thesis Wageningen University, the Netherlands.

Logan, J. (2001), 'China's Air Pollution Down Dramatically, But Can it Last?', *China E–News*, http://www.pnl.gov/china/polldown.pdf.

National Bureau of Statistics (NBS) (2000), *China Statistical Yearbook 2000*, Beijing: China Statistics Press.

National Bureau of Statistics (NBS) (2003), *China Statistical Yearbook 2003*, Beijing: China Statistics Press.

Natural Resources Defence Council (NRDC) (2001), 'Second analysis confirms greenhouse gas reduction in China', http://www.nrdc.org/globalwarming/achinagg.asp, 18 October.

OECD (2002), 'Environmental Priorities for China's Sustainable Development', in OECD, *China in the World Economy. The Domestic Policy Challenges*, Paris: OECD, pp. 579–622.

People's Daily Online (2000), 'China's Air Pollution Still Serious', 5 September, http://fpeng.peopledaily.com.cn/200009/05/eng20000905_49744.html.

People's Daily Online (2003), 'Cities sinking due to excessive pumping of groundwater', 11 December, http://english.peopledaily.com.cn/200312/11/eng20031211_130178.shtml.

Perkins, R. (2003), 'Environmental leapfrogging in developing countries: a critical assessment and reconstruction', *Natural Resources Forum*, **27**, 177–88.

Rothman, D.S. and S.M. de Bruyn (1998), 'Probing into the environmental Kuznet curve hypothesis', *Ecological Economics*, **25**, 143–5.

Sinton, J.E. and D.G. Fridley (2000), 'What goes up: recent trends in China's energy consumption', *Energy Policy*, **28** (10), 671–87.

State Environmental Protection Administration (SEPA) (2002 and previous years), *Report on the State of the Environment in China*, Beijing: Environmental Information Centre, http://www.zhb.gov.cn/english/SOE/soechina2001/.

Stern, D.I., M.S. Common and E.B. Barbier (1996), 'Economic growth and environmental degradation: the environmental Kuznets curve and sustainable development', *World Development*, **24**, 1151–60.

Stern, D.I. (2003), 'The Environmental Kuznet Curve', *Internet Encyclopaedia of Ecological Economics*, International Society for Ecological Economics, http://www.ecoeco.org/publica/encyc.htm.

Tsakok, Josephine M.H. (2003), 'Water management and infectious disease – Schistosomiasis in Hunan province', *The Sinosphere Journal*, **6** (2), November, 35–44.

United Nations (UN) (2001), *Population, Environment and Development*, New York: United Nations.

United Nations Development Programme (UNDP) (2001), *Human Development Report 2001. Making New Technologies Work for Human Development*, New York: Oxford University Press.

United Nation Population Division (UNPD) (2003), *World Population Prospects: the 2002 Revision Population Database*, http://esa.un.org/unpp/.

Wheeler, D., H. Wang and S. Dasgupta (2000), *Can China Grow and Safeguard its Environment? The Case of Industrial Pollution*, Centre for Research on Economic Development and Policy Reform, Working Paper No. 68, Stanford: Stanford University.

Wong, K.K. (1999), 'The Challenge of Sustainable Development', in David C.B. Teather and Herbert S. Yee (eds), *China in Transition. Issues and Policies*, Great Britain: Macmillan Press Ltd, pp. 171–93.

World Bank (1997), *China's Environment in the New Century: Clear Water, Blue Skies*, China2020 series, Washington, DC: World Bank.

World Bank (2001), *China: Air, Land and Water. Environmental Priorities for a New Millennium*, Washington, DC: World Bank.

World Bank (2002a), *World Development Indicators 2001*, Washington, DC: World Bank, http://www.worldbank.org/data/wdi2002/pdfs/table%203-13.pdf.

World Bank (2002b) *World Bank EdStats Database*, on line. http://devdata.worldbank.org/edstats/.

World Health Organisation (WHO) (1999), *Guidelines for Air Quality*, Geneva: World Health Organisation.

World Resources Institute (WRI) (1999), 'China's Health and Environment: Water Scarcity, Water Pollution and Health', *World Resources 1998–99*, Washington: WRI, http://www.igc.apc.org/wri/wr-98–99/prc2watr.htm.

Wu, Changhua, C. Maurer, Yi Wang, Shouzheng Xue and Devra Lee Davis (1999), 'Water pollution and human health in China', *Environmental Health Perspectives*, **107** (4), http://www.wri.org/health/prcwater.htm.

Wu Changhu (1999), 'The price of growth', *Bulletin of the Atomic Scientists*, September/October, **55** (5), 58–66.

Xu, Haigen, Liu, D. and Wu, H. (2001), 'Environmental regionalization for the management of township and village enterprises in China', *Journal of Environmental Management*, **63**, 203–10.

Xu, Haiqing (2000), 'Environment and China's entry to the WTO: urban sprawl', *The Sinosphere Journal*, **3** (3) Summer, 26–8.

Zhao, Jimin and K.S. Gallagher (2003), 'Clean vehicle development in China', *The Sinosphere Journal*, **6** (1), March, 20–28.

3. One, Two or Three Chinas? Evidence of Increasing Spatial Inequality from 1990 to 2000*

Vasco Molini

1. INTRODUCTION

Over the last 20 years, China has undergone rapid modernisation and steep economic growth. These important transformations have, however, not been homogeneously distributed across the country. Unlike in developed countries, regional inequality in China has risen in the past two decades. This is puzzling, as market oriented reforms started being implemented from 1978, and one would have expected these to facilitate resource flows that tended to equalise income and consumption across regions.

Recent research has demonstrated that high inequality is attributable to a large urban–rural income gap and growing macroregional (east/west/centre) or coastal inland disparity. The widening divide between rural and urban areas is a direct consequence of the urban-biased policies implemented before the reform period, but only from the 1980s did that divide become worrying, and assume a macroregional dimension. Since the end of the 1980s, per capita production and consumption started to diverge significantly across different macroregions, but also between rural and urban areas within provinces. At the end of the 1990s, the initially rich urban areas of coastal provinces were on average better off while the rural areas of interior provinces became relatively poorer. This chapter is an attempt to measure and understand the main determinants of rising inequality in China from 1990 to 2000.

2. METHODOLOGY AND DATA

Widening income disparity in China has been hotly debated in the last ten years. Analyses differ with regard to data interpretation, the methodology used, and even the type of data. Many authors have used stratified household surveys, provided by the World Bank or the Chinese government.

The problem with this type of data is the coverage. Most of the households accessible to researchers are representative of either urban (Fang et al., 2002) or rural areas, but not both. Some, more fully representative, surveys, are available only for few provinces (Chen et al., 1996) and with limited time series. We have decided to use a different approach, focusing our analyses on the average consumption data at provincial level, published by the Chinese State Statistical Bureau (SSB). It is widely recognised that in developing countries consumption data are more reliable, and have lower potential measurement errors (Deaton, 1997), than income data. This is particularly true in transition and developing economies, where most household income is not 'official', and in rural areas, where it is difficult to evaluate agricultural wages.

Two types of dataset for provincial per capita expenditures are provided by Chinese statistics: consumption per capita and living expenditures per capita. We used consumption per capita data first because real growth rates are available for rural and urban areas of every province. In China, in fact, the prices of goods are generally different in rural and urban areas. To obtain unbiased real consumption data, it is thus necessary to consider two different sets of prices for each province. Secondly, using consumption data, we included the value of housing and food subsidies, excluded in the computation of per capita living expenditures. By doing this, we obtained significantly higher results than the State Statistical Bureau (SSB) living expenditure data, and these higher results are closer to the real unobserved income data. The same dataset has been reconstructed by Kanbur and Zhang (2003), for 1952 to 2000. We limited our analyses to the period from 1990 to 2000.

Using rural average consumption data and urban average consumption data for 23 provinces, four autonomous regions (excluding Tibet) and three municipalities (Chongching is added to Sichuan province), weighted by population, we have been able to create a representative dataset that covers almost all rural and urban China[1] for ten years (with 58 observations each year). The definition of rural and urban areas is provided by the Chinese government.[2]

Of course, this level of data aggregation misses some important information. The inequality within each rural and urban area of every province is not included in the analysis. However, this does not reduce the validity of the dataset. We can consider the level of inequality calculated to be the lower bound of total inequality in China. This is due to the type of sample selected, and the fact that generally consumption data show less variance than income data (Deaton, 1997). Other studies (Chang, 2002; Lee, 2000), based on household surveys or on county level data, show higher levels of inequality, but the same trend over time, and the same proportions between the observations.

We used Theil's entropy measurement as an inequality index, which belongs to the class of decomposable generalised entropy indexes proposed by Shorrocks (1984). Our purpose is not only to calculate the magnitude of inequality, but also to understand its determinants. Decomposition is a useful method to evaluate the contribution of various determinants of inequality (the urban–rural gap, the macroregions gap, ethnicity and so on) and helps the policy maker by giving a very precise map of disequilibria in a country. The formula of the index and of the group decomposition is:

$$GE\ (0) = I(y) = \sum_{i=1}^{n} f_i \log\left(\frac{\mu}{y_i}\right) \tag{3.1}$$

where y denotes the vector of per capita consumption; $f_i = P_i/P$, where P_i is the population of the ith province and P is the total population; y_i is the value of the ith observation of y; $\mu = \Sigma_i f_i y_i$ is the mean of y_i, $i = 1, 2 \ldots, n$.

The index is then decomposed

$$GE\ (0) = I(y) = \sum_{g=1}^{G} w_g I(yg) + I(\mu_1\lambda_1, \ldots \mu_0\lambda_0), \ \ldots\ w_g = \frac{n_g}{n} \tag{3.2}$$

where G is the number of sample subgroups; y_g is the sub-vector of y or the consumption of the gth subgroup; μ_g is the population–weighted mean of the observations of the gth subgroup; n_g is the number of observations in the gth subgroup; λ_g is an n_g vector of ones; and $I(y_g)$ is the inequality index of the gth subgroup.

The first term on the right-hand side of (3.2) is the weighted sum of the group-specific inequality indices, the within-group inequality. The second term is the between-group inequality (BE in the tables) or inter-group component of inequality. The difference between I(y) and the first term gives the value of the second term. The within–group inequality represents the spread of distributions in the subgroups; the between-group inequality indicates the gap between the group means.

The provinces are grouped by urban–rural (Table 3.1); macroregions (Table 3.4), i.e. east, centre, and west;[3] and rural and urban areas of macroregions (Table 3.3). In the case of Table 3.4, for example, each group g may include the observations of a given macroregion that is either east (g_1), centre (g_2), or west (g_3). Then $I(y_1)$, $I(y_2)$, $I(y_3)$ are the inequalities within the eastern, central,

Table 3.1   Theil's Index and Urban–Rural Decomposition, 1990–2000

Year	GE(0)	BE Urban Rural	Within Rural	Within Urban	Gini
1990	0.12547	78.7	18.0	3,3	0.275
1992	0.14591	80.4	15.2	4.5	0.296
1994	0.18429	80.2	15.0	4.8	0.332
1996	0.18804	76.8	17.5	5.7	0.336
1998	0.20659	79.0	14.9	6.2	0.35235
2000	0.22315	80.4	13.3	6.3	0.36384

Source: *Chinese Statistical Yearbook* data, author's calculations.

and western macroregions, respectively. The weighted sum, $w_1I(y_1) + w_2I(y_2) + w_3I(y_3)$ is the within-macroregions inequality while $I(\mu_1\,\lambda_1, \mu_2\lambda_2, \mu_3\,\lambda_3)$ is the between-macroregions inequality.

2.1. Rising Inequality at the National Level

Comparing the situations in 1990 and 2000, we can observe the important transformations that occurred in the country. In 1990, the Gini index[4] was around 0.275 (Table 3.1), a low level typical of socialist economies, and GE(0) was around 12.54, while in 2000 the former had increased by 32.4 per cent, and the latter by 78 per cent (Table 3.1). Analysing the trend, the shape is quasi-monotonic, the inequality grows at different rates over the period or stabilizes but never declines. Inequality grew dramatically from 1990 to 1994, when foreign direct investment (FDI) rose to its peak and reforms accelerated, then stabilised during the mid-1990s, and resumed positive growth in 1998.

Figure 3.1   Evolution of Average Consumption per Capita among Chinese Provinces

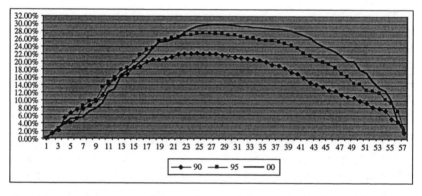

Notes: The curves here represent differences between the Lorenz curve and the 45° line, so that a lower curve corresponds to lower inequality.

Source: Our calculations based on *Chinese Statistical Yearbook* data (SSB).

As Figure 3.1 shows, the rate of growth of inequality was greater in the first half of the period than in the second. These results are consistent with other findings (Kanbur and Zhang, 1999, 2003), and the differences with the figures provided by other analyses are caused mainly by the use of different types of population definitions (compare Kanbur and Zhang, 2003 and endnote 2). As we will see later, the acceleration of state–owned enterprise (SOE) reform and the widening gap between the coastal provinces and the rest of the country caused the steep increase in inequality that occurred from 1998.

The general picture is an increased polarisation of consumption. The gap between the poorest and the richest increases, but in the middle the dispersion tends to widen as well. This implies that provinces which had a similar structure in 1990 have begun to show an increasing differentiation during the last decade. If we draw a normal distribution, we note that, by 2000, the standard deviation has increased by a factor of five, the distribution has flattened, and the median consumption has decreased to 67 per cent of the mean, compared to 71 per cent in 1990. Ninety per cent of the rural population (73 per cent of the total population) had a level of consumption under the mean in 1990; in 2000, this becomes 97 per cent, with a lower proportion of rural population (63 per cent). As the proportion of the total population with consumption under the mean remains around 65 per cent, it is clear that an increasing part of the urban population has started to have consumption levels lower than the mean. We now try to analyse the divergent forces that have worked behind this significant increase in regional inequality.

3. THE URBAN–RURAL DIVIDE

3.1. The Urban–Rural Divide before the 1990s

We first subgrouped our data into rural and urban, and then analysed the impact of rural and urban inequality on the total, as this dimension of inequality has always been dominant in the last 50 years (Kanbur and Zhang, 2003). Historically, industry-oriented development strategy has massively contributed to the increase of the divide. Pursuing a Soviet–style economic policy, based on the extraction of surplus from the agriculture sector in order to finance the embryonic industry, the government artificially lowered agriculture prices and hampered any form of labour mobility by imposing the household registration system (*hukou*). Urban areas had been favoured not only through planning, but also by *ad hoc* policies of subsidies, free housing, transfers and life-long employment. Although some attempts have been made to industrialise rural inland areas, path dependency condemned pre-reform China to a non-flexible (downward) urban–rural divide (Kanbur and Zhang, 1999, 2003). Moreover, since urbanisation varies across provinces, this divide translated immediately into a provincial divide (Yang, 2002).

Important changes occurred after the first wave of reforms. Immediately after 1979, and thanks to the introduction of the household responsibility system, agricultural output increased and the divide started to decline. The growth of Township and Village Enterprises (TVEs) played an important role in rural development. These small and medium enterprises, located in rural areas, helped first to absorb the agricultural labour force surplus creating higher productivity jobs and secondly increased the standard of living of a significant part of the rural population. During the golden period of TVEs, from 1985 to 1995 (Biggeri, 2001), the annual growth rate of gross output at constant prices was 24.7 per cent, with the number of employees increasing from 28 million in 1978 to 125 million in 1998.

However, most of the reform effects were short-lived. Upward pressure on urban prices and the increasing discontent of urban residents led the government to readjust the direction of the political economy. A set of new urban-biased monetary and fiscal policies were introduced, and the gap started to grow again. Yang (1999) argues that the increases in government expenditure and investment from 1986 to 1992 were disproportionately allocated to the urban sector. The share of the budget devoted to the urban sector, including SOE subsidies and all other expenses, ranged from 52 per cent to 62 per cent of total expenditure, for a share of the population of only around 24 per cent.

Monetary policies disadvantaged the rural population too. To control the high inflation of 1988/89, the government tightened investment credits to rural industries. As a direct consequence, many TVEs shut down, employment fell, and real rural output dropped by 3.66 per cent in 1989.

3.2. The 1990s Upturn

In the 1990s, the trend of the last part of the 1980s was consolidated. The rise of total inequality was accompanied by a widening of the urban–rural divide. On average, the urban–rural decomposition accounts for 80 per cent of total inequality (Table 3.1).

The rural population in 1990 had a share of 52 per cent of total consumption, and average consumption was one-third of urban consumption. The gap worsened in 2000, when rural mean consumption accounted for less than one-third of urban consumption (Table 3.2). The rural population, which by then had fallen to 63 per cent of the total, accounted for only 34 per cent of

Table 3.2   Urban–Rural Population and Average Per Capita Consumption, 1990–2000

Year	Location	Population Share	Average Consumption	Consumption Share
1990	rural	0.73	520.34552	0.52
1990	urban	0.26	1346.04468	0.47
1995	rural	0.70	1181.77710	0.43
1995	urban	0.29	3656.29468	0.56
2000	rural	0.63	2057.83740	0.34
2000	urban	0.36	6930.92334	0.65

Source: Our calculations based on *Chinese Statistical Yearbook* data (SSB).

total consumption (Table 3.2). Urban average consumption increased by a factor greater than four, while rural consumption rose by less than a factor of three over the period. Unlike the results of several authors (Kanbur and Zhang, 1999, 2003; Lee, 2000), our data confirm the key role still played by the urban–rural divide in explaining inequality.

There are several causes of the rural–urban divide. Chang (2002) argues that China is a typical example of a Lewis model economy, with a very modern urban sector, and an agricultural rural sector with an estimated 150 million units of surplus workers. While in the modern sector workers receive a wage close to their marginal wage, in agriculture the wage is close to subsistence level. This big divide is a natural consequence of the structure of the economy, and the only way to solve it is to expand the modern urban sector and encourage urbanisation.

Lu (2002), in explaining the causes of the urban–rural divide, agrees with this hypothesis. The author finds an inverse relationship between the urban–rural divide and per capita GDP in 1995. Using the Kuznets Williamson model (the inverted U-shape relation between growth and inequality), Lu affirms that urban–rural inequality is a temporary effect. At early stages of growth, the inequality tends to increase, but after a transition period, it decreases. Provinces with higher per capita income have a lower urban–rural divide.

The weak point of this analysis is the absolute faith in the autocorrective mechanism of the market, and the inability to predict the timing of corrections. The divide is actually generating a worrying social instability, and increasing mass migration from rural to urban areas. Many authors argue that this phenomenon, caused by the progressive relaxation of the *hukou* system, will in the long run have a positive effect on the urban–rural divide (Demurger et al., 2002; Lu, 2002; Kanbur and Zhang, 1999). As a matter of fact, inequality is attributed to the barriers to intersector reallocation of labour. Removing these barriers, and letting market forces operate, would permit the wage differential to decrease and rural unemployment to be absorbed.

Lu (2002) tries to quantify the labour market reallocation effect. Aggregate labour productivity growth is decomposed into sectoral growth of output per worker, and the Gross Allocation Effect (GAE), the contribution to aggregate labour productivity growth of employment shifts across sectors (primary, secondary and tertiary). Undertaking these calculations for all provinces over two subperiods (1990/95 and 1995/99), Lu finds interesting results. The GAE might be positive or negative, with the latter occurring when sectors with higher productivity fail to hire as many new workers as sectors with lower productivity growth. In the decomposition, the sign of the average provincial GAE is negative for the period 1995/99. This might mean that the industrial sector in this period did not absorb as much labour from agriculture as expected.

There are many causes for this result. Examples include SOE reform, and the introduction of more efficient labour-saving technologies. The key point, however, is that it is not guaranteed that the urban sector will create enough job opportunities to absorb the entire agriculture labour surplus. The Harris–Todaro (1970) model explains very clearly this empirical regularity of developing countries: rural to urban migration is persistent, despite the existence of widespread urban unemployment.

During this period of unemployment, or employment in the informal sector, migrants will not have any social welfare benefits, and will have lost the support of the traditional village structure. Thus, while from an economic point of view it may be correct to remove barriers, in a hypothetical social welfare function, it would be necessary to include the negative externalities of this decision. The lag in the absorption of the rural population might be too long and unsustainable; the mass migration would generate unexpected costs in infrastructure and housing, and environmental problems.

Lu (2002) obtains two other interesting results: provinces with higher per capita income tend to have more equal urban–rural consumption levels; and labour productivity gains from intersector labour mobility are only marginally significant in association with wider urban–rural consumption disparity, and more significant where the urban–rural divide is lower.

The positive correlation between per capita growth and decreased inequality between rural and urban areas does not imply that growth automatically generates a reduction in inequality. The 1999/2000 increase in the urban–rural gap in areas of the country with more relaxed controls on urban–rural migration and higher rates of growth (Table 3.3, east and central China) tells a different story.

Table 3.3 Theil's Index Calculated for Macroregions and Urban–Rural Decomposition, 1990–2000

	Year	GE(0)	BE Urban–Rural	Within Rural	Within Urban	Gini
East	1990	0.11249	79.2	16.4	4.4	0.25279
	2000	0.18973	83.2	10.5	6.3	0.32606
Centre	1990	0.10622	89.2	10.1	0.7	0.23464
	2000	0.16478	94.7	2.6	2.7	0.29360
West	1990	0.11187	92.1	7.3	0.6	0.22160
	2000	0.18967	90.9	8.4	0.6	0.30881

Source: *Chinese Statistical Yearbook* data, author's calculations.

3.3. The Importance of a Pro-rural Political Economy

It might be necessary to partially invert the direction of causality: the implementation of policies aimed to reduce the divide impacts positively on GDP. The richer, coastal (or eastern) provinces are the ones that historically were better endowed with infrastructure, and had dynamic urban areas linked to rural areas. In those provinces, the most successful policies to reduce the urban–rural gap were implemented: 55.3 per cent of TVEs and 60.2 per cent of the employees (Biggeri, 2001) are located in the east. In this part of the country, TVEs became, jointly with FDI, the engine of an export-oriented industrialisation. Rural industry produced a large proportion of China's exports, having started as a sub-contractor of foreign firms or SOEs.

Furthermore, most FDI in China up to now has been export oriented; FDI therefore prefers coastal provinces with easy access to sea transportation and links with local TVEs (Demurger et al., 2002). This rural industrialisation generated agglomeration effects and backward economic linkages that induced new rural enterprises (not necessarily export-oriented) to become established in eastern China. As a direct consequence, in 1990 the eastern urban–rural divide was the lowest of the three macroregions (Table 3.3). In central and western China, which are less favoured by geography, more urban-biased policies, such as investment in heavy industry, or subsidies to encourage Han Chinese to establish themselves in urban areas of Xinjian, have been pursued.

In our opinion, it is not correct to state that urbanisation and the support of the modern urban sector is the only solution. Experience has demonstrated that the creation of rural job opportunities and rural infrastructure (Fan et al., 2002) partially limited the mass migration of millions of peasants,[5] and also boosted GDP, establishing significant links between the modern urban sector and its rural counterpart. The second important result obtained by Lu (2002) shows that the lower the divide is, the more effective is the GAE. In coastal provinces, the presence of TVEs permitted the efficient reallocation of surplus labour from agriculture to more advanced sectors in the same rural area. Being in the same rural area helped not only the exchanges and interconnections between the two sectors, but also reduced the individual costs of mobility, such as moving house and leaving the village social security net, as well as the social costs.

The increase in the urban–rural divide at the end of the 1990s is thus the direct consequence of reduced efforts to lower that divide. The buoyant growth of China's industrial and service sector is severely urban-biased. Most economic activities are located in urban areas, prices and wages tend to grow faster, and urban areas offer generally more opportunities. While in the past central and local governments played a redistributive role, in particular urban to rural redistribution in the eastern provinces, during the 1990s this redistribution has been dramatically reduced, and a large part of investment has been focused only on the dynamic urban areas. In 1997, investment in electricity, roads, and telecommunications in rural areas accounted for only 19 per cent of government expenditure (Fan et al., 2002), while 50 per cent of GDP is produced by the rural sector. Moreover, the privatisation of TVEs led to the disengagement of local government from the management. This had an extremely positive effect on efficiency and productivity, but impacted negatively on the framework of rural society. Enterprises, in fact, abandoned their social roles (such as the creation of infrastructure, pension funds, and communal welfare programmes in housing and health care) in order to become private enterprises. The privatised firms, which produce 70 per cent of industrial output, now have to face all the problems of the private sector, such as cost reduction, finding credit, and facing strong competition that erodes profits. Between 1996 and 1998, the TVE sector underwent a minor recession, with a reduction in employment of 3.6 per cent per year (Biggeri, 2001).

3.4. Within Rural and Within Urban Inequality during the 1990s

The residual of the decomposition, around 20 per cent, is further decomposed into inequality within urban areas and inequality within rural areas. Inequality within rural areas is the largest component. Its relative contribution declines over the decade, in the face of a slight increase of inequality within urban areas (Table 3.1). In absolute terms, inequality within rural areas increased. In 1990, 68 per cent of rural provinces were below the rural consumption mean, but that became 71 per cent by 2000, with an increasing dispersion: the standard deviation increased by a factor of five and many provinces that were below but close to the mean clustered in the left-hand tail. In the rural areas, there is a clear macroregional divide, which we analyse in the following section. Six out of eight western rural areas belong to the ten poorest, while most of the richest are located in the east. This polarisation of the 1990s was consolidated in 2000.

In the urban sector, the standard deviation rose (by a factor of ten), but the situation of the poor improved: in 1990, 66.7 per cent of urban areas were below the urban mean, but in 2000 that fell to 63 per cent. Thirty-seven per cent of urban areas are above the mean and most of those areas are coastal provinces.

The macroregional diversification of urban areas is likely to be the direct consequence of the unbalanced development of the 1990s. In 1990, only a few coastal urban areas were richer than the central and western macroregions, while by 2000 almost all the richest urban areas belong to the eastern macroregion (except Hainan and Guanxi). These are followed by the central and then the western macroregions, even though some western urban areas are very close to the central ones.

Figure 3.2 provides a clear picture of the different performances of the urban and rural areas of the three macroregions. Compared to eastern rural

Figure 3.2 *Macroregional Average Consumption: the Urban–Rural Divide, 1990–2000*

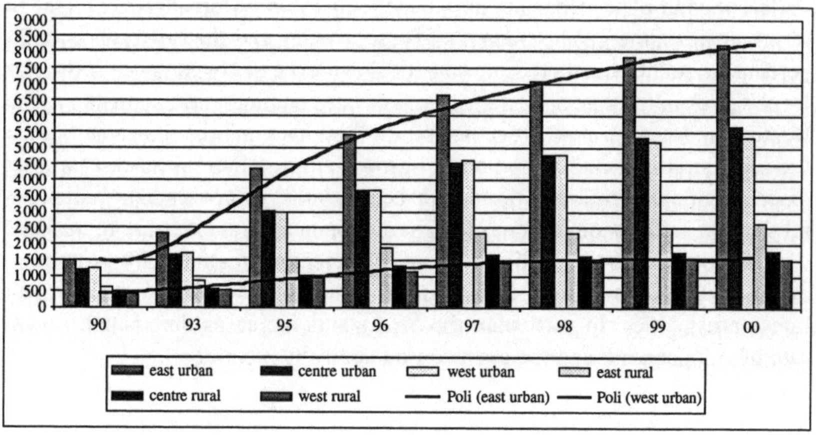

Source: *Chinese Statistical Yearbook* data, author's calculations.

areas, western rural areas show a sluggish trend, and in 2000 the disparity with central rural areas increased. The eastern rural area is the only rural area that might, in the long run, overcome the divide with less developed urban areas: in 2000 only the Beijing and Shanghai rural areas were richer than the central and western urban areas. The divide with coastal urban areas, however, is dramatically widening. Even though this astonishing development involved an increasing proportion of the population, urban coastal provinces account for less than 20 per cent of total population in 2000, and as we said before, we have limited information on the inequality within each province.

Two recent studies based on urban household surveys (UHS) shed light on a worrying situation in urban areas. Fang et al. (2002), studying urban poverty and inequality from 1992 to 1998, estimate that urban poverty first declined[6] from 13.74 per cent in 1992 to 8.41 per cent in 1996, but started to grow again as a result of urban reforms and increased unemployment, reaching 8.86 per cent in 1998, due to SOE reform. The main reason, stress the authors, is the increasing inequality that offset the positive effects of the rapid economic growth. The gains of growth, due to the loosening of redistributive policies and the inefficiency of safety nets, are not trickling down to the urban poor, in particular in western areas. There is a trade off between efficiency gain from a market reward system and worsening income distribution.

The abolition of the old welfare system has triggered a rapid increase in expenditure on education, healthcare and housing, making the poor more vulnerable to shocks. The authors calculate that, with a distribution of wealth at 1992 levels, the reduction of poverty from 1992 to 1998 would have been

42.28 per cent instead of 26.83 per cent. The increase in inequality has wiped out a potential 26.81 per cent more poverty reduction.

The second paper (Jones et al., 2003) focuses on different rates of growth of urban areas: the gap between the fastest growing and the slowest is over 24 percentage points and there is no statistical evidence of convergence at the city level. Cities in the east have higher growth rates and incomes compared to the western and central macroregions. While they have almost the same human capital, savings and population growth, cities in the east attract disproportionately more FDI, and are beneficiaries of government policies – all the Special Economic Zones (SEZs) and open coastal cities are in the east. The authors argue that policies giving preferential treatment by promoting openness (thus attracting FDI) account for most of the differences in growth rates across cities. In particular, the SEZ status increases the annual growth rate by 5.5 per cent, and the open coastal status by 3 per cent.

4. MACROREGIONAL INEQUALITY

4.1. Coastal Inland Divide or Macroregional Divide?

Our second step was to group the urban and rural provincial data into macroregions. We decided to decompose inequality into three groups (east, west, and centre), adopting the division proposed by the Chinese government. In our opinion, combining the west and centre into one unique inland area (Kanbur and Zhang, 1999, 2003) reduces the potential information available. The two areas show different characteristics regarding economic structure, infrastructure diffusion and level of urbanisation; nevertheless, before the mid-1990s, these differences, using consumption or GDP data, were not so clear. In a recent study on convergence between provinces in China from 1952 to 1997 (Zhang et al., 2001), the authors formulate the hypothesis of 'club convergence': divergence at national level but convergence between provinces belonging to the same macroregion.

First, the authors investigate whether there exists convergence between the three macroregions, but they reject this hypothesis. Secondly, they study the pattern of Chinese development. They identify the Cultural Revolution and the reform era as the structural break in the series that determined the divergence: the former impacted negatively on the east and accelerated the steep decline of the west; the latter widened the gap between the east and the other macroregions, and triggered the decline of the central region. Finally, analysing data on income distribution within each macro-region, the authors find robust evidence of divergence at national level, but convergence of each province to a regional steady state.

The divergence between the east and the other two groups is very significant, while the divergence between the centre and the west remained almost steady. The conclusions of the authors are that further study is needed to understand whether central provinces are joining the 'poor club' or will struggle to form their own 'club'.

A more robust support of the grouping into three macroregions is given by another study on convergence. Using a transition matrix derived from panel data of real rates of growth at provincial level from 1978 to 1998, Li (2003) demonstrates that there is a strong tendency to converge across provinces within macroregions, and that central and western provinces show a different pattern of growth. In 1978, the central provinces ranged from lower middle income[7] to highest income, with two thirds of them having incomes lower than the national average. In 1998, all the central provinces were clustered in the lower middle-income (four of them) or middle income (the remaining five) bracket. However, in 1978 two-thirds of the western provinces had real incomes below the national mean, while in 1998, seven out of nine were clustered in the lower middle income range, and one in the lowest. In conclusion, the comparison of the two regions shows that they are both worse off compared to the national average, but the relative decline of the western regions was more rapid and involved more provinces.

4.2. The New Dimension of Spatial Inequality and its Causes

Our data show a limited but constantly increasing gap between the western and central regions (Figure 3.2). The mean consumption of the two areas in 1990 was very close but diverged slightly over the decade, particularly in the second half of 1990s. The divide is clearer if we split the macroregions into rural and urban areas. The gap increased particularly in the rural areas, which accounted for about 70 per cent of the population of both macroregions: in 1990, western rural average consumption was 95 per cent of central average consumption, while in 2000 that had fallen to 83 per cent (Figure 3.2). In the urban areas in 1990, western average consumption was

Table 3.4   Theil's Index and Macroregional Decomposition, 1990–2000

Year	GE(0)	BE Macro-regions	Within east	Within centre	Within west
1990	0.12547	12.2	37.2	30.3	20.2
1992	0.14591	14.2	38.6	26.7	20.5
1994	0.18429	13.3	37.9	30.1	18.7
1996	0.18804	17.5	38.8	24.4	19.3
1998	0.20659	17.6	36.6	26.1	19.7
2000	0.22315	18.9	36.2	25.8	19.2

Source: Chinese Statistical Yearbook data, author's calculations.

higher than central average consumption, but in 2000, the situation became inverted.

Regarding the divergence between groups (Table 3.4), the increasing contribution of macroregion inequality to total inequality is clear. In the last decade, that contribution increased from 12.3 per cent of total inequality to 18.9 per cent in 2000, with a steep increase between 1994 and 1996 (Table 3.3). In 1990, 41 per cent of the total Chinese population was concentrated in the eastern region and controlled 50 per cent of total consumption, while the central region controlled only 31.5 per cent and the western region 18.5 per cent. In 2000, the distribution quickly worsened. The eastern population now accounts for 57 per cent of total consumption, compared to 28 per cent central and only 15 per cent western consumption. Even in terms of relative population, the decline of central and western provinces is continuing. Thanks to the loosening of the *hukou* system and to mass migration, the relative weight of the eastern population, and in particular the urban eastern[8] population, is increasing.

Calculating the average consumption by macroregion, we see that in 1990 western average consumption accounted for 67 per cent of eastern, and central 73 per cent of eastern. In 2000, the proportion changes drastically, with western falling to about 51 per cent and central to about 60 per cent of eastern mean consumption. In ten years, all three means have increased dramatically, but at different speeds: in the east, the mean has increased by a factor of 4.7, in the centre by a factor of 3.7, and in the west by a factor of three.

Looking at the causes of the increasing divide, we can distinguish between two groups: the natural or geographic, and the political. Geography has substantially influenced provincial income performance through two channels: agriculture and international trade. Most Chinese provinces, excluding the north-eastern, were agricultural economies with little diversification until the mid-1980s. The difference in land features, such as altitude and fertility, impacted on the performance of the provincial economy. Eastern (excluding some south-eastern) and some central provinces were better endowed with arable land (FASC NACO, 1999). Both groups have more rivers that are navigable and most eastern provinces are on the coast. The low cost of water transportation made these provinces the natural platform for producing and exchanging products.

When China reopened its doors to foreign exchange, the access to the sea allowed these provinces to take immediate advantage of the opening. Moreover, the eastern provinces were more urbanised than the central and western provinces. Demurger et al. (2002) attempt to estimate the role of geography in provincial income determination, and obtain important results. Topography is an important and significant determinant of province performance until 1978. Its coefficient decreased, while the proxies for easy coastal access[9] increased greatly in statistical significance and in magnitude after 1978. These results partially explain the increasing divide between all coastal provinces and some central provinces that were endowed with highly fertile land. The less that agriculture became relevant for the coastal provinces, the less topography determined economic performance.

After liberalisation, for example, the inland parts of the southern coastal provinces, characterised by rugged mountains, moved rapidly from agriculture to industry, performing better economically than the central provinces. After 1978, the proximity to the sea or to navigable rivers became, according to Demurger et al. (2002), the main determinant of high coastal growth, more than preferential policies, such as SEZs, implemented in these provinces. Finally, geographic location, as we stated above, explains why FDI is concentrated in these areas.

Many other contributions, without denying the role of geography, tend to blame unbalanced policies for the increasing macroregional inequality. Kanbur and Zhang (2003), for example, focus their attention on preferential policies. The creation of SEZs, and favourable tax breaks for coastal areas, inevitably speeded up the integration of coastal areas into the world market, but at the same time widened the coastal–inland disparity. Two solutions are proposed: the first, which is the more controversial, is to eliminate the preferences accorded to eastern provinces; the other, supported by many authors (Demurger, 2002; Kanbur and Zhang, 1999, 2003) is to extend preferential policies to the central and western areas. Demurger et al. (2002), for example, argue that 'preferential' is a misleading term and does not mean systematic subsidising, but rather deregulation and marketisation. The extension of this preferential treatment to other areas of the country is then possible without increasing public expenditure significantly.

The problem, we believe, is that at the outset, openness is insufficient. A significant investment in infrastructure is crucial too, and the latter in the last 50 years has been disproportionately concentrated in the eastern provinces.

The situation inherited after the revolution was an under-industrialised country, with most of the industry concentrated in the coastal areas. The Chinese leadership attempted, before 1978, to correct some clear imbalances between the three different areas of the country, but the results were controversial. The main guideline of Chinese policy was 'self-sufficiency'. Investment in infrastructure and industry was not guided by comparative advantage and economic efficiency, but by politics and security. The localisation of the military industry in the western provinces, for example, the so-called 'Third Front', was a completely uneconomic investment, and created an industrial complex that was disconnected from the local economy. The same attitude conditioned the development of transport. Before 1978, huge investments had been devoted to railways, and in particular, to connecting north-eastern industrial provinces with resource-rich provinces. This overlooked other modes of transport and within-province connections in less endowed areas, such as the western provinces (Demurger, 2001). The beginning of the reforms and in particular decentralisation, changed the sources of infrastructure funding (more local rather than central government expenditure was applied), and favoured investment more oriented to meeting the demand for public goods, but caused the concentration of infrastructure investments in coastal provinces.

Average transport network density in 2000, for example, reflects precisely the economic division of the country. In particular, the road network density, developed in the last 20 years, decreases from eastern to inland areas and from south-eastern to upper north–eastern provinces (Liaoning, Hebei, and Shandong). Public investment has also been severely coast-biased in irrigation, telephones, electricity, and human capital. Fan et al. (2002) estimated the impact of infrastructure investment on inequality and poverty in different areas of the country. In terms of poverty reduction, any investment in agricultural R&D, education, roads, telecommunication and electricity, would have a greater impact in the western provinces than in other areas of the country. Looking at inequality, and using agricultural, non-agricultural and total labour productivity of the three areas, they estimated the contribution of input factors to regional disparity. All the public investment in the western provinces would have a strong impact on inequality reduction. The gap (Fan et al., 2002) in agricultural productivity would reduce by 9 per cent upon investing 100 additional yuan per capita in education, and by 5 per cent when investing the same additional amount in agriculture R&D. The gap in non-agricultural productivity would be reduced by 40 per cent through investing 100 additional yuan in education, and by 6 per cent by investing the same additional amount in telephones. Now the problem is how to finance this *refocusing* of public investments.

The differing capacities of provinces to raise funds, and the reduced role played by central government, limit the capacity to redress the trend in the provision of infrastructure. Zhang et al. (1998) find a strong and significant negative correlation between decentralisation (measured as per capita budget and extra-budget local expenditures divided by central expenditures) and economic growth, suggesting that the process of decentralisation has been too quick compared to overall economic development in China. At the early stages of development, the central government is in a better position than local governments to undertake public investment with nationwide externalities, while local public investments are sometimes uncoordinated and overlapping. These results are consistent with an important section of public economics literature that underlines, for transition and developing economies, the risks of a decentralisation that is too accentuated and uncontrolled, in particular its negative impact on spatial inequality (Prud'homme, 1995).

There is an increasing consensus that macroregional (or coastal–inland) inequalities are becoming a key issue for the Chinese government. Their contribution to total inequality is limited compared to the urban–rural divide, but their contribution to *changes* in inequality has increased dramatically (Kanbur and Zhang, 2003).

However, there is no consensus on the main causes and solutions. Tsui (1996) blames the decentralisation process and the inability of central government to correct the disequilibria generated by coastal-biased growth. The solution might be a recentralisation of fiscal revenues and a more decisive role for the state in pump priming the economy in poor areas. Demurger et al. (2002), although they do not deny the important role played by this policy, tend to focus more on the geographic dimension and on the positive effects of liberalisation. The pro-coastal polices were important at the beginning, but now what makes these provinces successful is their openness and a positive attitude to the market.

4.3. The Within-Macroregion Inequality

The residual of the decomposition, the within-macroregion inequality, explains 80 per cent of total inequality, but the relative contribution of the macroregions is different, due to the different population sizes (Table 3.3). The eastern and western provinces faced greater increases of within-inequalities: the Gini indices reached 0.32 and 0.30 respectively (Table 3.3). However, the increasing within-inequality does not invalidate the 'club convergence' hypothesis. Li (2003) used only provincial aggregated GDP data, while we used consumption data for rural and urban areas, and this difference matters. Decomposing the within-macroregion inequality into rural and urban (Table 3.3), we can see that more than 80 per cent of inequality within each macroregion is explained by the urban–rural divide. The residual is lower than that at the national level, suggesting that there is a stronger macroregional homogeneity among rural areas or among urban areas,[10] and confirming the hypothesis of regional clustering.

As we mentioned before, the urban–rural divide is, surprisingly, increasing in areas that are more dynamic. In both eastern and central areas, compared to 1990 the gap has risen, while there is convergence between rural areas, particularly in the centre. In the east, the urban–rural divide is the lowest of the three macroregions, which is combined with a small but relevant rural divide and an increasing urban divide. The eastern provinces seem to be less homogeneous than the other two groups. Examining the data more closely, we can distinguish between two subgroups, the south-east (excluding Guizou and Hainan) and the north-east (excluding the three municipalities). The two subgroups share common features, though the South-east has a more open economy with a greater concentration of FDI, while the north-east is characterised by the presence of SOEs and less competitive industries. During the 1990s, Liaoning province in particular lagged behind, having to face problems such as the reform of SOEs, rising unemployment and difficulties in re-training.

5.   CONCLUSIONS

In the last decade in China, spatial inequalities increased very fast, creating severe disequilibria between different areas of the country. Using data on average consumption for urban and rural areas of each province, we calculated Theil's index and the Gini index. We decomposed Theil's index into subgroups in order to understand the contribution of different types of inequality on total inequality. Our index has been subgrouped first into urban and rural; secondly, into macroregions; and finally, into rural and urban areas inside each macroregion.

The main contributor to inequality turned out to be the urban–rural divide. This has been a key problem for modern China and it remains unresolved. Important reforms were implemented during the 1980s. These temporarily reduced the gap, but in the 1990s it started to grow again. We identified the main cause to be the reduced effort in counteracting the side-effects of too much urban-biased growth. Local and central governments progressively abandoned redistributive policies, and the economic growth in urban areas attracted most of the investment, private and public. This led to a renewed increase of the divide and to increasing concerns about the social sustainability of this development.

The residual of the decomposition, the inequality within rural areas, and the inequality within urban areas, shows an increasing divide in the urban areas and a declining divide in the rural areas. The decomposition in macroregions has shed light on another important aspect of the unbalanced growth in China. Starting from the end of the 1980s, the three macroregions have grown at different paces, and there is no evidence of convergence to a common steady state. The eastern provinces, favoured by their geographic location and infrastructure endowments, managed to integrate into the world market, while the central and western provinces, where about 60 per cent of the total population is located, seem to lag behind.

Central and local government policies, instead of correcting the disequilibria, have accentuated them. Nonetheless, in 2000 there are positive signs of a changing attitude towards inland areas. To encourage the development of the western provinces, the government launched the *Great Western Development Strategy* or *Go West Strategy*, a campaign of public investment in infrastructure (in particular transport and energy), and the creation of special economic zones similar to SEZs. The aim of this policy, since China's accession to WTO, is to foster the competitiveness of western regions and create opportunities for foreign investors.

Finally, we investigated the inequality within each area, finding that the urban–rural divide is increasing, and that, even in the more dynamic eastern provinces, it is the main determinant of inequality. This result confirms that there is no automatic trickle-down effect from urban to rural areas, and significant policy changes are needed to reduce the gap.

NOTES

* The author is grateful to Maria Weber, Bocconi University, Milan; Mario Biggeri, University of Florence; Giovanni Andrea Cornia, University of Florence; and Giacomo Boati, ISPI, Milan for useful comments and discussions. The author thanks Mark Elsner, Oxford Analytica, Oxford for the editing and Michela Gessati, Bocconi University for invaluable research assistance in the data collection. All remaining errors are mine.

1. The dataset does not include the two Special Administration Regions, Hong Kong and Macao.
2. We used the population by provinces data. These do not include military personnel and 1.05 million persons without settlement registration. Data for the urban and rural populations have been adjusted in several provinces, so the sum of the figures by province is not equal to the national total computed in the aggregated tables of the *China Statistical Yearbook*. Data from 1980 to 1999 used the *permanent residence* definition for urban and rural populations: urban population refers to the total population of districts under the jurisdiction of a city with district establishment, the population of street committees under the jurisdiction of a city without district establishment, the population of resident committees of towns under the jurisdiction of a city without district establishment, and the population of resident committees of towns under the jurisdiction of a county; rural population refers to total population except urban population. Data from 2000 are classified according to the *Regulation of statistics classification on urban and rural population* (draft), formulated by the National Bureau of Statistics in 1999. Data for rural and urban populations at regional levels are available in the *China Statistical Yearbook* only for 1990 and 2000, while for the other years only the total populations of each region, and the total rural and urban populations, are available. To solve this problem, we calculated the missing values as a weighted mean of the two censuses (i.e. for years closer to 1990 a greater weight was assigned to the 1990 urban–rural breakdown at provincial level), controlling with the total rural and total urban populations of every year. The sum of our provincial rural and provincial urban populations from 1991 to 1999 is exactly the same as the national urban–rural division from 1991 to 1999, provided by Table 4.1 of the *China Statistical Yearbook 2002*.
3. We use the definition of the three macro-areas used by Biggeri (2001). East: Beijing, Tianjin, Hebei, Liaoning, Shanghai, Jiangsu, Zhejiang, Fujian, Shandong, Guangdong, Guangxi, Hainan. Centre: Shanxi, Inner Mongolia, Jilin, Heilongjiang, Anhui, Jiangxi, Henan, Hubei, Hunan. West: Sichuan, Guizhou, Yunnan, Shaanxi, Gansu, Qinghai, Ningxia, Xinjiang.
4. The Gini index measures inequality over the entire distribution of income or consumption. A value of 0 represents perfect equality, and a value of 1 perfect inequality. According to the *2003 Human Development Report*, the most unequal country is Namibia (0.70) and the most equal is Denmark (0.24). Using income data, China has a Gini index of 0.40.
5. Many authors estimate that the floating population composed of migrants from rural to urban areas is around 100 million units.
6. This excludes urban migration, which might be high. The authors argue that their estimates are the lower bound.
7. In the transition matrix, Li considers five states and measures them as the real rate of growth of GDP per worker at provincial level divided by the national average. The states are the following: lowest income (range 0–0.5); lower middle income (range 0.5–0.85); middle income (0.85–1.15); upper middle income (1.15–1.5); and highest income (> 1.5).
8. Thirteen per cent of the total population in 1990, and 19 per cent in 2000, according to our calculation based on the *China Statistical Yearbook*.
9. Distance from the coast, and proportion of a province within 100 km of the coastline or an ocean-navigable river in 1994.
10. Li (2002) uses provincial GDP that is a weighted average of rural and urban GDP.

BIBLIOGRAPHY

Biggeri, M. (2001), *The Township and Village Enterprises: the Success of Small and Medium Enterprises in Rural China*, Third draft, Isesao–Bocconi Working Paper.

Chang, G.H. (2002), 'The cause and cure of China's widening income disparity', *China Economic Review*, **13**, pp. 335–40.

Chen, S. and M. Ravallion (1996), 'Data in transition: assessing rural living standards in Southern China', *China Economic Review*, **7** (1), pp. 23–56.

Deaton, A. (1997), *The Analysis of Household Surveys: A Micro–econometric Approach to Development Policy*, Baltimore and London: Johns Hopkins University Press.

Demurger, S. (2001), 'Infrastructure development and economic growth: an explanation for regional disparities', *Journal of Comparative Economics*, **29**, pp. 95–117.

Demurger, S., J.D. Sachs, W.T. Woo, S. Bao and G. Chang (2002), 'The relative contributions of location and preferential policies in China's regional development: being in the right place and having the right incentives', *China Economic Review*, **13**, pp. 444–65.

Fan, S., L. Zhang, and X. Zhang (2002), *Growth, Inequality, and Poverty in Rural China*, IFPRI Research Report 125, Washington DC: IFPRI.

Fang, C., X. Zhang and S. Fan (2002), 'The emerging urban poverty and inequality in China: evidence from Household Survey', *China Economic Review*, **13** (4), pp. 430–43.

FASC, NACO (1999), *Abstract of the First National Agricultural Census in China, National Agricultural Census Office of China*, Food and Agricultural Statistics Centre, China Statistics Press, Beijing: FASC, NACO.

Harris, J. and M.P. Todaro (1970), 'Migration, unemployment and development: A two sectors analysis', *American Economic Review*, **60** (March), pp. 126–43.

Kanbur, R. and X. Zhang (1999), 'Which regional inequality? The evolution of urban–rural or coast inland inequality in China', *Journal of Comparative Economics*, **27**, pp. 686–701, December.

Kanbur, R. and X. Zhang (2003), *Fifty Years of Regional Inequality in China: A Journey through Revolution, Reform and Openness*, Paper prepared for the UNU/WIDER Project Conference on Spatial Inequality in Asia, Tokyo, 28/29 March 2003.

Jones, D.C., C. Li, and L. Owen (2003), 'Growth and regional inequality in China during the reform era', *China Economic Review*, **14**, pp. 186–200.

Lee, J. (2000), 'Changes in the source of China's regional inequality', *China Economic Review*, **11**, pp. 232–45.

Li, H. (2003), 'Dynamics of income distribution across Chinese provinces during 1978/98', *Journal of Chinese Economics and Business Studies*, **1** (2), pp. 145–7.

Lu, D. (2002), 'Urban rural income disparity: impact of growth, allocative efficiency and local growth welfare', *China Economic Review*, **13**, pp. 419–29.

Prud'homme, R. (1995), 'The danger of decentralization', *World Bank Research Observer*, **10** (2), pp. 201–20, Washington, DC: The World Bank.

Shorrocks, A. (1984), 'Inequality decomposition by population subgroups', *Econometrica*, **52** (6), pp. 613–25.

State Statistical Bureau (SSB) (various years), *China Statistical Yearbook*, Beijing: China Statistical Publishing House.

Tsui, K. (1996), 'Economic reforms and inter-provincial inequalities in China', *Journal of Development Economics*, **50**, pp. 353–68.

Yang, D.T. (1999), 'Urban-biased policies and rising income inequality in China', *The American Economic Review*, **89** (2), May, pp. 306–10.

Yang, D.T. (2002), 'What has caused regional inequality in China?', *China Economic Review*, **13**, pp. 331–4.

Zhang, T. and H. Zou (1998), 'Fiscal decentralization, public spending, and economic growth in China', *Journal of Public Economics*, **67**, pp. 221–40.

Zhang, Z., A. Liuc, and S. Yaoc (2001), 'Convergence of China's regional incomes 1952–1997', *China Economic Review*, **12**, pp. 243–58.

4. US–China: A New Balance of Power in East Asia

Maria Weber

Since the end of the Cold War, the collapse of the Soviet Union and the deconstruction of the bipolar model of the international system, the change in the perception of China has been the major shift in East Asia (Swaine and Tellis, 2000; SIIS, 2000). The rise of Beijing and the evolution of the balance of power in the Asia–Pacific Region issue a challenge to the US leadership of security provisions in East Asia. A possible future conflict with China is emerging as a threat in the eyes of US military planners. In its planning document called Joint Vision 2020, for the first time the Pentagon listed China as a potential adversary or a 'peer competitor' (US Government, 2000). Furthermore the document foresees a closer coordination with Japan, projects US troop presence in Korea even after unification, and concludes that Asia will replace Europe as the key focus of US military strategy over the next 20 years.

1. SINO–US RELATIONS SINCE THE COLD WAR

On the one hand, since 1980 the US Department of State has several times explicitly theorized that it will be crucial to implement a policy of containment towards China. The supporters of such an approach consider that the Chinese economic growth and the resurgence of nationalism will encourage China to develop a hegemonic role in Asia. Hence they assert the necessity of an international effort to contain China. On the other hand, the growing importance of Chinese business and the huge potential of its market has increasingly interested the Americans. Witness Clinton's long trip to China in July 1998, during which China achieved a new normalization of relations with Washington. Besides, the Americans acknowledged the need to 'involve' Beijing in a constructive mode in the administration of Asian problems and, more generally, in the management of the international system. Nonetheless, it would be excessive to state that the balance of power has shifted from the Washington–Tokyo axis in favour of China, for the connection between the

United States and Japan is a relationship between countries bound by a bilateral agreement of security, and between two economies of the G-7 (Trombetta and Weber, 2001).

The war in Kosovo and the incident of the bomb attack on the Chinese embassy in Belgrade in May 1999 seemed to have deteriorated the friendly Sino–American relationship which, after Clinton's trip to China in July 1998, had been described as a 'strategic partnership'. The Chinese reacted harshly to the bombing of its embassy in Belgrade. For four days, President Jiang Zemin refused to answer the telephone to President Clinton who was calling to apologise. Beijing's government suspended any bilateral discussion on human rights and postponed the date of the bilateral consultation on armament control and nonproliferation of nuclear weapons. The Chinese did not believe that the bomb had fallen by accident, as a results human error. The spontaneous pickets in front of the American embassy in Beijing recalled the anti-American political climate of the seventies. Zhang Zhaozhong, a famous Chinese armaments expert, declared that for a power like the United States, so advanced technologically, the use of a four-year-old map was unthinkable. A public survey published by the *China Youth Daily* revealed that not even one of the 800 interviewees believed the American version of the incident. Various conspiracy theories appeared at the time in the Chinese newspapers. Some articles hypothesized the intrusion of the CIA to outface President Clinton, whereas others argued that the bomb attack on the embassy could have constituted a test to sound out the Chinese reaction in the case of a possible American intervention to defend Taiwan. Others, conversely, conjectured an explicit desire of the Americans to destabilise China and its modernisation programme.

The sum of those hypotheses, all containing more or less convincing accusations, contributed to overshadow Sino–American relations. Nevertheless, the relationship between China and the USA has such a strong base of mutual economical interest that in October 1999 an American delegation resumed the dialogue with Beijing's representatives to agree in principle to China's entry into the World Trade Organization (WTO). The Clinton Administration was able to create consensus among the European allies in the integrationist strategy (Shambaugh, 2002), which became the core driver of the US policy of engagement with China. As a result, China first acceded to the Comprehensive Test Ban Treaty (CTBT), the Non-Proliferation Treaty (NPT), the Chemical Weapons Convention (CWC), and the Biological Weapons Convention (BWC). Next, it joined the ASEAN Regional Forum (ARF) and the Committee on Security and Co-operation in the Asia-Pacific (CSCAP). Then, Beijing signed the two United Nations human rights covenants, participated in Asia–Europe Meeting (ASEM) and the ASEAN plus 3 (China, Korea, Japan) forums. Finally, it promised to actively study the joining of the Missile Technology Control Regime (MTCR).

The Bush Administration's policy towards China has rapidly transformed the relationship from strategic partnership to strategic competition. Much more than the previous US government, the Bush Administration is actively attempting to construct and consolidate an East Asian security system with the USA as the sole superpower. The USA is actively seeking to use the Theatre Missile Defence (TMD) as a vehicle for the establishment of minilateralism in North East Asia – including Japan, South Korea and Taiwan – as a means of containing China. Certainly, Beijing will interpret it differently and this may result either in an escalated cross-straits arm race, in a security conflict or in a political negotiation between the USA, China and Taiwan. In the foreseeable future it is likely that the issue of East Asian security, focused on the China–Taiwan relations will serve to stimulate the evolution of a new East Asian security framework.

The Sino–US tension grew once more on 1 April 2001, when an American E-P3, a spy-plane crossing Chinese territorial air space, crashed with a Chinese jetfighter. The Chinese pilot died, the American spy-plane was obliged to land on Hainan Island and the crew (24 members) was held as hostage. Both President Bush and President Jiang Zemin asked for official excuses; while the tension was mounting, many observers feared a dramatic evolution of the crisis. Colin Powell took the first step towards the negotiation, by expressing sympathy for the death of the Chinese pilot. After a few days President Bush sent a letter to the pilot's widow expressing his regret. Beijing's answer was to loosen the restrictions on the access of American diplomats to the EP-3 crew. Meanwhile, diplomats were working to find a peaceful solution: the result was an official letter, in which the Bush Administration apologised for the pilot's death and regretted that the E-P3 spy plane failed to send a signal on entering Chinese air space. This letter proved to be the solution to the crisis: on 12 April, the American crew was allowed to

Table 4.1   US Arms Sales to Taiwan in 2001

Arms sales Four Kidd–class destroyers, to be ready by 2003.
12 P-3C Orion aircraft.
Eight diesel-powered submarines.
Paladin self-propelled artillery system.
MH-53E minesweeping helicopters.
AAV7A1 amphibious assault vehicles.
MK 48 torpedoes without advanced features.
Avenger surface-to-air missile system.
Submarine-launched and surface-launched torpedoes.
Aircraft survivability equipment.
Technical briefing on the Patriot antimissile system the island has been developing.

Source: *New York Times*, 24 April 2001, p. 6.

leave China. In spite of the peaceful resolution of the crisis, the tension between China and the USA remained high. On 25 April 2001, the Bush Administration decided to sell arms to Taiwan on a scale unprecedented since 1979 (see Table 4.1). This decision reaffirmed a further pro-Taiwan policy of US security, prompting Beijing's reaffirmation that Taiwan is considered by the Chinese authorities as a rebel province, and not as a protectorate of a foreign power.

2. THE TAIWAN ISSUE

Talking of the Taiwan issue means touching a raw nerve in China: not only because since 1949, the governments of both Taipei and Beijing have constantly claimed to be the only legitimate representatives of the whole of China, but also because a nationalist spirit is growing in Taiwan. In the nineties a progressive democratic party emerged which asserted the right, in the name of the Taiwanese people, to proclaim the island's independence from mainland China.

The Taiwan issue is neither only an old problem of civil war frozen by the Cold War nor a question of a divided nation, as it is tempting to be view it. As Manning argues, Taiwan is also an emblematic symbol of East Asia's strategic problems. First, Taiwan's massive trade with and investment in mainland China are an emblematic symbol of the growing tensions between globalization and nationalism, connected with the emerging Taiwanese identity. In this sense, it raises the question of whether it is geopolitics or geo-economy that most shapes international behaviour in the current new and uncertain historical period (Manning, 2000). Second, the Taiwan issue symbolises the emergence of China as a great power, which is 'demonstrating nationalist passion to right the historic injustice of Western and Japanese imperialism that left China weak and divided' (Manning, 2000). Finally and most ominously, Taiwan may be the ultimate symbol of the clashing interests and values of the USA and China.

In 1993, bilateral talks, aimed at establishing mechanisms for regular contact between the two sides to be based on the one-China principle, began in Singapore. The semi-official talks were suspended in mid-1995 following Taiwan's President Lee Teng-hui's private, but high-profile, visit to the United States. Following the visit and in the run-up to the island's presidential election in March 1996, China held extensive military exercises opposite Taiwan, including missile launches into the ocean just off Taiwan's northern and southern coasts. Moreover, in April 1996, just one month after the third Taiwan Straits Crisis, the USA began working on new Revised Guidelines for US–Japan Defense Cooperation, which link directly the security of Taiwan with the US–Japan Security Pact in East Asia with reference to situations in surrounding areas and problems defined as situational in nature. This revealed a significant change by the USA and Japan in their way of considering the security of Taiwan (Soong, 1999; Yang, 1998).

At the beginning of 1998, after three years of ostracism, Jiang Zemin himself proposed to establish bilateral talks between Taipei and Beijing to normalise their relations. In addition, Beijing offered to extend the principle of 'one country, two systems', already experimented within Hong Kong. Under that system, Taiwan would enjoy a wide-ranging autonomy, would have its own legislative, executive and judiciary bodies as well as its own armed forces, and would retain its own political and economic system, but would have to recognise the sovereignty of the PRC and submit to its rule. It has been suggested that if such a reunification should occur it might be proper to rename the PRC – perhaps calling it simply 'China' – and modify its flag and symbols. Someone has even courted the idea that the Chinese state could be restructured (Soong, 2002).

2.1. Beijing's Perception of the Taiwan Issue

For Beijing, the minimal requirement is that the notion of 'one China' is accepted in some way and that some form of reunification is not becoming less likely. Beijing has many domestic problems and its leaders would consider politically appealing any opportunity to remove Taiwan as a pressing issue without the regime losing face. For Taipei, buying time would allow China's historic transformation to unfold before it decides whether any form of political association with the mainland is desirable, or whether a future regime in Beijing might adopt a different posture towards Taiwan. In that scenario the most intricate question is whether Taiwan's quest for international political space can be accommodated in a one-China framework. If the concept of one-China becomes more elastic, Taipei's aspirations for more international political space could be calibrated by new understandings, under which, for example, Taiwan defines its political space by joining the UN system, the IMF, the World Bank, the WHO, and the IAEA, with observer status or even with full membership (Manning, 2000).

On the other hand, Taiwan is the last vestige of a century of humiliations and Beijing's position is that China has experienced disunity and invasions during the last 5000 years, but it has always reverted to a united state (Klintworth, 2000, p. 14). This has made Taiwan like a sacred mission, especially after the return of Hong Kong and Macao. Moreover, showing weakness with Taiwan might set a precedent for potentially rebellious parts of China such as Tibet or Xinijang (Klintworth, 2000, p. 14). Finally, Taiwan is perceived as a key element in the regional equilibrium, particularly as the inclusion of Taiwan in the proposed theatre defence missile system could affect it.

2.2.   Taipei's Perception of the Taiwan Issue

After half a century of hostilities between the PRC and Taiwan, for some years conditions have appeared suitable for resuming, once again, a dialogue between the two sides of the Straits. Economic convergence is now widespread and has caused powerful economic changes which require a peaceful solution to the dilemma concerning the future of the two republics. It is in this context that one should read the recent proposal by the Taiwanese to the PRC, to create a federation similar to the CIS which would unite the two Chinas while respecting both sovereignties. The federation project will probably be accomplished in the coming years, thus saving both governments' faces and maintaining the autonomy of Beijing and Taipei. The fact that in May 2000, the two governments officially proposed to the United States that they should intervene in the question as a mediator and help to 'throw a bridge of dialogue' between Beijing and Taipei, is a signal in that direction.

Nonetheless, the democratisation process taking place in Taiwan is hampering the rapprochement between the two. Since Lee Teng-hui came to power, the Nationalist party (*Guomindang*, GMD) has been working to democratise its institutions and those of the state. Martial law was revoked in 1987 and in the following years the formation of political parties and opposition groups was allowed, while police control over the opposition was curbed. The first democratic parliamentary elections were held in 1992. Since 1996, the President and Vice President – the two highest positions in the country – have been directly elected. This process is deeply important in the political history of East Asia since, for the first time, part of China has put representative democracy into practice and has begun to choose its rulers freely. Taiwan could become an innovative model of enormous importance for the People's Republic of China, and this is an additional threat to the Communist Party and a challenge to its ideological roots. However, the presidential elections held in 2000 and in 2004 have designated as President the candidate of the Progressive-Democratic Party (PDP), which represents that key minority of Taiwanese who believe that the time has come to be bold and to proclaim complete independence – not only *de facto*, but also *de jure* – from mainland China. On 20 May 2000, in his inaugural address, President Chen Shui–bian explicitly declared his basic position of maintaining the dignity and security of his country. The President also declared the 'five no's' policy (not declaring independence, not changing the national title, not pushing forth the inclusion of the so-called State-to-State description in the Constitution, not promoting a referendum to change the status quo regarding the question of independence or unification, and not abolishing the National Reunification Council or the Guidelines for National Unification). Furthermore, he affirmed that the government would follow the basic principles of 'goodwill reconciliation, active cooperation, and permanent peace' in handling cross–strait relations. Finally, Mr. Chen proposed that the question of 'one China' could be jointly resolved through a cross-strait dialogue.

President Chen Shui-Bian declared that the formula 'one country, two systems' used for Hong Kong and Macao was unacceptable for the Republic of China, but added that he was willing to 'work out' a form of reconciliation with mainland China. The people of Taiwan cannot bear the 'one China' precondition or the 'one country, two systems' formula proposed by mainland China, and designed to downgrade Taiwan. Several surveys have shown that over 70 per cent of the Taiwanese finds the mainland's 'one country, two systems' policy unacceptable. In addition, in his address 'Bridging the New Century' delivered on 31 December 2000, President Chen pointed out: 'The integration of our economies, trade, and culture can be a starting point for gradually building faith and confidence in each other. This, in turn, can be the basis for a new framework of permanent peace and political integration.'

Since 2000, increasingly liberalised procedures have played a pivotal role in the qualitative upgrading and quantitative expansion of cross-strait academic, cultural and educational exchanges. These measures included the easing of residence and naturalisation restrictions on mainlanders serving teaching or specific public functionary positions in Taiwan, the recruitment of mainland technological experts through relaxed restrictions on periods of stay and entry procedures into Taiwan, and permission for Taiwan athletes to become members of or render services to mainland sports groups. In addition, the residence quota of the mainland spouses of Taiwan residents has been increased and restrictions have been eased to grant them conditional work permits. In order to avoid social disorder, given that national security is of utmost importance in Taiwan's mainland policy, guidelines have been established to review the problems arising from mainlanders' engagement in activities in Taiwan and the countermeasures thereof. In particular, as part of an effort to attain the policy objective of positive cross-strait interactions, interrelated regulations will be revised and Taiwan's entry procedures for economic and trade related personnel from the mainland will be simplified.

On 26 August 2001, the cross–strait affairs panel of the Economic Development Advisory Conference (EDAC) reached a consensus on the basic principles for cross-strait economic and trade development and the promotion of various economic and trade liberalisation measures. These valuable accomplishments are attributable to the integration of diverse opinions between governing and opposition parties as well as among all sectors of society. Surveys have found that over 60 per cent of the people support the consensus achieved by the Supra-party Task Force and the cross-strait policy of 'active opening and effective management' proposed by the EDAC.

In October 2001, with the approval and implementation of an action plan to liberalise the commodity customs clearance and to expand the function and scope of offshore shipping centres, cross-strait shipping measures have also been strengthened. On 1 January 2002, the government partially deregulated tourist visits by mainlanders to Taiwan on a trial basis. Moreover, on 1 May, Taipei announced that the plan would be extended to a wider category of visitors. In December 2001, in response to the formal WTO accession by both Taiwan and the mainland, the government formulated a new cross-strait economic and trade action plan to define the direction for adjustment of mainland investments policies in Taiwan's services sector. On 1 January 2002, President Chen emphasised again his willingness to promote a constructive cooperation as the new framework for positive, reciprocal, and mutually beneficial cross-strait relations after formal accession to the World Trade Organization (WTO) by both sides. In his remarks on cross-strait negotiations on 10 May 2002, President Chen set forth three firm principles: Taiwan will not be downgraded, localised, or marginalised. His effort fully underscores the government's consistent and basic stand on national sovereignty.

2.3. China–Taiwan Economic Convergence

Taiwan's economic prosperity is connected with that of the southern Chinese region: Taiwanese investments in China might amount by now to over $40 billion and 54 000 companies sponsored by Taiwanese capital were registered in 1999. While political integration may be as far away as ever, the integration of the two economies continues apace. Unfortunately, there is no reliable data on Taiwanese investments in China, as different figures are provided by different institutions. Sources in Hong Kong set the value of contracts signed by Taiwanese entrepreneurs on the mainland between $10.5 billion and $20.4 billion by the end of 1992 up to 1997 (*China Perspectives*, May–June 1998). Japanese sources have estimated $15 billion for the same period and, more recently, the American and Taiwanese Press mentioned a figure of over $40 billion invested by 45 000 firms (Weber, 2001). Contractual investment by Taiwan on the mainland amounted to $6.9 billion in 2001, with $3.2 billion actually invested and with a total of 4 100 investment items, an increase of 73 per cent, the highest percentage increase since 1995 (Cheng Bifan, 2002).

This mix of economic interdependence and neo-institutionalism might be the prescription for handling the China issue. Richard Rosecrance has explained how direct investments and the transnational production of goods can create a web of commercial ties that discourages war (Rosecrance, 1986). The economic integration of Taiwan and China is so deep-rooted that it makes the possibility of an armed conflict unrealistic and rather 'inconvenient'.

Following renewed efforts by various parties, there was a proposal, made in March 2002 by the vice-chairman of the Guomindang, Vincent Siew Wan-chang, for a free trade area (FTA) and a common market between the two sides. There is an important difference between Vincent Siew's 'common market' proposal and Chen's concept of integration through economic, cultural and political stages.

Siew argued that to realize a common market ideal there must be a basis acceptable to both sides – 'One China, separate interpretations' – without necessarily having to face the sovereignity issue directly. As Cheng Bifan (2002) points out:

> Economic Union between the two sides is not a matter between two countries but an internal matter of a divided country. In this way the sovereignty issue would temporarily be made abstract while both sides will enjoy equal status... If a 'Chinese Economic Community' will be formed this will reduce, even eliminate, the military confrontation between the two sides.

On the other hand, President Chen was referring to cooperation between two states each enjoying sovereignty and independence.

3. CHINA'S RESPONSIBLE BEHAVIOUR AFTER SEPTEMBER 11

The tragedy of September 11 has radically changed US–China relations. Immediately after the terrorist attack on the United States, China decided to play a responsible role. The Chinese government expressed its strong disapproval of international terrorism and its strong support of the American people (Weber, 2002). Behind Chinese support for the war against terror, there was not only the intention to mantain good relations with the USA but also Beijing was looking to the USA to provide political support in its fight against the Uighurs, China's Muslim minority, predominant in the province of Xinjiang.

The region of Xinjiang is huge and scarcely populated by different ethnic groups (60 per cent of which are not Han, and made up mostly by Uighur Muslim Turks, as well as Kazakhs and Hui), and is the region which causes the greatest concern to the Chinese leaders. Alongside the usual problems between the locals and the Han, which have been exacerbated in this particular case by a strong Uighur (and partly Kazakh) independence movement, Xinjiang is also the scene of a worrying spread of Islamic fundamentalism, which is rife among all the main minorities and even attracts the Uighur and Kazakh cadres of the CCP. The Pan-Turk independence movements began to make their voice heard in 1990, at the time that the Soviet Union was disintegrating, through riots and clashes, which were kept secret by official sources. In the last five years pro-independence groups have been responsible for setting off bombs in Urumqi, the region's capital, and even in Beijing, killing and injuring a number of people. According to Beijing, a Uighur independence organisation, the East Turkestan Islamic Movement (ETIM) is an Afghanistan-based group that has been involved in more than 200 terrorist acts in recent years. Some of the terror strikes ascribed to ETIM were deadly bombings, others were protest riots or attacks on police stations.

The Bush Administration declared the ETIM a terrorist organisation that had committed acts of violence on civilians. The United States was inspired by China's efforts to strike against terrorist activities jointly with the USA and will cooperate with China in cracking down on terrorist forces, especially to cut off their financial sources. In this way, the price that the Bush Administration had to pay for Beijing's support to the American 'war on terror' was to allow the Chinese government to repress the independence movement in Xinjiang. The US State Department persuaded the United Nations to add ETIM to its list of international terrorist groups. The US Administration made a diplomatic deal so that Beijing would not use its UN Security Council veto to block the invasion of Iraq. China in return can crack down on Uighur dissidents as terrorists with less risk of censure for human rights violations.

Since September 11 the overall relationship between China and the United States has seen sound progress. The first signal was the Apec (Asia–Pacific Economic Cooperation) meeting in Shanghai in October 2001. On that occasion President Bush declared: 'China is a great power. America wants a constructive relationship with China. We welcome a China that is a full member of the world community, and that is at peace with its neighbours. We welcome and support China's accession to the World Trade Organization (WTO).' The Bush Administration's reluctance to pursue the integrationist strategy vis-à-vis China does not apply to the realm of trade: the US Trade Representative Robert Zoellick brought to a conclusion China's accession to WTO (Shambaugh, 2002, p. 7).

Events during 2002 were rather positive for US–China relations. In February 2002, during a meeting in Beijing, President Bush and President Jiang Zemin stressed the cooperation between the two countries. Meanwhile, President Jiang Zemin mentioned China's strong opposition to any military action against North Korea, Iran or Iraq. On the Taiwan issue the tone was less conciliatory: President Jiang Zemin emphasised Clinton's 'one–China policy', while President Bush reminded him of American involvement with Taiwan. On the other hand, visiting US Deputy Secretary of State Richard Armitage reiterated in Beijing on 27 August 2002 that the USA does not support Taiwanese independence. He made the remarks at a press conference, saying that such a stance had always been made clear by White House spokespersons before. After reiterating the US government stance on Taiwan, Armitage said he did not think Chen Shuibian's 'one country on each side' statement would interfere with the third summit meeting between President Bush and President Jiang Zemin. In September 2002, in a meeting with Sandra Day O'Connor, associate justice of the US Federal Supreme Court, President Jiang said the two countries share extensive and important common interests, although some differences still remain. Jiang said the two sides should strengthen mutual exchanges and understanding in consideration of their different domestic circumstances. He said a constructive and cooperative relationship between the two nations is beneficial to the practical interests of the two peoples, and is also conducive to peace, stability and prosperity in the Asia–Pacific region and in the world at large.

4.   CHINA'S MEDIATION IN THE NORTH KOREAN CRISIS

The North Korean nuclear crisis started on 12 December 2002, when North Korea declared its intention to restart its power plants and restore the nuclear schemes frozen by the agreement signed in 1994 between Washington and Pyongyang, providing for the freezing of all nuclear schemes and for the acceptance of checks by the International Atomic Energy Agency (IAEA) in exchange for a reduction in American sanctions. In order to cope with the North Korean energy crisis, the agreement included a project called Kedo (Korean Peninsula Energy Development Organization) for the supply of fuel and of two nuclear power plants, not to be used for military purposes. This project should have been completed by 2003 but was then extended until 2007; this delay was interpreted by Pyongyang as an infringement of the 1994 agreement.

Pyongyang's reaction was assertive: on 31 December 2002 it turned out the IAEA inspectors; on 10 January 2003 it announced its withdrawal from the non-proliferation treaty signed in 1985 and asked the USA to sign a bilateral non-aggression treaty. On 5 February Pyongyang announced the reopening of the Yongbyon nuclear power plant, officially for the production of power, although it could reprocess 8 000 spent fuel rods already in store to produce five nuclear devices in six months. A few days later Colin Powell suggested holding a multilateral meeting mediated by China and Russia. Pyongyang repeatedly rejected the proposal and kept asking for a bilateral dialogue with the USA, threatening to resort to war. In order to make its threat credible, North Korea did not hesitate in adopting aggressive attitudes against its neighbouring countries, the main allies of the USA in Asia: South Korea and Japan. On 20 February, a North Korean ship crossed the border to the south and on 25 February, the day the newly elected president Roh Moo-hyun took office, a North Korean missile crashed near Seoul. A few days later another North Korean missile was launched in Japan's territorial waters.

The North Korean strategy is nothing new. For years now Pyongyang has been adopting a simple and tested negotiation style: trigger a crisis in various ways (military accidents, threats, missile launches, propaganda, withdrawal from negotiations, and so on) and then turn it to its advantage by promising to settle it in exchange for diplomatic benefits and economic aid. To this end a credible enough threat had to be made to the regional counterparts. The most effective tools were the missile deterrent and the nuclear threat, which turned North Korea into an example of a minor power capable of bearing weight in international politics. For some time this has been the strategy selected by Pyongyang to avoid yielding to the economic troubles that overwhelmed the country after the end of the cold war.

This time the crisis was different from the previous ones and the explanation should mainly be sought in the international context and in the fact that President Bush, since his opening speech in January 2002, has been including North Korea in the 'axis of evil', together with Iran and Iraq. The American policy of the wall against wall in the attempt to keep the actual risk posed by North Korea's nuclear power under control produced the opposite effect.

The North Korean crisis offered China the opportunity to demonstrate its ability to act as a responsible player in the international political scenario. Indeed, the behaviour adopted by the People's Republic of China with respect to the North Korean matter seemed quite smart and earned it an image of reliability. While being the power closest to Pyongyang, China clearly stated it does not share the preferences of Kim Jong–il. Beijing sent several top-level emissaries to Pyongyang to convince the North Koreans to pursue the way of negotiations. In order to apply pressure, Beijing even closed for some time – officially for 'technical reasons' – an oil-duct conveying much-needed oil to North Korea. After that, during the summer it withheld a North Korean cargo boat, and operated troop transfers along the border. In January 2003, the President Jiang Zemin denounced North Korea's decision to withdraw from the nuclear non-proliferation treaty. Even the new Chinese President Hu Jintao, as soon as he was appointed in March 2003, asked the Pyongyang government to dismantle its nuclear programme, suggesting that, otherwise, China might stop granting economic aid to North Korea.

Today, as at the time of the Ming dynasty, China is pursuing two strategic objectives with respect to the Korean peninsula. First, it aims to prevent Korea from turning into a direct threat. To this end, since 1992 China has been implementing a policy of reconciliation with Seoul. For Beijing, it is certainly very positive and encouraging to see that South Korea has abandoned the old strategy adopted during the Cold War, consisting in the containment of North Korea and, through North Korea, of China. Similarly, closer economic relations and diplomatic initiatives, such as the intention jointly expressed by both countries on 12 November 1998 to build a 'cooperative partnership' in view of the approaching new century, seem highly promising. Second, China wants to prevent Korea from turning into a 'catwalk' for a third-party power, capable of invading the country. This makes it even clearer why it would be strategically useful for Beijing to see South Korea's political and military links with America loosened, something that should be achieved, however, without openly challenging the United States, but rather by creating a peaceful and stable environment, where a guarantee for security from America would no longer appear to be necessary.

China, together with Russia, opposed the adoption by the UN Security Council of a resolution on North Korea, but voted within the International Atomic Energy Agency in favour of reporting North Korea's breach of the Non-Proliferation Treaty to the same UN Security Council. On the other hand, so far Beijing has though it appropriate for Washington to formally undertake on a multilateral rather than a bilateral basis, not to invade North Korea, which would obviously be to Pyongyang's advantage. It is clear then that China has an interest in a prompt and peaceful settlement of the matter, possibly also achieving Pyongyang's nuclear disarmament. This would mitigate the impact that the current situation is having on a strategic level. The opportunities for Washington to strengthen its alliance with Japan and South Korea and, on the other hand, the unrest that North Korea is causing, which could lead new regional players – including Tokyo, Seoul, and even Taiwan – to equip themselves in turn with atomic weapons, certainly do not represent positive developments from China's point of view, since they all limit its influence. Moreover, Beijing has a more general interest in avoiding severe tensions in East Asia, simply because these could negatively influence the economic dynamics of the region and, thus, China's economic relations with the rest of the world.

For Beijing, the North Korean crisis represents a trial. If conflict occurred, China would end up with the American troops just close to its border, and would even have to accept the *de facto* rearming of Japan. Moreover, a unified Korean peninsula would be a strong economic competitor. China is looking forward to the current regime remaining in Pyongyang, as well as to the inception of an economic liberalisation process promoting foreign investments and, possibly, a gradual reform of the regime. By succeeding in curbing the crisis, Beijing would demonstrate its ability to act constructively and would increase its role in increasing security in North East Asia. In this respect, the multilateral meeting organized in Beijing in late August 2003 marked a point in favour of China's diplomatic status and paved the way to the lessening tension that resulted, in January 2004, in the 'private' visit by an American delegation of nuclear experts to the nuclear power plant of Yongbyon. While this may not be the end of the crisis, these multiple signs of relaxation mostly point to an improvement in the diplomatic weight of Beijing.

BIBLIOGRAPHY

Alagappa, M. (1997), 'Systemic Change, Security and Governance in the Asia–Pacific Region', in Chan Heng Chee (ed.), *The New Asia–Pacific Order*, Singapore: ISEAS.

Bernstein, R. and R. Munro (1997), *The Coming Conflict with China*, New York: Knopf.

Campbell, K.M. and D.J. Mitchell (2001), 'Crisis in the Taiwan Straits?', *Foreign Affairs*, July–August.

Chang, P.H., and M. Lasater (eds) (1994) *If China Crosses Taiwan Strait: The International Response*, Lanham, MD: University Press of America.

Caporaso, J.A. (1992), 'International Relations Theory and Multilateralism: The Search for Foundations', *International Organization*, **46** (3), pp. 599–632.

Cheng Bifan (2002), *Interaction between Political and Economic Factors in Relations across the Taiwan Strait*, paper presented at the Monash Asia Institute's Prato Security Conference, 17–18 May.

Commings, B. (1996), 'The World Shakes China', *The National Interest*, **43**, pp. 28–41.

Cossa, R.A. (1999), *Security Multilateralism in Asia. US Views Toward Northeast Asia Multilateral Security Cooperation*, Policy Paper no. 51, University of California Institute on Global Conflict and Cooperation.

Cossa, R.A. (2000), 'Coming of Age and Coming Out: Shifts in the Geopolitical Landscape', *Comparative Connections*, **2** (2), pp. 9–19.

Cossa, R.A. and J. Khanna (1997), 'East Asia: Economic Interdependence and Regional Security', *International Affairs* (2).

Economy, E. and M. Oksenberg (eds) (1999), *China Joins the World: Progress and Prospects*, New York: Council of Foreign Relations.

Foster-Carter, A. (2001), 'North Korea and the World: New Millennium, New Korea?', *Comparative Connection*, **2** (4), pp.102–13.

Goldstain, A. (1998), 'Great Expectations: Interpreting China's Arrival', *International Security*, **22** (3).

Garver, J.W. (1997), *Face Off. China, the United States and Taiwan's Democratization*, Seattle; London: University of Washington Press.

Hong Nack Kim (2000), 'The 2000 Parlamentary Election in South Korea', *Asian Survey*, **XL** (6), November/December.

Klintworth, G. (2000), *China and Taiwan – From Flashpoint to redefining One China*, Parliament of Australia Research Paper no. 15.

Lampton, D.M. (2001), *Same Bed, Different Dreams: Managing US–China Relations, 1989–2000*, Berkeley; London: University of California Press.

Manning, R.A. (2000), 'Taiwan and the Future of Asian Security', *Politique Internationale*, Summer.

Mearsheimer, J.J. (1993), 'A Realist Reply', *International Security*.

Mearsheimer, J.J. (2001), *The Tragedy of Great Power Politics*, Milano per la traduzione italiana; New York and London per la versione originale, Norton (Italian translation, *La logica di potenza*, Università Bocconi Editore, Milano, 2003).

Myers, R., M. Oksenberg and D. Shambaugh (eds) (2001), *Making China Policy: Lessons from the Bush and Clinton Administrations*, Lanham, MD: Roman and Littlefields.

Naidu, G.V.C. (2000), 'Mutilateralism and Regional Security: Can the ASEAN Regional Forum Really Make a Difference?', *Asia Pacific Issues*, **45**.

Nathan A.J. and R.S. Ross (1997), *The Great Wall and The Empty Fortress*, New York: W.W. Norton & Co.

Noerper, S. (2000), 'US–Korea: Looking Forward, Looking Back', *Comparative Connections*, **2** (2), pp. 35–41.

Nye, J.S. (1998), 'China's Reemergence and the Future of the Asia Pacific', *Survival*, **39** (4).

Robinson, T.W. and D. Shambaugh (eds) (1995), *Chinese Foreign Policy: Theory and Practice*, Oxford: Clarendon Press.

Rosecrance, R. (1986), *The Rise of the Trading State*, New York: Basic Books.

Ruggie, J.G. (ed.) (1993), *Multilateralism Matters: The Theory and Praxis of an Institutional Form*, New York: Columbia University Press.

Rupprecht, K. (2001), 'European and American Approaches toward China as an Emerging Power', *China Aktuell*, Institut für Asienkunde, Hamburg, February.

Scalapino, R.A. (1998), 'The Changing Order in Northeast Asia and the Prospects for US–Japan–China–Koreas Relations', Policy Paper No. 47, University of California Institute on Global Conflict and Cooperation.

Segal, G. (1996), 'East Asia and the Containment of China', *International Security*, **20** (4), pp. 107–35.

Shambaugh, D. (2002), 'European and American Approaches towards China: Different Beds, Same Dreams?', *China Perspectives*, **42**, July–August.

SIIS (Shanghai Institute of International Studies) (2000), *The Post Cold War World*, Shanghai.

Simon, A. (1995), 'Realism and Neoliberalism: International Relations Theory and Southeast Asian Security', *The Pacific Review*, (1).

Soong, H. (1999), 'Taiwan's Security Strategy Towards PRC: from the Perspective of The Revised "US–Japan Defense Guidelines" and the 'Three No's Policy'", *Journal of Strategic and International Studies*, **1** (4), October, pp. 21–54.

Soong, H. (2002), *The Implications of America's Liberal Egemony on Taiwan's Future*, paper presented at Monash Asia Institute's Prato Security Conference, 17–18 May.

Stueck, W. (1995), *The Korean War*, Princeton: Princeton University Press.

Swaine, M.D. and A.J. Tellis (2000), *Interpreting China's Grand Strategy*, Washington: RAND publ.

Trombetta, M.J., and M. Weber (2001), *Shifts in East Asia Regional Security: Old Issues and New Events amidst Multilateral–Bilateral Tensions*, ISPI: Global Watch Paper no. 7.

US Government (2000), *Joint Vision 2020*, available from http://www.dtic.mil/jointvision/jvpub2.htm.

Wang, F. (1998), 'To Incorporate China: A New Policy for a New Era', *The Washington Quarterly*, **21** (1), pp. 67–81.

Weber, M. (ed.) (2000), *After the Asian Crises. Perspectives on Global Politics and Economy*, London: Macmillan.

Weber, M. (ed.) (2001), *Reforming Economic Systems in Asia*, Cheltenham, UK: Edward Elgar.

Weber, M. (2002), 'I nuovi alleati nella lotta al terrorismo: la Cina', in B. Biancheri (ed.), *Il nuovo disordine globale dopo l'11 settembre*, Università Bocconi Editore, Milano.

Yang, Y. (1998), 'US–Japan Security Alliance and Asia–Pacific Security', *NTU Political Science Review*, **9** (June), pp. 275–304.

PART II

THE REFORM OF THE WELFARE SYSTEM

5. State-owned Enterprises Reform and Rising Unemployment*

Giacomo Boati

1. BACKGROUND INTRODUCTION

Full employment is quoted by some scholars as the most important source of human welfare (Barr, 1998; Xing, 2000). In the last few years China has adopted a number of reforms in order to move towards a capitalist-oriented economy, and has succeeded in adapting its economy to the market. In the Tenth Five Year Plan, a viable social security system is said to be the basis for the development of a socialist-style market economy. Conversely, the Human Development Report by the UNDP (United Nations Development Programme) (1999)[1] suggests that while these market–oriented reforms have solved many problems, they also pose a variety of challenges, among which increasing unemployment is one of the most prominent social issues (Kaijie, 2003, p. 37). The dynamics of unemployment has in fact been gathering momentum of late: labour protests and demonstrations are so frequent that for many observers and party leaders unemployment is the biggest threat to social stability in China today (Ching Kwan Lee, 2000, p. 41; Lee and Warner, 2003, p. 16).

In this chapter we will attempt to understand the extent of the unemployment problem in the urban context and to discover how far it can be considered a threat to social stability. To do this we will first need to examine some peculiarities of the employment system which, despite being created mainly in the pre-reform period, have continued to affect the dynamics of unemployment up to the present day.

When considering employment in China, the main characteristic is the difference between the rural and the urban. In our overview of unemployment we are going to concentrate on the urban kind. During the *Maoist* period, following a Soviet model, the economy was divided into urban and rural, a division that also applied to the labour market and the social welfare system. The distinction in social security benefits between rural and urban reflected the policy makers' assumption that, given the nature of traditional farming techniques, the marginal rate of technical substitution between land and labour was relatively high.[2] As it was easier to avoid unemployment in the agricultural sector, policy makers felt they were justified in leaving agricultural concerns out of social benefits (Xing, 2000). This division was rigid: mobility from rural to urban areas was strictly forbidden and mobility in general was linked to the household registration system (*hukou*), an internal passport that granted all social benefits (Mallee, 2000; Rocca, 2003; Leung, 2003). Migration was prohibited, any mobility in the factors of production being seen as disobedience with respect to the planning system, according to which rural residents were forbidden to move to the city without official approval. Mobility across sectors was planned by labour and personnel public administrative departments. Since the 1990s labour mobility has, however, been encouraged or at least tolerated.[3] In 1998 the Ministry of Public Security issued new provisions that relaxed *hukou* regulations: persons joining parents, spouses or children could gain an urban *hukou*. But even if the household registration system has gradually been relaxed, many restrictions still affect peasants.[4] Notwithstanding relaxations in the immigration control system, the rural–urban divide is being kept alive through various laws and regulations, involving differences in statistics and the social security systems.

As a matter of fact, the dual nature of the labour market was followed by dualism in the social security system. In rural areas social security was limited to basic necessities. In urban areas workers were paid a basic wage but had more benefits than rural workers; in addition to food, housing, medical care, clothing, burial expenses, they also received pre-school child care, schooling and pensions.

Another key point was the particular treatment reserved for State-Owned Enterprises (SOEs),[5] which played a mixed political and economic role. Their budget was an integral part of the government's budget and the profitability of a sector was considered as a whole and without any disaggregation to demonstrate the profitability of any single enterprise. They combined low wages with over-employment and lifetime employment but, most importantly, the work-unit, (*danwei*) acted as a primary locus of political organisation and social control (Hussain, 2000, p. 14), providing work for SOEs' employees, education for their children, social benefits for their families, and pensions after retirement. A job was for life and there was an option, called *ding ti,* of passing it on to the child of a retiree (Wong, 1998, p. 66; Hochraich, 2001). In 2000, 40 per cent of the hospitals and 30 per cent of schools were operated by SOEs (Leung, 2003, p. 77). SOEs, in fact, could not dismiss workers unless they had committed criminal acts.

When China started to open its market to the world, and take its first steps away from a centre-based economy towards a socialist market system (with deep social repercussions), the SOEs became more dynamic and the labour market started the long march towards a capitalistic labour market model. The SOEs' crucial social role collapsed and the country was flooded with the 'new' category of the unemployed: people with hardly any social benefits.

In this chapter we overview:

1. SOEs reform, in order to have a look at the origins of today's unemployment;
2. the unemployment generated and its evaluation in China, in an attempt to grasp its implications for social stability;
3. the unemployment policies conducted by the government in the last few years.

The concluding part of the research aims to understand the implications of unemployment on social stability.

2. SOE REFORM AND THE RISE OF UNEMPLOYMENT IN CHINA

In 1979, at the beginning of the open door policy, the SOE system revealed various problems relating to production efficiency, the social welfare burden and behaviour distortions in managers and workers. Workforce privileges discouraged a professional attitude: lifetime employment encouraged shirking and low productivity (Hochraich, 2001), and the wage grade system from the 1950s evaluated employees, depending on their education and age rather than judging them on their productivity (Xing, 2000 p. 81).[6] For SOE managers, group harmony was often more important than maximising profit (Solinger, 2002).

When the authorities started to open up the economy and move toward a capitalist-oriented model in 1979, the SOEs' role appeared unsuited to compete with the challenges posed by a market economy. From the start, the authorities conceived reforms to allow SOEs to acquire more efficiency and become more competitive. During the 1980s, the Economic Responsibility System (ERS) was introduced, so as to enable SOE managers to be more independent. With the new rules managers could draw up production plans, they could sell their surplus to other enterprises and they could retain a share of the profits in their SOE. It was the first move towards economic efficiency, but one peculiar aspect of the SOEs was left untouched: employees' privileges.

In 1986 came the formal turning point in the labour market, a radical change in the treatment reserved for workers employed by the state, and employment conditions in China as a whole. Four important regulations were released by the State Council: the 'Temporary Regulation on the Implementation of Labour Contract and Regulation in State Owned Enterprises' removed the lifetime-employment guarantee; the 'Temporary Regulation on the Recruitment of Workers in State-Owned Enterprises' opened up recruitment through competitive examination and eliminated the option of replacing a parent who left a work-unit with an adult child (*ding ti*); the 'Temporary Regulation on the Dismissal of Workers in State Owned Enterprises Who Violated Discipline' made it possible to dismiss workers for the first time; and the 'Temporary Regulation on Unemployment Insurance for Workers in State Owned Enterprises' legalised unemployment insurance (Wong, 1998, p. 66).

The breakthrough regulation that had the greatest impact was the advent of the option to recruit employees with limited-term labour contracts,[7] for a period of one to five years and without an automatic provision for renewal. New workers' categories were created: non-fixed workers, including temporary workers and extra-plan workers. These categories earned much less than fixed workers, the average wage being 70 per cent of the normal, or more, depending on the sector (Nolan, 1993, p. 279). In this period the wage–setting system was also reformed, linking the total wage system to the profitability and productivity of enterprises (Xing, 2000, p. 83). The bulk of dismissals in China was, however, based on the 'Law of Enterprises Bankruptcy' (1988), which made it possible to discharge workers simply for economic reasons. Although the Bankruptcy Law and other regulations were not fully implemented until the mid-1990s, they constituted the main pillar for the subsequent SOE reforms and dismissals.

Figure 5.1   Registered Unemployed in Urban Areas

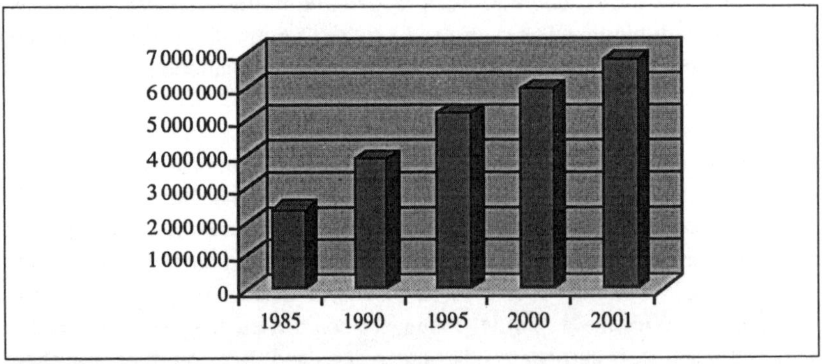

Source: *China Statistical Yearbook, 2002.*

With the new regulations on labour contract and the law on bankruptcy the SOEs had, for the first time, the power to dismiss workers for economic reasons. In actual fact, at the beginning of the 1990s' labour market reforms, dismissals for economic reasons were only aimed at loss reduction. The dismissal of SOE workers was also linked to the social welfare financial burden and the lack of sustainability of benefits systems; enterprises discharged workers in order to reduce deficits that had been created above all by welfare benefits (Yaohui and Jianguo, 2002, p. 396).

Political legitimacy for dismissal in the name of efficiency and profitability was given in November 1993 by the Fourteenth Central Committee of the CCP with the 'Decision on Issues Concerning the Establishment of a Social Market Structure', and with a 50 point agenda to create a modern enterprise system. The points on the agenda were aimed at improving SOEs' efficiency, diversifying the ownership structure, creating a competitive market and reforming the social system.

In 1997, after the SOEs reform stated by the Fifteenth National Congress of the Communist Party of China, the use of the regulation to dismiss SOEs workers began to be aimed at improving the enterprise's profits (Hochraich, 2001). It is since that period that dismissals began to aim at the attainment of enterprise profitability (Hochraich, 2002) and have been taken on a massive scale, involving great cutbacks in the number of SOE employees (see Figure 5.1). According to the *White Paper on Labour and Social Security in China* (2002), 25.5 million people were laid off from state enterprises between 1998 and 2001 alone and the SOEs' workforce fell from 112 million in 1994 to 75 million in 2002 (with a growing urban workforce). SOE reform has had a strong impact on society and this is one of the main issues the Chinese government has been obliged to face in the last few years. As a matter of fact, a huge labour pool reserve spread in China during the 1990s, people basically lacking in social benefits (Hochraich, 2001). Among the categories that have helped to increase the number of jobless, in addition to SOE dismissals, we can count a growing number of new entrants to the urban labour market. According to Leung, the working population will reach a peak in 2010 (Leung, 2003, p. 75). Among the jobless categories we should also count workers

Figure 5.2   Number of Staff and Workers in State-owned Units (10000)

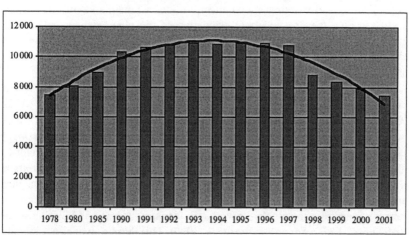

Source: China Statistical Yearbook, 2002.

dismissed on account of the downsizing of public administration and demobilisation of the armed forces: dismissals by the armed forces numbered 500 000 during the Ninth Five Year Plan, and others are envisaged in the Tenth Five Year Plan. We should then count people migrating from rural areas: the official rate of urbanisation was around 37 per cent in 2001 but some scholars estimated it to be at 50 per cent (Hussain, 2000, p. 9), the difference being made up of migrants who are not registered. This labour pool reserve is difficult to quantify but accounts for the core of Chinese unemployment.

3.   DISUNITY AMONG THE UNEMPLOYED

3.1.   The Misleading Evaluation of Urban Unemployment in China

It is generally agreed that the official calculation of the urban unemployment rate in China has to be reviewed, and various Chinese scholars and government departments[8] are considering new ways of doing this, as reported by the *South China Morning Post*. Many scholars also argue that the official rate cannot be taken as a sound economic indicator (Brooks and Ran, 2003; Gu, 2003; Yang Guang, 1999; Hussain, 2000; Xing, 2000; Rocca, 2000; Solinger, 2001). The literature is full of attempts to estimate and evaluate the real urban unemployment rate (Yang Guang, 1999), though for some authors it is actually impossible to come to any kind of statistical agreement about the current state of unemployment in China (Solinger, 2001, p. 671). The attempts, therefore, seem to be of scant significance, since the evaluations start from unsound Chinese data[9] and the results vary considerably. In Table 5.1 we provide a background framework and conservative calculation of unemployment simply by collecting and working out data from official Chinese sources. We are not trying to give the one and only evaluation of the phenomenon, but we are interested in suggesting a possible dimension, starting from the common denominators of the analysis of unemployment in China, and trying to understand their implications.

The main point quoted by scholars in evaluating unemployment data is that registered urban unemployment does not consist of many categories of the *de facto* unemployed. There are a variety of definitions for people who are out of work in China. The definition of registered urban unemployed person (*shiye*) is quite restrictive: the registered unemployed persons in urban areas refer to those persons who are registered as permanent residents in the urban areas engaged in non-agricultural activities, of working age, capable of labour, unemployed but desiring employment and registered at the local employment service agencies as available for work ('Explanatory Notes on Main Statistical Indicators', *China Statistical Yearbook*, 2000). This definition does not include laid-off workers (*xiagang*), that is workers from SOEs who have been dismissed but maintain a link with the enterprise that decided to eliminate their job.[10] They are a relatively privileged category of the unemployed, having the right to receive a basic living allowance and health care benefits, while re-employment centres have to pay their unemployment insurance. The *xiagang* have to meet three requirements to enter the category (Solinger, 2001, p. 677):

1. they should have been working before the contract system was instituted in 1986, having had a permanent job in the state sector;
2. they have to be not employed but still linked to the state enterprise;
3. they may not have any other job.

The number of laid-off is higher than the number of unemployed and, if added to the number of the officially unemployed in the unemployment calculation, the ratio doubles, reaching 8.4 per cent, according to data from the *Chinese Statistical Yearbook* (Table 5.1). For some authors, official figures of the laid-off are decidedly too low (Solinger, 2001, p. 672), since the official category only includes people in the reemployment services, omitting those not entered in a re-employment service or those who are laid-off from enterprises that have gone bankrupt and have insufficient funds to open a re-employment centre. On the contrary, some scholars argue that the number of *xiagang* is overestimated, on account of the benefits enterprises are receiving from the State (Brooks and Ran, 2003, p. 16).

Table 5.1   Unemployment in 2001

	Registered urban unemployment[a]	Laid-off workers[b]	Unemployed and laid-off
Total amount	6 810 000	9 108 700	15 918 700
% labour force	3.6	4.8	8.4

Source: a. *China Statistical Yearbook, 2002*; b. *China Labour Statistical Yearbook, 2002.*[11]

Moreover, unemployed immigrants (*dagong mei*) are not counted in the registered unemployment urban ratio. The system of immigration control founded on the certificate of residence (*hukou*), even if it has been relaxed in the past few years, continues to exist (Rocca, 2003; Leung, 2003, p. 79; Mallee, 2000). Peasants entering the cities from rural areas are not counted in any statistic until they reach resident status, even though these unregistered peasants seem to form the main manpower in some sectors, such as housing and restoration work (Rocca, 2000, p. 8). Some estimates indicate that their number could be as high as 100 million.

Another category of workers that is not listed in the unemployed statistics comprises workers with wage arrears problems (*touqian gongzi*). The extent of this problem seems very large: some sources argue that in 2001 the total wage arrears across the country amounted to 36.7 billion RMB ($4.4 billion).[12] Much of the unrest in the country in recent years is strictly connected with the wage arrears problem (Rocca, 2000, p. 8; Hurst and O'Brien, 2002, p. 346).

In order to have a correct overview of the state of unemployment in China we should then consider workers in excess, or *fuyu renyuan* (Solinger, 2001, p. 680). Many scholars argue that, even after SOEs reforms and dismissals, there is a large number of superfluous workers in the state sector. An IMF survey (Brooks and Ran, 2003, p. 17) argues that if SOEs labour productivity could be raised to non-state levels, 10–11 million SOEs workers would have to be considered redundant. Other categories often taken into consideration in unemployment surveys are the *tiqian tuixiu*, people obliged to accept early retirement, who often fail to receive a pension for a long time, and the amount of money they do receive is very limited (Rocca, 2000, p. 8).

3.2. Subdividing the Unemployed and its Consequences

From this simple survey of unemployment statistics we can see that the unemployed neither belong to one unified category nor enjoy the same treatment by the government (for a classification of the unemployed in accordance with their benefits see Solinger, 2001).[13] Reasons for the subdivision of the unemployed can basically be found in two main factors:

1. lack of freedom of association: the All-China Federation of Trade Unions (ACFTU) is the only way for workers to join together, and there is no other means of association. The ACTFU is integrated in the political structures of the Party and the State, and the main task of the workers' representatives is to contain labour unrest rather than voice it;
2. the implications of the State's role in the partitioning. We can understand this by observing the authorities' attempt to control (and perhaps conceal) the real situation where unemployment is concerned. The State has created different categories of unemployed, allotting benefits and making definitions; it defines new policies for unemployed categories and basically denies the workers' freedom of association (Rocca, 2000).

Returning to the main focus of the chapter, the threat to social stability in China due to unemployment-related concerns and difficulties, we see that dividing up unemployment has had some interesting results. First of all, the government finds it easy to complicate efforts to measure unemployment. Ever since the beginning of the reform, the State Council and the authorities have gone on denying there is a problem. While high government officials publicly admit that the problem does exist, stating that it is in the common interest to solve it, official statistics on unemployment underestimate its extent. Secondly, dividing the unemployed into separate categories has led to them having less social impact: demonstrations and protests by workers and the unemployed themselves tend to involve people claiming benefits from a single enterprise. Thirdly, the authorities can rely on this fragmentation to repress and control the category: the failure of the unemployed to unite in a homogeneous class has made it easier for officials to scale down demonstrations. Indeed, the most favourable outcome for the authorities has been the inability of Chinese workers and the unemployed to stage a structured protest. This inability to unite in a single class reduces their chances of demonstrating *en masse* and, as a result, the contractual strength of the unemployed is lowered.

The results we have described are significant where the mushrooming of protest by the unemployed and former workers is concerned. We have identified elements that have given the government excuse to intervene in order to safeguard social stability by controlling demonstrations of unrest, and we have defined some of the elements that can lessen the impact of demonstrations, not stopping them but diluting protest and depriving it of the weight needed for the conduct of good negotiations. In the last few years, however, following the radical reform of the SOEs, action in defence of rights, especially work-related ones, has gained visibility. There has also been improvement as a result of China's openness to international commitment in terms of civil rights guarantees: political leaders have been obliged to resort less frequently to repressive measures, and leaders of movements feel freer and more protected by international institutions (Minxin Pei, 2000).

According to a variety of sources,[14] there has been an upward trend in workers' demonstrations, although the number of participants is still very limited. The collective action of Chinese workers, including all the categories we quoted earlier, is often based on individual initiatives on a limited scale (Kernen, 2002, p. 23). From a survey of Chinese and foreign newspapers (*People's Daily, Workers' Daily, The New York Times, The Washington Post* and *AP News Service*) from 1996 to April 2001 on popular action linked to protest, we can seize on the unemployed and workers' protest division; the bulk of the episodes refers to retirees' pension arrears problems (42 per cent), and the others refer to laid-off workers (29 per cent) or to workers claiming wage payments (34 per cent) (Hurst and O'Brien, 2002, p. 346). Almost all the information quoted on demonstrations, however, points to a remarkable number of demonstrations with a small participation. For instance, *Jane's Intelligence Review,* in 2001, quoted a survey on 26 collective actions by laid-off workers: 88 per cent had more than 500 participants but few of them reached thousands.[15]

The surveys on the number and the scale of workers' and unemployed demonstrations reveal that most of the protests were made by laid-off workers from a single enterprise or, at most, the biggest protests simply unite people from the same unemployment class or category. The ability of the unemployed to unite in a homogeneous class is virtually non-existent and labour activism is finding it hard to agree on a single way to protest (Ching Kwan Lee, 2000, p. 58). It is surely true that on account of their subdivisions, the workers, the laid-off and the unemployed in China today lack the organization they need for effective negotiating power.

4. UNEMPLOYMENT POLICIES

The great increase in unemployment, begun in the late 1980s, reached a peak with the massive dismissals from SOEs starting from the 1990s. Since the mid-1980s the government has introduced a number of policies aimed at reducing the impact of unemployment on society and managing this relatively new problem. One of the effects of the transition was the creation of the laid-off,[16] a category of *de facto* unemployed but not identical to formal unemployment, which appeared suitable for all the social and economic actors: government, enterprises, managers and employees (Gu, 2003, p. 12). The laid-off workers maintain labour relations with their work unit, which is expected to provide a range of services for them, including assistance in finding a new job. The aim of creating this category was to find a way to ease the transitional institutional arrangement.

The number of laid-off workers varies in accordance with the sector and the geographical region. While lay-offs take place all over the country, massive

Figure 5.3   Number of Laid-off per Region

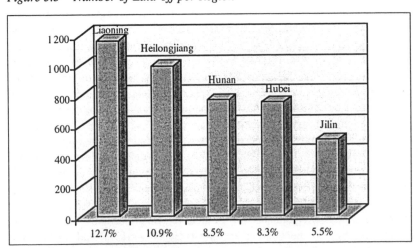

Source: China Statistical Yearbook, 2002.

lay-off is a regional phenomenon (Gu, 2003, p. 5). In fact, massive lay-off is concentrated mainly in provinces where SOEs are inefficient and less productive, operating in the so-called 'sunset industries'. Among the provinces most affected is the north-eastern part of the country, and especially Liaoning. In Figure 5.3, showing the provinces with the highest number of lay-offs, we can notice that Liaoning, together with Heilongjiang and Jilin, also in the north-eastern part of the country, are among the top five. The Liaoning province, once famous for its primary and mining industries, is certainly experiencing the worst conditions. The poor performance of this region recently persuaded the government to use Liaoning as a starting point in trials for renewing the social welfare system, the pension system and unemployment insurance: the Liaoning Social Security Pilot Programme.

4.1. The Re–employment Project and Re-employment Centres

In order to tackle the unemployment and lay-off issue, the re-employment project was launched, with the aim of improving re-employment through job replacement, job training and job creation programs. The project was introduced in 1994 in 30 cities and later (in 1995) coverage was extended to urban areas in the entire country. It involved a broad range of policies focused on improving the chances of the laid-off to find work.

The re-employment project was first implemented in Shanghai as a pilot municipality, combining welfare provision, employment services and re-training programs (Lee and Warner, 2003, p. 2).[17] The main characteristics of the project hinged on the employment policies carried out by the government in order to cope with the problem of youth unemployment during the early stages of the reform era (Gu, 2003, p. 13). The biggest challenge, however, was to deal with the transition in the labour market from a system where unemployment was virtually non-existent to a system in which unemployment was conceivable, accepted and fought.

To face up to the issue, the State Council created re-employment centres as 'transfer stations' from the concept of being laid-off to that of being unemployed. In 1998, the Central Committee of the CCP and the State Council issued the 'Circular on fully implementing the work of ensuring a minimum standard of living and re-employment of laid-off State workers' (Lee and Warner, 2003, p. 9). In order to eradicate unemployment in China, a 'two-guarantee policy' was indicated, including:

1. a basic livelihood for laid-off workers through re-employment centres;
2. a basic livelihood for all retirees and recipients of pensions in full and on time (*White Paper on Labour and Social Security in China*, 2002).

The creation of re-employment centres was meant to provide a basic living allowance and train laid-off workers through specialised training, making it easier for them to find a new job; and to contribute to the pension, medical and social security fund of the laid-off workers whom the centre is responsible for (Solinger, 2000, p. 12). The centres provide a minimum standard of living for the laid–off workers (a basic living allowance) and assist them in finding re–employment. They also pay for the workers' unemployment insurance premium for a maximum of two or three years.[18] After this time workers who have not yet found a job become simply unemployed and can apply for the basic living allowance paid to urban residents. The funding of the re-employment centres is shared equally between the government (one third), the province (one third) and the SOEs (one third). If the SOEs are unable to pay their share, it is taken up by the local government (Lee and Warner, 2003, p. 14).

Re-employment centres are intended to be a bridge between a welfare system based on SOEs and a system based on a capitalistic labour market, but scholars[19] have criticised it, stating that re-employment centres are not enabling workers to leave the SOEs and that the cost of keeping them is damaging the SOEs' finances. According to Solinger, re-employment services are of doubtful effectiveness in re-employing people, and are surely under-funded (Solinger, 2000, p. 31). Since 2001 re-employment centres have no longer been mandatory for SOEs, and since 2002 laid-off workers have started to appear in the unemployment figures. From 2004, the laid-off category is supposed to disappear and people will simply be classified as unemployed (even though many argue that the plan is unlikely to keep to schedule, as the implementation of reforms is still lagging behind). At that point, the unemployed could only be covered by unemployment insurance.

4.2. Unemployment Insurance and Minimum Living Standard Guarantee

In 1986 the State Council released the 'Temporary regulations on unemployment insurance for employees from State Owned Enterprises' and unemployment insurance was introduced (Kaijie, 2003, p. 40). To solve the problem of the livelihood security of the unemployed, in 1993 the State Council released the 'Regulations on unemployment insurance for the employees of SOEs'. The central government policy was directed towards involving local governments in providing livelihood security for the unemployed and in providing social insurance. In 1999 the State Council revised the 1993 Regulations and released the 'Regulation on unemployment insurance', which made unemployment insurance mandatory (Kaijie, 2003, p. 40). In the Tenth *Five Year Plan for the National Economy and Social Development* an advisory note of the Chinese Communist Party noted 'further improvement of unemployed insurance, and the input into the fundamental living security of laid-off workers from SOEs into unemployment insurance on the basis of trials' (Kaijie, 2003, p. 41).

Today unemployment insurance is mandatory for urban employees and is financed by 3 per cent of the wage, to be shared between employers (2 per cent) and employees (1 per cent). The provinces and municipalities must fund the unemployment insurance deficits. Workers, to have benefits, should have paid the premium for at least one year. If they have paid for one to five years, they have the right to 12 months' payment. If they have paid from five to ten years of unemployment insurance, they can enjoy 18 months' payment and if they have been paying for more than ten years the payment lasts up to 24 months. For the first 12 months they receive 70 per cent of the minimum standard wage (higher than the minimum living standard for urban residents). For the subsequent 12 months they receive half of the payment made for the first 12 months (Xing, 2000).

The application of the unemployment insurance scheme is raising a variety of problems, among which the more serious concern the scheme's ineffectiveness in collecting contributions from small non-state enterprises (Solinger, 2000, p. 12). This implies that, combined with relatively low coverage in the private sector, the effectiveness of unemployment insurance as income maintenance is extremely weak (Hussain, 2000, p. 21). Also relevant is the purpose for which unemployment funds are used: until recently, authorities financed other social benefits with unemployment funds that were extremely high because, since its creation in 1986, only a few workers were accorded unemployment benefit. These distortions are made worse by the fact that the unemployment insurance is now going to absorb the transition from the laid-off toward a more capitalist-oriented unemployment class, as re-employment centres close and the laid-off merge with the unemployed. In 2001, 102 million employees participated in the programme, 42 per cent of the urban workforce (*China Labour Statistical Yearbook*, 2003, pp. 10–33): the dilemma is then whether the unemployed will really be covered by unemployment insurance benefits and to what extent (Gu, 2003, p. 17). Current low coverage of employees reflects an inequitable division between SOE workers, with a high coverage, and non-state sector employees with a coverage lower than 10 per cent (Hussain, 2000, p. 18).

In order to cope with the low coverage in support for the growing numbers of unemployed, a minimum basic income was implemented: in 1993, with growing unemployment and SOE bankruptcy that generated the problem of unpaid pensions and wages for many workers and pensioners, the traditional social assistance programme was restructured, with the aim of extending the coverage to a larger part of the population and raising the level of benefits for the recipients (Yang, 2003, p. 35). The new reforms, called the Minimum Living Standard Guarantees, included targets called 'the three nos' (Leung, 2003, p. 83): people with:

1. no source of income;

2. no capacity to work;
3. no family support.

Also covered were people with problems related to unemployment such as families with financial problems due to unemployment, unemployed people ineligible for unemployed benefits and pensioners with inadequate income.

The programme provided assistance to registered urban households. In 1997, the State Council recommended that the programme be implemented in all cities by 1999. The number of recipients rose from 2 million people in 1997 to 4.16 million people in 2001 but the number of people eligible for assistance was 14.8 million (Leung, 2003, p. 83). Another problem has been the deficit that unemployment insurance funds are now facing in provinces in which the laid-off class has already been pushed into unemployment (*China Labour Statistical Yearbook*, 2003, pp. 10–34); the deficit has to be covered from the municipal budget but the trend is not sustainable in the long term. A further rise in income tax for unemployment insurance could reduce the deficit but will increase the problem of low coverage.

The transition from SOE-centred social welfare units to a market-based social safety net has almost been put in place. Unemployment Centres have been constituted as a 'transition instrument' and unemployment insurance is intended to be the new collector for the unemployed. Alternatives to the SOE system have thus been created, but implementation is still lagging behind.

5.   CONCLUDING REMARKS AND POSSIBLE SCENARIOS

China's labour market dynamics seem to be one of the major challenges to the social stability of the nation in the near future. Our overview of Chinese unemployment highlights a labour market in transition from an SOE-centred social welfare unit, to an independent system with a comprehensive social safety net.

The country, after the reforms of the public sector, has still to re-absorb millions of SOEs redundant workers. Estimation of future entrants into the labour market based on IMF studies (Brooks and Ran, 2003) indicates that the working-age population will grow by 10–13 million annually until 2010 and that today there is still a surplus labour force in SOEs. If SOEs enhanced labour productivity to the level experienced by the non-state sector, there would be 10–11 million redundant workers, in addition to the millions already dismissed since the 1980s (Wang, 2001). Projections made by IMF studies[20] indicate that, under some defined hypothesis, there are three possible scenarios: in an optimistic one, with a GDP growth of 8 per cent of the non-agricultural sectors (and the assumption that most of the new jobs are to be taken by new entrants to the labour force), the labour market could absorb two thirds of the total labour surplus in the next few years. In the middle scenario (with 7 per cent growth, SOEs' dismissals taking place by 2005, and assuming six million rural migrants will move to urban areas annually in this period), the IMF projections predict an increase in the urban unemployment rate reaching a peak of 10 per cent by 2005, and slowly declining to 8.2 per cent by 2010. In the worst scenario, with an average GDP growth rate of 6 per cent, the labour market will undergo strong pressure by new entrants into the labour pool reserve.

In any case, even on the most optimistic hypothesis, the negative effects of unemployment will spread throughout society, jeopardising social stability. If we look at the growing number of protests in Chinese cities, social stability already seems to be threatened by labour-related problems. Nevertheless, the number of workers' protests in China is of uncertain meaning: the atomisation of the labour market and the unemployed does not facilitate the identification of the unemployed as a single class which could deal more profitably with State authorities. According to Cai, the main causes for the limited scale of mobilisations are that workers and the laid-off from various enterprises believe they have different goals and find it difficult to share and spread information (Cai, 2002, p. 341). We also identified other elements relevant to the dividing up of the unemployed: the lack of freedom of association and the State's determination to separate workers with the aim of controlling and concealing the truth about unemployment.

Many authors argue (Solinger, 2000, pp. 16–23; Minxin Pei, 2000),[21] and we are convinced, that the atomisation suffered by the labour market until now, has played an important role in stopping the protests of the working class and in keeping them at a level that can be managed by the State.

In Chinese society today and in the labour sector in particular we can identify the coexistence of various tensions that are struggling against each other: the drive toward reforms clashes with the need to maintain stability, and the need to have sound statistical data on unemployment clashes with the tendency to rely on unsound macroeconomic data and with the need to preserve social stability (Rocca, 2000, p. 3).

In the future, the impact on social stability of worsening unemployment conditions in China will depend very much on the ability of the working class to unite in a single body. Paradoxically, if the labour market reforms that have been implemented succeed in standardising the status of employees and the unemployed in the different provinces and sectors instead of leaving them divided and unable to form a united category, the future of demonstrations and protests will be more powerful and destabilising for the Chinese authorities. Whatever happens, this process of standardisation of the labour market will have a long-term effect: much of the actual effect of unemployment conditions and China's social stability during the next few years will be decided by the outcomes of labour market reforms. We are reasonably confident that, even if unemployment is to be a great threat to the Chinese authorities, social stability will be preserved over the next few years and the peak of instabilities created by redundant workers will be surmounted. The State will then have the instruments to manage the unemployment issue and to preserve social stability in the country.

NOTES

*   I am thankful to Maria Weber for her support; I would like to thank Vasco Molini, Anna Stenbeck, Benedetta Trivellato and Marco Rossi for their comments and discussions. Many thanks also to Daphne Hughes, for her editing assistance. Obviously I take the entire responsibility for all I have written.
1.   China, United Nations Development Programme, 1999.
2.   In other words, with the same capital resources, the government could create more employment in the agricultural sector than in the industrial one.
3.   For instance, in some cities, *hukou* was given to people who could pay a certain amount of money.
4.   For instance, rural households are obliged to fulfil government agricultural production quotas, but there are also restrictions on social benefits: rural migrants are not entitled to the social safety net in urban areas without the possession of a *hukou* and if families with children go to urban areas they have to pay extremely high fees to enable their children to have an education. The result of these restrictions is that the main category of immigrants consists of young people without children.
5.   State-Owned Enterprises are situated in urban areas: when considering the effect of unemployment generated by SOE-dismissal, we are considering urban statistical aggregation.
6.   Wages in the urban areas were centrally determined and controlled by the Bureau of Labour and Personnel on criteria such as educational levels and work experience: the State Ministry of Labour and Personnel assigned an employment quota to each provincial or city government (Xing, 2000, p. 5). The local authorities then determined a wage for each person.
7.   In 2000, 50 per cent of SOEs had workers with terminal contracts.
8.   Even a senior research fellow of the Academy of Macroeconomic Research under the State Development Planning Commission said it was widely acknowledged in China that the official unemployment rate, which only includes urban residents who register for unemployment handouts, did not reflect the real situation. See *China Economic Review online* (2003), available at http://www.chinaeconomicreview.com/htm/n_20030301.482613.htm.
9.   Chinese statistical data in general are notoriously inaccurate. See Rawski (2000), available online at http://www.pitt.edu/~tgrawski/papers2000/REVD00.HTM; and 'What's Happening to China's GDP Statistics?', *China Economic Review*, 12 (4), December 2001, pp. 347–54, online at http://www.pitt.edu/~tgrawski/papers2001/gdp912f.pdf.
10. For a comprehensive description of the laid-off categories see Solinger, 2000, pp. 16–23 and Gu, 2003.
11. Data from the labour statistical yearbook are considered less misleading because they are not official but they are just a 'sample survey' (Yang Guang, 1999).
12. *Beijing Evening News*, 2001.
13. There is general agreement in recognising that the Chinese jobless have been broken into numerous, variously defined subdivisions (among others Solinger, 2001; Rocca, 2000; Cai, 2002).
14. Among others: *China Labour Bulletin*, www.china–labour.org, various reports; Human Rights Watch, www.hrw.org/press; IHLO, www.ihlo.org; 'Is Social Security the "Solution" to the Labour Protests in North–Eastern China?', Ching Kwan Lee, 2000.
15. 'Beijing's struggle to ride the tiger of liberalisation', *Jane's Intelligence Review,* January 2001, pp. 26–30.
16. 'Laid–off workers are those who lose their jobs as their employing units encounter economic difficulties, while still maintaining their nominal employment relationship with the enterprises' (Gu, 2003, p. 2).

17. For instance local government subsidised the employment of laid-off and unemployed and employers could employ people for 3 or 6 months without signing a labour contract for them (Gu, 2003, p. 13).
18. Depending on the province, the period of permanence in the re-employment centre can last up to a maximum of three years.
19. For further information on re-employment centres and for an analysis of problems related to this subject, see Solinger, 2000, p. 12.
20. See Brooks and Ran, 2003.
21. Solinger (2001) and Rocca (2000, p. 3), after an exhaustive overview of the existing class of unemployed or laid-off workers and their relative classification in accordance with the quality and quantity of benefits they receive from the authorities, suppose it to be most useful for the government to have the unemployed divided into categories, in order to repress any unified mobilisation.

BIBLIOGRAPHY

ADB (2002), *The 2020 Project: Policy Support In The People's Republic Of China*, available at http://www.adb.org/Publications/country.asp?id=47&wp=12.

Barmé, G. (2000), 'The Revolution of Resistance', in Elizabeth J. Perry and Mark Selden (eds), *Chinese Society: Change, Conflict and Resistance*, London, Routledge, pp. 198–220.

Barr, N. (1998), *The Economics of the Welfare State*, Oxford: Oxford University Press, 3rd edition.

Brooks, R. and Ran, T. (2003), *China's Labor Market Performance and Challenges*, IMF Working Paper WP/03/210.

Cai, Y. (2002), 'The Resistance of Chinese Laid–off Workers in the Reform Period', *The China Quarterly* (170), June, London: Cambridge University Press, pp. 327–44.

Cai, Y. and Wang, D. (2003), *What Can We Learn from China's 2000 Census Data?*, paper presented at Shanghai Conference 11–13 September 2003 avalaible at http://www1.msh-aris.fr/reseauemploi/Shanghai/ListeconferencesShanghai.html.

China data centre: http://chinadatacenter.org/chinadata/guest/yb2001/indexe.htm.

China Economic Review (2003), March, p. 4, available at http://www.chinaeconomicreview.com/htm/n_20030301.482613.htm.

China Labour Bulletin, www.china-labour.org.

China Labour Statistical Yearbook (2003), Beijing: China Statistical Publishing House.

China Statistical Yearbook: various issues, Beijing: China Statistical Publishing House.

Ching Kwan Lee (2000), 'Is Social Security the "Solution" to the Labour Protests in North-Eastern China?, Hong Kong Liason Office (IHLO), 24 April 2002, available at: http://www.ihlo.org/item1/chinasocsec.pdf.

Ching Kwan Lee (2000), 'Pathways of Labour Insurgency', in Elizabeth J. Perry and Mark Selden (eds), *Chinese Society: Change, Conflict and Resistance*, London: Routledge, pp. 41–61.

Chow, G. (2002), *China's Economic Transformation*, Malden, MA: Blackwell Publishing, USA.

Gu, Edward, May 2003, *Labour Market Insecurities in China*, Geneva: International Labour Office.

Hochraich, Diana (2001), *Labour Mobility and Unemployment in China*, French Ministry of Finance, Paris. Paper presented at the International Workshop on the Chinese Economy, Shanghai.

Hong Kong Liaison Office (IHLO), www.ihlo.org.

Human Rights Watch, www.hro.org/press.

Hurst, W. and O'Brien K. (2002), 'China's Contentious Pensioners', *The China Quarterly* (179), June, London: Cambridge University Press, pp. 345–60.

Hussain, A., Leisering, L. and Sen G. (2002), *People's Republic of China. Old–Age Pensions for the Rural Areas: From Land Reform to Globalization*, Manila: Asian Development Bank, September.

Hussain, Athar (2000), *Social Welfare in China in the Context of Three Transitions*, Center for research on economic development and policy reform, working paper No. 66, Stanford University.

ILO employee dismissal regulation: http://natlex.ilo.org/scripts/natlexcgi.exe?lang=E.

ILO, 'China: Labour Market and Income Insecurity', http://www.ilo.org/public/english/protection/ses/info/publ/labour_china.htm.

Kaijie, D. (2003), 'The Crucial Role of Local Government in Setting Up a Social Safety Net', *China Perspectives* (48), July–August 2003.

Kernen, A. (2002), 'State Employees Face an Uncertain Future, the Predictament in North-East China', *China Perspectives*, Special Edition China–WTO (part 1) (40), March–April, pp. 21–7.

Kernen, A. and Rocca, J. (1998), 'La réforme des entreprises publiques en Chine et sa gestion sociale: Le cas de Shenyang et du Liaoning', *Les Etudes du Ceri* (37), January.

Lee, G. and Warner, M. (2003), *From Local Experiment to Nationwide Labour Market Policy? The Shanghai Re–employment Model*, mimeo, paper presented at LVMH conference, INSEAD Euro–Asia centre, Fontainebleau, France, 7 and 8 February.

Lee, V. (2000), *Unemployment Insurance and Assistance Systems in Mainland China*, Research and Library Services Division, Legislative Council Secretariat, Hong Kong.

Leung, J. (2003), 'Social Security Reforms in China: Issues and Prospects', *International Journal of Social Welfare* (12), pp. 73–85.

Mallee, H. (2000), 'Migration, Hukou and Resistance in Reform China', in Elizabeth J. Perry and Mark Selden (eds), *Chinese Society: Change, Conflict and Resistance*, London: Routledge.

Ministry of Labour, State Economic and Trade Commission and the Ministry of Finance (1997), *Notice on Establishing Re–employment Service Centres at Experimental Cities with Enterprises of 'Optimized Capital Structure'* (Lao Bu Fa [1997] Document No. 252), Herald Translation Service, Chinalaw Web – http://www.qis.net/chinalaw/prclaw63.htm.

Minxin Pei (2000), 'Rights and Resistance: The Changing Context of the Dissident Movement', in Elizabeth J. Perry and Mark Selden (eds), *Chinese Society: Change, Conflict and Resistance*, London: Routledge, pp. 20–40.

MOLSS (Ministry of Labour and Social Security)(2002), *White Paper on Labour and Social Security in China*, The State Council Information Office, http://www.china-embassy.org/eng/29539.html, April.

Nolan, P. (1993), *State and Market in the Chinese Economy*, London: Macmillan Press.

Nolan P. (1994), 'Large Firms and Industrial Reform in Former Planned Economies: The Case of China', *Cambridge Journal of Economics*, **20** (1), pp. 1–29.

Rawski, T. (2000), *China by the Numbers: How Reform Affected Chinese Economic Statistics* (revised 20 December 2000), available online at http://www.pitt.edu/~tgrawski/papers2000/REVD00.HTM.

Rawski, T. (2001) 'What's Happening to China's GDP Statistics?', *China Economic Review*, **12** (4), December 2001, pp. 347–54, online at: http://www.pitt.edu/~tgrawski/papers2001/gdp912f.pdf.

Rocca, J. (2000), 'L'évolution de la crise du travail dans la Chine urbaine', *Les études du CERI* (65), April.

Rocca, J. (2003), *The Invention of Social Policies in Marketizing China: The Cases of Migrant Workers and Precarious Urban Workers*, paper presented at Shanghai Conference 11–13 September, available online at http://www1.msh–paris.fr/reseauemploi/Shanghai/ListeconferencesShanghai.html.

Solinger, Dorothy J. (2000), *Labor in Limbo: Pushed by the Plan Towards the Mirage of the Market*, Irvine: University of California.

Solinger, Dorothy J. (2001), 'Why We Cannot Count the "Unemployed"', *The China Quarterly* (167), September, London: Cambridge University Press, pp. 671–88.

Solinger, Dorothy J. (2002), 'Labour Market Reform and the Plight of the Laid-off Proletariat', *The China Quarterly* (179), June, London: Cambridge University Press, pp. 304–26.

United Nations Development Programme (UNDP) (1999), *Human Development Report China*, Beijing.

Wang, G. (2001), *Projections of China's Population from 2001–10*, Working Paper Presented at Conference of China Labour Markets in Transition.

Wang Xiao-qiang (1998), *China's Price and Enterprise Reform*, London: Macmillan Press.

Wong, L. (1998), *Marginalization and Social Welfare in China*, London: Routledge.

Xing, Meng. (2000), *Labour Market Reform in China*, Cambridge: Cambridge University Press.

Yang, D. (2003), 'Leadership Transition and the Political Economy of Governance', *Asian Survey*, **XLIII** (1), January–February, pp. 25–40.

Yang Guang (1999), *Facing Unemployment: Urban Layoffs and the Way Out in Post–reform China (1993–1999), An Empirical And Theoretical Analysis*, Working paper 308, Institute of Social Studies, The Netherlands, December.

Yaohui, Zhao and Jianguo, Xu (2002), 'China's Urban Pension System: Reforms and Problems', *Cato Journal*, **21** (3), pp. 395–414.

6. Dealing with an Ageing Population in China

Maria Weber and Anna Stenbeck

1. INTRODUCTION

In the early 21st century China formally became an ageing society as the share of elderly aged 65 or above reached 7 per cent of the population. The ratio is still low by international standards, but the size of the country implies that China already has more elderly than any other country in the world, and the population is ageing rapidly. Industrialised countries have experienced the same demographic transition, due to declining birthrates and rising life expectancies. While it took most OECD countries 80–100 years to double their old-age dependency ratios,[1] China was expected to double its ratio in little over 30 years (World Bank, 1997, p. 14). Between 1978 and 2002, the share of elderly grew by a half, more rapidly than most developed countries with the exception of Japan (see Table 6.1).

China's exceptionally rapid ageing is attributed to the combination of longer life expectancy and the government's population-control policy. Life expectancy increased from 36.3 years in 1960 to 66.8 years in 1980, and reached 70.7 years in 2002 (World Bank, various years). The number of births per woman has declined constantly since the mid 1970s until reaching the current average of 1.9 in 1995, below the UN's estimated natural population replacement rate of 2.1. Since the 1970s, China has promoted family planning to slow down the population growth-rate, by encouraging late marriage and childbearing and advocating the practice of 'one couple, one child'. The policies, which remain in place, are enforced through a system of financial and administrative rewards and sanctions. Family planning is carefully coordinated with labour and social security policies, as part of a comprehensive sustainable development plan. According to the government's targets, the population size should not exceed 1.33 billion in 2005, 1.4 billion in 2010, and reach a peak of 1.6 billion in 2050 followed by a gradual decline as the age-structure matures (CPIRC, 2000).

The ageing process that inevitably accompanies a stabilisation of population growth has begun to generate concern as the long-term

Table 6.1   Comparative Population Ageing

	Ageing 1978–2002	Population 2002			Labour participation	GDP per capita
	≥ 65[a] (% change)	Total (million)	≥ 65 (% of total)	Old–age Depend.[b]	Ratio[c]	(PPP, US$)
Japan	110.5	127.1	18.0	34.2	1.02	25 650
China	56.2	1 281.0	7.2	13.5	1.13	4 475
Italy	46.9	57.9	18.6	35.5	0.85	25 570
Russia	33.5	144.1	12.9	22.6	0.95	7 926
France	16.9	59.4	16.1	33.6	0.95	26 151
US	14.8	288.4	12.5	25.3	1.04	35 158
UK	9.8	58.9	16.1	34.1	1.06	25 672
Germany	9.2	82.5	16.8	31.3	0.93	26 324
India	2.9	1 048.3	5.0	13.2	1.18	2 571

Notes:
a. change in the share of ≥ 65;
b. ratio of ≥ 65 to working age population;
c. ratio of labour force to working age.

Source: World Development Indicators (various years).

sustainability of any old-age provision, whether public or private, depends on the proportion of elderly relative to the working population. Though longer life expectancies are appealing, funding long retirements becomes ever more burdensome as the proportion of elderly increases. Many Western countries are currently experiencing rising pension costs and large estimated implicit pension liabilities. Pension-system reform is one of the most urgent and politically sensitive issues on the agenda of developed countries today.

This chapter aims to present an overview of China's public provisions for old-age security, historically exclusive to urban enterprise workers and government employees. China has no rural pension system but recent demographic and socio-economic developments have raised the demand for rural old-age security and the eventual establishment of a national system.

2.   EVOLUTION OF PUBLIC HEALTHCARE

2.1.   The Era of Mao Zedong

China's first pension system was introduced in 1951 by the State Council (SC)[2] Regulations on Labour Insurance.[3] Enterprises contributed 3 per cent of the total wage bill to labour-insurance funds administered by the local All-China Federation of Trade Unions (ACFTU), under the supervision of the

Ministry of Labour (MOL). The retirement age was high relative to life expectancy; 60 years for male and 50 for female workers,[4] and the ratio of retirees to workers was as low. The system generated a surplus, and part of the revenue was transferred to a national fund to provide a degree of pooling and pre-funding. However, this modern organisation suffered a severe setback during the Cultural Revolution when trade unions were dissolved and all accumulated labour-insurance funds were dissipated. Local and national pooling and pre-funding were suspended and individual enterprises became *de facto* responsible for financing their pension liabilities and paying the benefits directly to retirees. The social insurance model was not re-established after the end of the Cultural Revolution, and in 1978 the SC formally assigned the responsibility for pensions to the single enterprises (Dixon, 1981, pp. 247–59; CPIRC, 2000, pp. 1–2; World Bank, 1997, p. 16).[5]

2.2. The Era of Deng Xiaoping

The Deng era comprised two periods of reform, a first period from 1978 to 1988, and a second period from 1988 to 1992 which continued and accelerated in the post-Deng era. Economic and industrial reforms were accompanied and complemented by social security reforms, with the aim of stimulating a turnover of the workforce and raising the productivity of SOEs. The SC document of 1978 included two separate pension regulations, respectively for public personnel and urban enterprise workers. State employees received a 'merit-based' pension,[6] financed by the State budget on a pay-as-you-earn basis.[7] Pension benefits ranged from 60 to 75 per cent of the monthly standard wage, depending on the years of employment. In addition, each retiree in the state-owned sector could secure a fully salaried position for one child upon his or her retirement.

The 1978 regulations effectively encouraged early retirement at a time when life expectancy rose substantially. The number of retirees jumped fivefold between 1978 and 1985, and the ratio of workers to pensioners fell from 30.3:1 in 1978 to 6.4:1 in 1988 (World Bank, 1997, p. 16; Whiteford, 2003). Yearly pension expenditures took up an ever-larger share of enterprises' total costs, in aggregate rising from 2.8 per cent to 10.6 per cent of the urban wage bill. As each enterprise was responsible for its own retirees, the pension burden was unevenly distributed across enterprises, with the oldest and least profitable sustaining the highest costs relative to turnover (INPRS, p. 1). The solution was to 'socialise' old-age provision, by transferring its administration to local governments and separate public bodies, and to distribute the costs more evenly. The seventh five-year economic plan (1986–1990) was the first to adopt the term 'social security system' officially.

2.3. The Post–Deng Era

In 1986 China introduced the 'labour contract system',[8] and set up a separate pension system for contract workers, with local administration and pooling of funds and, for the first time, individual contributions. The system proved a precursor for the subsequent 1990s reforms, establishing the principles of socialised administration, limited State liability, and individual responsibility (Chow, 2000, pp. 36–7; Chow and Xu, 2001, p. 40). The urban social security system was reformed continuously during the 1990s, but three main documents (1991, 1995 and 1997, see endnote references below) outlined the framework for the current system.

In 1991 the SC presented a plan for a comprehensive system that would cover all enterprise workers, and be financed according to the principle of shared responsibility between the government, employers and individual workers.[9] The 1991 Resolution introduced county/city-wide pension pooling, and envisaged future pooling at the provincial level. Social insurance agencies (SIAs) were given the task of collecting contributions, administering and managing the funds, and disbursing benefits to pensioners.[10] The benefit calculation method remained defined on the years of service and the standard local wage. Contribution rates were set by local governments to cover current expenditure and generate a small surplus for fund accumulation. Enterprises and workers were also encouraged to set up voluntary schemes to supplement the basic state benefit, thus establishing the principle of a three-tiered structure. Local governments were allowed a wide margin of discretion within the national guidelines, as the pension burden varied between localities, sectors and large individual enterprises. In areas with many retirees, contribution rates reached 30 per cent (compared to a national average of 20 per cent), deterring non-state enterprises with few retirees from participating. Coverage varied; over 95 per cent of SOEs participated, little over 50 per cent of COEs, and less than a third of other enterprises (Chow, 2000, pp. 76–9; Chow and Xu, 2001, pp. 40–4; INPRS, p. 2; World Bank, 1997, p. 17).

In 1995 an SC Circular adopted the principle of combining social pooling with individual accounts and introduced the principle of defined contributions.[11] Cities and provinces were given a choice between two models but could also combine elements of the two. Though the Circular aimed to unify standards and ensure a rapid expansion of coverage, it had the unintended consequence of encouraging local governments to adopt a wide array of different models with different proportions of pooling and individual accounts. The resulting fragmentation was detrimental to labour mobility and competitiveness, and became an obstacle to subsequent attempts to unify the system and raise the level of pooling (Chow, 2000, pp. 84–5; Chow and Xu, 2001, pp. 44–7; Leung, 2003, p. 79).

In 1997 the government announced its intention to unify the urban system and presented the conceptual framework for a three-tiered system with uniform eligibility criteria, uniform contribution and benefit rates, and uniform standards for provincial administration and pooling.[12] At the Fifteenth Party Congress in September 1997, Party Secretary Jiang Zemin inaugurated a new phase of reforms, aiming to turn SOEs into modern competitive enterprises, and advancing social security reform was seen as necessary and complementary, to provide for the new waves of laid-off workers and avoid popular unrest, to increase pension portability and thereby labour mobility between the SOEs and the non-state sector, and to smooth pension costs across enterprises. It was also imperative to address the apparent deficiencies of the latest reform attempts. The enterprise-based welfare system had become a heavy burden on the newly profit-oriented SOEs, squeezed between the growing costs of social obligations and market pressure on prices and revenues. By unifying contribution rates across enterprises and localities the 1997 Decisions removed the link between the size of a single enterprise's contributions and the size of its pension liabilities. Pension benefits were also unified and reduced, to yield an average replacement rate[13] of 60 per cent. This reduction, from the previous 80–100 per cent, would be compensated by voluntary supplementary employer and individual savings (Chow, 2000, p. 86; Leung, 2003, p. 79; CPIRC, 2000, pp. 2–3).

Implementing the reform proved neither quick nor uncomplicated. Large regional income disparities, the close relationship between local governments and enterprises, and difficulties in extending the coverage in the non-state sector, hampered the unification process. In 1998 approximately half of the urban workforce was covered, only a third of retirees received their pensions through 'socialised delivery' instead of directly from the work unit, and the balance between revenues and expenditures was fragile.

As the financial position of SOEs deteriorated, many insolvent enterprises interrupted or delayed their social welfare payments, causing the compliance rate to fall below 80 per cent in 1999. Only a few provinces, including the provincial level municipalities (Beijing, Shanghai, Chongqing and Tjanjin), had unified standards and administrations, while the majority transferred funds from municipal schemes in surplus to those in deficit. Inevitably, municipal governments were reluctant to harmonise standards and hand over the surpluses required for the adjustment transfers. On balance, pension schemes were in deficit in 17 of the 31 provinces (Chow and Xu, 2001, p. 53).[14]

The problems prompted the government to issue further regulations in 1998–9 to transfer eleven sector-specific pension schemes[15] to the relevant local administrations, to clarify the mechanisms for socialised collection and delivery of pension benefits, and to insist on the transfer of pension administration and pooling to the provincial level. In 2001, the government launched a series of pilot projects, in the Liaoning province and in selected cities of other provinces, to experiment with modifications to the scheme that, if successful, might be used to amend the national guidelines (Zhu, 2002, p. 44; Gounaris and Chao, 2002).[16]

3.   THE MAIN FEATURES OF THE URBAN PENSION SYSTEM

3.1.   Regulation and Administration

The foundation of China's current social security system rests on a few basic principles expressed in the 1995 Labour Law, but mainly on administrative regulations, rules, decisions, measures, guidelines and orders, issued by the SC or its various pertinent ministries, and subsequently elaborated and adapted by local governments to local conditions. A number of ministries and commissions under the SC are directly and indirectly involved in pension policies, including the Ministry of Labour and Social Security (MOLSS), the Ministry of Finance (MOF), the State Development Planning Commission (SDPC),[17] and the MOCA (Zhu, 2002, p. 40; ADB, 2002).

The MOLSS has the overall administrative and management responsibility for all social insurance programs, including pension schemes, which implies overseeing pension records, revenues and expenditures, as well as the investment of pension funds. The daily handling of social insurance affairs, which used to be the responsibility of the single enterprises, is gradually being transferred to Social Insurance Agencies (SIAs) at the provincial or city/county levels.[18] SIAs collect contributions from enterprises, including the workers' withheld contributions, and disburse pensions to the beneficiaries' bank or postal accounts. SIAs also administer and manage revenues and expenditures so that accounts are kept separate and funds are used for their specified purposes only. Supervisory organs within the labour and social security departments oversee the collection, management and payment of social insurance funds, and investigate and punish enterprises that violate the regulations.

Under the previous enterprise-based system, the actual amount of contributions paid depended on the persuasiveness and the personal relationship between local governments and the single enterprises. When enterprises kept the records and disbursed benefits it was common practice to 'remit the difference' between the contributions owed and benefits due for their own retirees. This officially unlawful practice effectively relegated the local administrations to act as clearing-houses for transfers between net-contributing and net-benefiting enterprises. Since net contributors had no incentives to comply, and instead sought to avoid or delay payments, the local government's capacity to distribute pensions fully and on time was severely undermined. A number of coercive measures have been introduced to improve compliance such as making evasion a punishable offence, withholding certain renewable business permits until contributions are paid, forcing large enterprises to sign special payment agreements, and even publicising the names of the enterprises with the largest arrears. Experiments with delegating the collection of social insurance fees to local tax organs seem successful; the practice was extended to 16 provinces in 2002 and accounted for the collection of one third of the basic pension contributions (NBS, 2003; ADB, 2002; Chow and Xu, 2001, pp. 53–4; Frazier, 2002; Zhao and Xu, 2002, p. 402).

3.2. System Design

The design of the urban pension system follows closely the World Bank's recommendations of a multi-pillared partially-funded system. The system has three tiers: a mandatory basic pension, voluntary employer-sponsored supplementary schemes and individual voluntary saving schemes (see Table 6.2).

Table 6.2   The Urban Pension System

Tiers	World Bank's Pillars	Financing	Benefits
1. Basic Pension (mandatory)	I. Social pool (pay-as-you-go)	Employer max 20% of wage bill	Defined benefits 20% local average wage
	II. Individual accounts (fully-funded)	Worker 8% of wage	Defined contributions per month: 1/120 of total accumulated funds
2. Employer supplementary scheme (voluntary)	IIIa. Individual accounts (fully-funded)	Employer limits, tax breaks (a) Worker ≤ half of total (a)	Defined contributions lump sum or regular withdrawals
3. Individual supplementary (voluntary)	IIIb. Individual accounts (fully-funded)	Worker local rules, tax breaks (a)	Defined contributions lump sum or annuities

Note: Summarised from various sources. Under defined benefits (DB) schemes, benefit levels are fixed at the time of retirement, as a function of past earnings (individual or average) and the years of contribution. Under defined contribution (DC) schemes, benefits are calculated as an annuity based on the individual worker's accumulated balance of contributions, accumulated returns, expected future returns and life expectancy. The investment risk is born by the worker in DC schemes and by the pension fund in DB schemes. (a) Regulations both endorse and limit employer and worker financing of supplementary schemes.

The first tier, hereafter referred to as the Basic Pension, is guaranteed by the State and consists of two pillars, a social pool (Pillar 1) and a system of individual accounts (Pillar 2).[19] Enterprises should contribute no more than 20 per cent of the wage bill and workers no less than 4 per cent of the individual wage (rising by 1 percentage point every two years until reaching 8 per cent in 2005). Eleven per cent of each worker's wage is accredited to the individual account while the remainder goes to the social pool. Pillar 1, the social pool, operates on a pay-as-you-go basis distributing defined benefits equal to 20 per cent of the local average wage to workers who have contributed for at least 15 years. Pillar 2, the individual accounts, operates with defined contributions and pays a monthly benefit equal to 1/120 of the value accumulated at the time of retirement.[20] Pillar 2 should generate a wage replacement rate of 38.5 per cent for a worker with 35 years of contributions, assuming that the return on investment equals the growth rate of wages.[21] Together the two pillars should guarantee a basic pension yielding a wage replacement rate close to 60 per cent.

The second and third tiers of the urban system, together forming Pillar 3 envisaged by the World Bank, consist of voluntary supplementary programs initiated respectively by employers and individuals and administered by local governments. Employer-sponsored schemes may be set up by enterprises that comply with the mandatory contributions of the first tier. Employers and workers can jointly finance them, but the worker cannot be required to pay more than half of the total contribution. Employers may select fund managers from government-run financial management agencies, commercial insurance companies or other financial institutions with the approval of the MOLSS, or choose to manage the funds internally (Gounaris and Chao, 2002).[22]

In line with the central government's policy of shared responsibility, workers should contribute to third-tier individual voluntary schemes managed by local governments or SIAs. However, by the end of 2003, the regulatory framework for individual schemes remained vague and coverage was limited. Though the schemes should offer higher returns than the interest rate on bank deposits, they also compete with commercial insurance and savings products, as well as with alternative uses of capital.

3.3. Financing

The Basic Pension is financed from three sources: employer and worker contributions, investment earnings from accumulated funds, and fiscal revenue, since the government guarantees the financing in case of shortages. Despite the favourable picture depicted by the aggregate statistics (see Table 6.3), expenditures under Pillar 1 have on average exceeded revenues from contributions, forcing local governments to 'borrow' funds formally accredited to the individual accounts. Thus individual accounts are largely notional; they figure in the pension records but are not backed by any tangible financial assets. In addition, the funds accumulated under the Basic Pension system have only been invested in government bonds or State-bank deposits, implying that Pillar 2 is in effect a hybrid of a defined benefit and a defined contribution scheme since the size of the pension benefit varies with the amount contributed by the single worker but the rate of return is fixed administratively (Takayama, 2002).

Table 6.3   The Basic Pension System

	1999[a]	2000	2001	2002
Contributors (million)	95.02	104.48	108.02	111.29
Beneficiaries	29.84	31.7	33.81	36.08
System dependency ratio[b]	31.4%	30.3%	31.3%	32.4%
Revenue (billion yuan)	196.51	227.81	248.9	317.15
Expenditure	192.49	211.55	232.13	284.29
Accumulated surplus	73.35	94.71	105.41	160.8

Notes:
a. institutions and State organs included from 1999;
b. ratio of pensioners to workers.

Source: *China Labour Statistical Yearbook*, 2002; NBS, 2003.

The transition to a partially funded system, and the 'empty' individual accounts, has evidenced the existence of a large implicit pension debt. Since 1997 the MOF has transferred funds from the central budget to provinces with pension deficits. The fiscal transfers for 2001 were estimated to reach 35–40 billion yuan, equal to 15 per cent of the total revenue from contributions and more than twice the stated surplus for that year (Frazier, 2002, p. 3; *China Statistical Yearbook*, 2002).

In September 2000 the SC established the National Social Security Fund (NSSF) to serve as a supplementary adjustment tool to meet shortfalls in the provincial Basic Pensions, and as a reserve of last resort to cover future social security expenditures. The NSSF is funded from budgetary allocations, proceeds from issuing government bonds and selling State assets,[23] and from earnings of State lotteries. The NSSF Council currently manages the accumulated funds while the MOF and the MOLSS are jointly responsible for the expenditure policy. By the end of 2002 the fund had accumulated 124.2 billion yuan,[24] less than half the yearly expenditure under the Basic Pension, invested mainly in bank deposits and government bonds. In December 2002 the SC announced that part of the fund's assets would be invested in stocks, corporate bonds and other fixed-income instruments, according to predetermined risk criteria, and in June 2003 the NSSF Council selected six domestic fund-management companies through competitive biddings.[25] At the end of 2003, NSSF funds could neither be invested in foreign assets, officially due to the inconvertibility of the yuan, nor by foreign managers (Gounaris and Chao, 2002; *Shanghai Evening Post*, 2 June 2003).

3.4. Problems and Sustainability: Implicit Debt and Future Adjustments

The Basic Pension system clearly suffers from a number of problems including excessive fragmentation and insufficient pooling, low coverage in the non-state sector, low compliance rates among participants, a large implicit liability, and a structural imbalance between current revenues and expenditures.

In 1997 the system simply inherited the accumulated liabilities of the previous arrangements, and no specific measures were taken to finance the transitions costs. Pillar 1 (the social pool) should generate a surplus sufficient to compensate for pensions owed to workers who accumulated their (generous) rights under the old system, and, ideally, also to reintegrate the 'empty' individual accounts.[26] Recent estimates of the implicit pension debt range from 20 per cent of GDP according to a Chinese study[27] to 71 per cent according to a World Bank paper (Wang et al., 2000, p. 26). Opinions also differ on the feasibility of financing accumulated shortfalls through current revenue since contribution rates are already high enough to cause considerable evasion. Alternative suggestions include financing the liabilities by issuing long-term government debt, selling state assets, or by raising general taxes. Though the central government recognized these options, and indeed established the NSSF, it has cautiously preferred to keep the direct responsibility for pension liabilities with local governments, and off the central government's balance-sheet.

Views also differ on whether the 'notional' accounts under Pillar 2 should be fully replenished or not. The traditional view supporting fully-funded accounts assumes that pension funds can be invested profitably and that domestic savings contribute positively to the development of financial markets (Ma and Zhai, 2001; Zhao and Xu, 2002; Feldstein, 2003). However, recent studies have pointed to encouraging experiences of countries that have combined defined contribution schemes with purposefully 'notional' accounts. In this view, fully replenishing the accounts may be sub-optimal because it lays an unfair burden on current contributors and because large amounts of savings cannot always be absorbed and channelled towards productive investment (Williamson and Zheng, 2003).

Whether the accumulated liabilities are funded or not, the Basic Pension system will eventually need readjustments to avoid future deficits. In 2002, 111.28 million contributors and 36.03 million retirees participated, providing almost complete coverage of SOEs and urban COEs. However, despite continuous efforts to extend the coverage in the non-state sector, many small enterprises avoid contributions and local authorities lack resources to pursue evaders. Private and foreign-invested enterprises have no economic incentives to participate in social pooling: since their workforces are relatively young, their pension costs are significantly lower than the contribution rates. In 2001 the coverage rate was 85 per cent of enterprises with a specified ownership, but only 45 per cent when including the self-employed and unspecified employment (*China Labour Statistical Yearbook*, 2002; NBS, 2003; *China Statistical Yearbook*, 2002) (see Figure 6.1).

Figure 6.1   Employment in Urban Areas

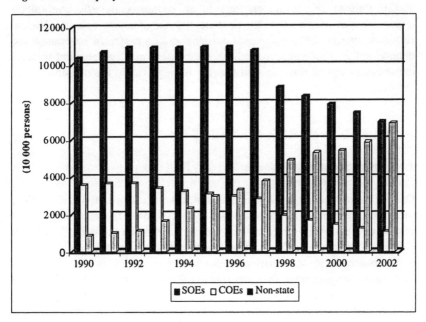

Note: Non-state refers to all other enterprise forms, including private, and self-employed.

Source: *China Statistical Yearbook*, 2003.

In the short term there is plenty of scope to improve financial sustainability, by encouraging new entrants and enforcing compliance with existing regulations. However, as the scheme matures and the sources of new entrants are exhausted, key parameters such as benefit levels, contribution rates or the retirement age, may need readjusting. For example, in the 1950s when the ratio of workers to retirees was 400:1 the system required a contribution rate of only 3 per cent to finance pension benefits as high as 80 per cent of the average wage. By contrast, in 2000 when the ratio was 3.1:1 the required contribution rate had increased to 22–4 per cent despite reduced benefit levels.

In the longer term, as the population ages and real-wage growth outpaces GDP growth it may become necessary to lower benefits, for example by shifting from wage- to price-indexation, or raise the retirement age. Wage-indexation implies that retirees share the growing prosperity of current workers, but price-indexation can cap the growth of pension costs when, as in China during the 1990s, real wages grow faster than prices. The present system assumes an average retirement length of ten years though pensioners now live on average more than 13 years after retirement, and the life expectancy of insured urban workers is likely to exceed the national average. According to the population census in 2000, there were at least 19 million elderly aged 70 or above living in urban areas (*China Statistical Yearbook*, 2002). Raising the retirement age is an economically effective, albeit unpopular, way of improving the financial balance of pay-as-you-go schemes. However, in China the retirement policy is also a preferred instrument for managing the labour supply, and the government may be reluctant to raise the statutory age at this moment for fear of aggravating the unemployment problem.

4.   OLD AGE IN RURAL AREAS

4.1.   Tradition of Self-reliance

Despite the rapid socio-economic development and urbanisation in the 1990s, there are over 807 million Chinese residents (64 per cent of the total population) living in rural (*nongcun*) areas, including an estimated 56 million elderly. China has no public old-age provisions for rural citizens, except for a patchwork of local initiatives, pilot schemes, and a number of social assistance programmes that also benefit the elderly.[28] The notion of retirement did not exist in rural areas until recently, and most elderly rely on the traditional system of land- and family-based support, living in multigenerational households and working the land or in related family businesses for as long as their health permits. The question of rural pensions is not self-evident, there is no consensus whether a rural system is desirable and feasible, and whether such a system could be integrated with the urban pension system (ADB, 2002).

In 1991 the SC reiterated its policy on rural old-age security, reaffirming the principle of land- and family-based support,[29] and the government's residual role as provider of last resort. The Ministry of Civil Affairs (MOCA) encouraged county governments to set up voluntary pension-insurance schemes for farmers and rural workers. In practice these were merely organised savings-schemes, operated with defined contributions and fully-funded individual accounts, and entailed neither pooling nor redistribution. Farmers and workers contributed according to their momentary savings capacity, while local governments and township and village enterprises (TVEs) subsidised their contributions proportionally. After retiring at 60 years of age, beneficiaries were entitled to a monthly annuity calculated as a share of the accumulated funds, assuming a guaranteed ten-year delivery (World Bank, 1997, p. 19; ADB, 2002).

By the end of 1997 nearly all the counties and prefectures had established administrative organisations to operate rural pension schemes, and an estimated 82 million peasants and workers participated. However, the MOCA schemes suffered from a number of problems including very low coverage in poor areas, minuscule average contributions, high administrative costs, and occasional mismanagement by local government officials. Though participation was supposed to be voluntary, the methods used to 'encourage' new entrants were sometimes excessive, compelling the SC to issue a warning to local governments affirming that the schemes should not become a burden to farmers. The legitimacy of the schemes was frequently challenged by the 'tax-relief policy', which undermined local governments' ability to provide social services and establish social insurance schemes since they could not mandate contributions or raise local taxes. In late 1997 a Rectification Group, set up to review commercial insurance products, scrutinised the MOCA schemes and issued a negative evaluation. The SC transferred the responsibility for rural pension schemes from the MOCA to the MOLSS at all levels of government as part of the 1998 government reorganisation.

In July 1999 an SC Decision effectively settled the issue of rural pensions by stating that conditions were insufficient to establish a comprehensive social insurance scheme. Therefore, any further development of such schemes would be discontinued and the existing MOCA/MOLSS schemes would be rectified and commercialised (ADB, 2002). Though the MOLSS put forward two proposals to this effect, and Premier Zhu Rongji repeatedly called for rectification, no consistent measures were implemented and certain local governments continued to operate the schemes on an experimental basis. At the end of 2003, after the instalment of a new government and despite appeals from local government officials, scholars and international organisations, there was no consensus on a rural pension system.

On the one hand, a rural pension system could help to ease the dependence of the elderly on their children, reduce the inequity between rural and urban residents, lessen distortions in the labour market, and sustain the modernisation of agriculture. On the other hand, establishing a universal rural system represents a daunting task likely to require considerable government subsidies. Sceptics stress the risk of undermining traditional values of family- and community-based support, and of creating excessive reliance and expectations on the government. After several feasibility studies in connection with the tenth five-year economic plan (2001–2005), the central government appeared favourable in principle while acknowledging that the time may not yet have come.

3.2. Unification and Coordination with the Urban System

According to a study by the Asian Development Bank (ADB), on balance, rural pensions are both desirable and feasible and the MOCA/MOLSS schemes are judged useful and their problems solvable. However, the principle of fully earnings-related savings based on individual accounts is inadequate for the poor (ADB, 2002). The uneven economic development across regions requires a differentiated strategy ranging from heavily government backed schemes with very low contribution and benefit levels in poorer areas, to more advanced two-tiered schemes approaching the urban model in richer areas.

Though a national pension system covering both rural and urban areas is unrealistic at this time, there are reasons why a future gradual unification is advantageous and inevitable. Recent socioeconomic developments, including the rapid growth of rural industries and the extensive migration to cities, are eroding the traditional distinction between rural and urban (ADB, 2002). In China's well-off East-coast provinces a growing share of the rural population is employed in non–agricultural activities in towns and townships under conditions that closely resemble urban areas. According to the Ministry of Agriculture, in 2002 TVEs employed 130 million farmers and accounted for 47 per cent of China's manufacturing value added, while 92 million farmers had migrated to urban areas (Xinhuanet).

The role and place of TVEs in China's social security structure is currently ambiguous; in some localities they participate in the urban system; in others they sustain rural schemes directly by enrolling their employees, and indirectly by contributing to local fiscal revenue. To compel TVEs to join the urban system would be impractical since rural and urban average wages still diverge too much, many TVE-employees are seasonal workers and remain part-time farmers, but above all because TVEs are instrumental to the development of rural schemes. A separate pension system for farmers only, common in many European countries, could not be self-sustaining considering the continuous downsizing of employment in the primary sector, but would necessitate substantial subsidies from local or central governments (ADB, 2002).

After two decades of continuous migration in spite of administrative restrictions, China has a large 'floating population' of rural migrant workers living in the cities without official urban registration and therefore excluded from social welfare benefits. The 'household registration' (*hukou*) system has been gradually relaxed, more exemptions are allowed and new categories of temporary residency have been introduced. In 2001 the government announced that migrant workers with a stable job should be granted permanent residency, and thereby the same access to social welfare programmes as urban workers. Provinces are encouraged to allow free intra-provincial movements; all citizens should have the right to live and work in any small- or medium-sized city within the province (Xinhuanet).

Large-scale migration and the increasing interdependence between rural and urban areas contribute to invalidating the old principle of entitlement based on registration, raising instead the issue of equity and fairness among individuals and enterprises. Official labour mobility requires transferable entitlements, and an efficient market economy requires free and fair competition where no enterprise can avoid social contributions to lower production costs. As a national pension system remains unfeasible for the foreseeable future, the primary concern is gradually to set up compatible and workable rural schemes, which can be coordinated with the urban schemes to reduce inequities and distortion in the labour market.

5. CONCLUSIONS

China has adopted a model of social insurance to provide the social safety-nets that are required by a market economy. Compared to the old policy of life-time employment in urban areas, and land- and family-based support in rural areas, a new social order has created a new set of uncertainties. Social insurance models assume that risks (old age or ill health) affect all members of a social group with probabilities that can be estimated in the aggregate. Key characteristics are compulsory participation, redistribution, and 'socialised' administration. The rationale behind compulsory social insurance includes benefits from risk-pooling, the assumption that people don't always plan ahead, and the fact that growing individualism or socioeconomic changes may undermine family-based provision. China has adopted similar schemes for pensions, healthcare and unemployment, based on a combination of social pooling and individual accounts. The social insurance model is advantageous because it should be self-sustaining and allows the government to maintain a residual role as regulator, supervisor, and occasionally as lender-of-last-resort, instead of assuming large explicit commitments.

China's admission to the WTO in 2001 has created a number of new opportunities for the government to import foreign expertise in pension administration and fund management. The combined total of domestic savings deposits reached more than 8 trillion yuan ($964 bn) in 2002, as the level of personal savings had doubled since 1995 (NBS, 2003). This accumulation suggests that China lacks a mechanism for channelling domestic savings into productive investments. In rural areas commercial life-insurance products have competed with local government savings schemes since 1991, but have only proved viable in well-off areas, where transaction costs are lower and profit potential higher, while remaining unprofitable in remote and poor areas (ADB, 2002). Commercial insurance and other savings-related products represent a valid complement to, but cannot substitute for, a social-security system.

At present China's accumulated pension liabilities seem manageable, considering the high rate of economic growth and the low coverage of entitlement to benefits. In the short term China is likely to continue the steady expansion and continuous and incremental reform of its social-insurance schemes, experimenting with modifications and new alternatives locally before they are applied nationally. However, in the long term the government might consider revising the urban pension system and investing more resources in the establishment of a rural system.

NOTES

1. The ratio of elderly to working-age individuals.
2. The executive organ of the PRC with legislative powers conferred by the constitution.
3. Amended in 1953, 1958 and 1978. In 1955 a separate system was set up for government and party employees such as cadres, civil servants, and servicemen. In 1958 coverage was extended to all enterprises irrespective of size.
4. Average life expectancy in 1955–60 was 43.1 years for men and 46.2 years for women (Whiteford, 2003). The 1997 Decisions raised the statutory retirement age for women in professional and managerial work to 55 years, while it remained 50 years for female production or supplementary workers.
5. SC (1978), June.
6. Proportional to individual wages and the years of service.
7. The State scheme, excluding military personnel, covered around 30 million public sector employees and retirees in 2000.
8. The Labour Law and Insurance Regulations did not apply to contract workers, who were not guaranteed lifetime employment or the same benefits as permanent workers.
9. SC (1991a).
10. SIAs are non-profit making agencies affiliated to the district level Labour bureaus of the MOL (Chow, 2000, p. 78).
11. SC (1995).
12. 1997 SC 'Decisions on the Unification of the Basic Pension Insurance for Enterprise Workers' (SC Document 26, 1997). Retirees continued to receive benefits according to the old system, financed from the social pool, while a transitional mechanism applied to current employees.
13. The ratio of the pension benefit to the reference wage.
14. Including autonomous regions and municipalities directly under the central government.
15. National industries such as railways, banks, civil aviation, and telecommunications had separate pension pools.
16. SC (2000).
17. In October 2002 reorganised into the State Development and Reform Commission (SDRC).
18. Since the transfer of pension administration and management to provincial level authorities is not completed, we will hereafter refer to local governments in wide sense.
19. This text distinguishes 'tiers' from 'pillars' to be consistent with both the World Bank's and the Chinese definitions. Different authors use different distinctions and may occasionally refer to what we call tiers as pillars.
20. The ratio is based on the assumption of retirement at 60 years and an average life-expectancy of 70 years.
21. If pensioners outlive the expected ten years and exhaust their individual accounts they continue to receive benefits as before and the entire amount is taken from the social pool. If pensioners pass away earlier the funds left over in their accounts are transferred to their dependents.
22. In summer 2003 the draft guidelines 'Trial Measures on Enterprise Annuity' outlined objectives and requirements.

23. In June 2001 the government attempted to raise funds by requiring that ten per cent of the funds raised during the public listing of SOEs should be transferred to the NSSF. The requirement was abolished in October the same year after a sharp fall in share prices.
24. Premier Zhu Rongji's 'Report on the Work of the Government' at the Tenth National People's Congress, March 2003.
25. Southern, Boshi, Penghua, Changsheng and Harvest Fund Management Companies and China Asset Management Company. (*China Daily*, 7 July 2003).
26. Pillar 1 should also cover the 'mortality drag', the losses accrued under Pillar 2 because accumulated benefits are inheritable and cannot be used to cross-subsidise annuity payments to those who outlive average life expectancy.
27. The SC Office for Restructuring Economic System estimates the pension debt from the old system as 1.8 trillion yuan under the most optimistic scenario (China Daily Online, July 2003).
28. Poor relief, disaster relief and the 'five guarantees' provide temporary and urgent aid to people with no other means of sustenance. Recently the Minimum Living Standard Support (MLSS) has been extended to rural residents.
29. SC (1991).

BIBLIOGRAPHY

Asher, Mukul G. and Newman, D.D. (2002), *The Challenge of Social Security Reform in Transition Economies: The Case of China*, Research Report No. 3, Singapore: International Centre for Pension Research, National University of Singapore.

Asian Development Bank (ADB) (2002), *People's Republic of China Old-Age Pensions for the Rural Areas: From Land Reform to Globalization*, Manila: Asian Development Bank.

Chan, C.L.W. and Chow, N.W.S. (1992), *More Welfare After Economic Reform: Welfare Development in the People's Republic of China*, Hong Kong: University of Hong Kong.

Chang, G. (2002), 'The Capital Needs of the People's Republic of China (2001–2005)', *Contracted Research Papers*, US–China Economic and Security Review Commission.

Chen Liwen and Mei, J. (2003), 'Recent Developments in the Chinese Financial Industry', *Research Report June 2003*, Beijing: O'Melveny & Myers LLP, Topics in Chinese Law.

China Population Information and Research Center (CPIRC) (2000), *White Paper on Population*, http://www.cpirc.org.cn/en/eindex.htm.

Chow, N.W.S. (2000), *Socialist Welfare with Chinese Characteristics: The Reform of the Social Security System in China*, The University of Hong Kong: The Centre of Asian Studies.

Chow, N.W.S. and Xu, Yuebin (2001), *Socialist Welfare in a Market Economy: Social Security in Guangzhou, China*, Aldershot, UK: Ashgate.

Cook, S. (2002), 'From Rice Bowl to Safety Net: Insecurity and Social Protection during China's Transition', *Development Policy Review*, **20** (5), Oxford: Blackwell Publishing Ltd, pp. 615–33.

Dixon, J.E. (1981), *The Chinese Welfare System, 1949–1979*, New York: Praeger Publishers.

Feldstein, M. (1999), 'Social Security Pension Reform in China', *China Economic Review*, **10**, Orlando: Elsevier Science, pp. 99–107.

Feldstein, M. (2003), 'Banking, Budgets, and Pensions: Some Priorities for Chinese Policy', *Remarks for China Development Forum 2003*, Beijing: State Council, Development Research Centre.

Frazier, M.W. (2002), *The Unfunded Mandate of Heaven: The Center, the Cities, and the Politics of Pension Reform in China*, working paper presented to the American Political Science Association, Boston (August).

Gounaris, N. and Chao, H. (2002), 'Capital Flows within China and the Creation of Chinese Institutional Investors', *Research Report May 2002*, Beijing: O'Melveny and Myers LLP, Topics in Chinese Law.

Hao Yan (1997), 'Old-age Support and Care in China in the Early 1990s', *Asia Pacific Viewpoint*, **38** (3), Oxford: Blackwell Publishers, pp. 201–17.

International Network of Pensions Regulators and Supervisors (INPRS), 'Social Insurance in China', *Country Reports*, INPRS, Paris: OECD Secretariat.

James, E. (2001), *How Can China Solve its Old Age Security Problem? The Interaction Between Pension, SOE and Financial Market Reform*, paper for Conference on Financial Sector Reform in China, Cambridge, MA: Harvard University, September 2001.

Kang Jia (2003), 'Contingent Debt in China's Public Sector', *China & World Economy*, **3**, Beijing: Chinese Academy of Social Sciences (CASS), Institute of World Economics and Politics.

Leckie, S.H. (2003), 'Pension Reform in China', article www.chinaonline.com, 25 June 2003.

Leung, J.C.B. (2003), 'Social Security Reforms in China: Issues and Prospects', *International Journal of Social Welfare*, **12**, Oxford: Blackwell Publishing, pp. 73–85.

Lu Aiguo (1996), 'Welfare Changes in China during the Economic Reforms', *Research for Action*, **26**, Helsinki: UNU/WIDER.

Ma Jun and Zhai Fan (2001), *Financing China's Pension Reform*, paper for Conference on Financial Sector Reform in China, 11–3 September.

National Bureau of Statistics (NBS) (2002a), *China Labour Statistical Yearbook*, Beijing: China Statistical Publishing House.

National Bureau of Statistics (NBS) (2002b), *China Statistical Yearbook*, Beijing: China Statistical Publishing House.

National Bureau of Statistics (NBS) (2003), *Statistical Communiqué 2002*, February 2003.

Saunders, P. and Shang Xiaoyuan (2001), 'Social Security Reform in China's Transition to a Market Economy', *Social Policy and Administration*, **35** (3), Oxford: Blackwell Publishers Ltd, pp. 274–89.

Takayama, Noriyuki (2002), *Pension Reform of PRC: Incentives, Governance and Policy Options*, paper for ADB Conference on Challenges and New Agenda for PRC, Tokyo, December.

Tang, K.L. and Ngan, R. (2001), 'China: Developmentalism and Social Security', *International Journal of Social Welfare*, **10**, Oxford, UK: Blackwell Publishing Ltd, pp. 253–9.

Wang Yan, Xu Dianqing, Wang Zhi and Zhai Fan (2000), *Implicit Pension Debt, Transition Cost, Options and Impact of China's Pension Reform*, working paper no. 2555, Washington, DC: The World Bank.

White, G. (1998), 'Social Security Reforms in China: Towards an East Asian Model?', in Goodman, R., White, G. and Kwon Huck–ju (eds), *The East Asian Welfare Model*, London, New York: Routledge, pp. 175–98.

Whiteford, P. (2003), 'From Enterprise Protection to Social Protection, Pension Reform in China', *Global Social Policy*, **3** (1), London: SAGE Publications, pp. 45–77.

Williamson, J.B. and Zheng Bingwen (2003), 'The Applicability of the Notional Defined Contribution Model for China', *China & World Economy* (3), Beijing: Chinese Academy of Social Sciences (CASS).

World Bank (1997), 'Old Age Security, Pension Reform in China', *China 2020 Series*, Washington, DC: The World Bank.

Zhang, Lijia (2000), 'China's Grey Peril: The Crisis Facing The Elderly Population', *China Review* (Summer) (16), Hong Kong: The Chinese University Press.

Zhao, Yaohui and Xu, Jianguo (1999), *Alternative Transition Paths in the Chinese Urban Pension System*, paper for CCER–NBER joint conference, Beijing University, China Centre for Economic Research (CCER).

Zhao, Yaohui and Xu, Jianguo (2002), 'China's Urban Pension System: Reforms and Problem, *Cato Journal*, **21** (3), Washington, DC: Cato Institute Publications (Winter), pp. 395–413.

Zhu, Yuken (2002), 'Recent Developments in China's Social Security Reforms', *International Social Security Review*, **55** (4), Oxford, UK: Blackwell Publishing Ltd.

7. In Search of an Inclusive Public Health Care System

Maria Weber and Anna Stenbeck

1. INTRODUCTION

Over time, China's public health policy seems to reflect the dominant political ideologies; egalitarianism and central planning under Mao Zedong, pragmatism and liberalisation under Deng Xiaoping, and gradual adaptation under Jiang Zemin.

The health status of China's population began to improve rapidly during the 1950–60s when a period of relative stability followed the end of the civil war. Economic liberalisation since the 1970s has created the preconditions for two decades of impressive growth and raised millions of Chinese out of absolute poverty, improving living standards and public health in the process. However, the partial liberalisation of the healthcare sector has left three main problems: inefficiency, insufficient funding, and a marked inequity in access to healthcare.

Two recent shocks, the WTO accession in November 2001 and the SARS epidemic in 2003, highlighted the shortcomings of China's healthcare system, and created additional pressure for its reorganisation. The extensive socioeconomic transformation, in particular factors associated with large-scale migration to the cities, has mandated a series of public healthcare reforms in a continuous effort to obtain more equitable access to medical services and to control the spread of infectious diseases.

2. DEVELOPMENT OF A PUBLIC HEALTHCARE SYSTEM

2.1. The Era of Mao Zedong

Upon establishing the People's Republic, public healthcare was organised according to guidelines announced at the first National Health Congress (NHC) in 1950.[1] The population's health status improved dramatically during the 1950–70s; life expectancy rose, mortality rates declined, and diseases such as cholera, typhus and plague were completely eradicated. International scholars and organisations acclaimed China's health achievements, often attributing them to the public provision of preventive and primary healthcare, though they also owed much to the improved nutrition, housing and sanitary conditions that followed the end of the civil war (Sidel and Sidel, 1982, p. 72).

Urban workers received free healthcare at their workplace clinics and healthcare costs incurred in public facilities were reimbursed. Two national insurance schemes were established in 1951: the Government Insurance Scheme (GIS, *gongfei yiliao*) for government employees, and the Labour Insurance Scheme (LIS, *laobao yiliao*) for employees of large state-owned enterprises (SOEs). Smaller SOEs and collectively owned enterprises (COEs) could participate in the LIS or provide their own health benefits. Public hospital fees were regulated at levels far below actual cost, and even without insurance healthcare was relatively affordable (Liu et al., 1999, p. 507; Liu et al., 2002, p. 6).[2]

In rural areas, village health stations staffed by part-time 'barefoot doctors'[3] (*chijiao yisheng*), and township health centres staffed by full-time physicians and nurses, provided preventive and primary care. Patients were referred to county hospitals for more specialised and advanced care. Village and township facilities were financed from collective-farm revenue and the cooperative medical system (CMS), a community-based insurance scheme funded by individual premiums, collective welfare funds, and local government subsidies. During the collectivisation of farming in the 1950s and 1960s most agricultural communes (*gongshe*) adopted the CMS, and by the late 1970s nearly 90 per cent of the rural population was covered (World Bank, 1997, p. 49; Yu et al., 1998, p. 3; Liu et al., 2002, p. 7).

2.2. The Era of Deng Xiaoping

The deaths of Mao Zedong and Zhou Enlai in 1976 signalled the beginning of a period of radical ideological change. The Dengist reforms of the early 1980s, apparently in line with international ideologies favouring decentralisation and economic liberalisation, nevertheless had a diametrically opposite effect on the organisation of China's healthcare system. While other countries privatised hospitals and increased the share of financing to be provided by the State, China largely maintained public ownership and management of hospitals while 'privatising' the burden of financing (Bogg, 2002, p. 55). The share of total population without health insurance jumped from 29 per cent in 1981 to almost 80 per cent in 1993 while out-of-pocket[4] spending rose from 20 per cent of health-sector revenue in 1978 to 42 per cent in 1993 (World Bank, 1997, pp. 14, 19).

Three aspects of the reforms influenced the healthcare sector particularly. Firstly, the responsibility for providing and financing social services, including healthcare, was devolved to local governments at provincial and county level. Secondly, hospital managers were made financially responsible for their budgets and instructed to raise their own revenue. Thirdly, the pricing of medical services was partially deregulated enabling hospitals to raise the prices of new services and technologies in order to generate a profit margin (Dong, 2001, pp. 5–8; Bogg, 2002, p. 34; Huang, 2002).

In urban areas, the reforms had a significant redistributive effect: the insured spent ever more on expensive and specialised treatments while the uninsured could no longer afford basic services. In Shanghai, China's biggest city, health expenditure under the state insurance schemes jumped by a quarter following the reforms, evidencing the lack of demand-side cost consciousness inherent to insurance mechanisms (Dong, 2001, p. 12). Health spending under the GIS, which covered 2 per cent of the total population, increased from 14 per cent of the public health budget in 1978 to 46 per cent in 1993 (World Bank, 1997, p. 20). The LIS covered less than 12 per cent of the population but accounted for a quarter of national health expenditure. Many loss-making SOEs were unable to finance their healthcare benefits, and the number of urban uninsured swelled as a consequence of state sector restructuring, rural-to-urban migration, and the expansion of the non-state sector (Bitran and Yip, 1998, p. 4).

In rural areas, the dissolution of agricultural communes caused CMS schemes to collapse and left rural residents who were paying for healthcare completely out-of-pocket. Between 1978 and 1993 CMS coverage fell from 90 to 7 per cent of the rural population while CMS spending fell from 20 to 2 per cent of national health expenditure (World Bank, 1997, p. 19; Dong, 2001, p. 5). Village and township health centres were either privatised or turned over to the new township governments while 'barefoot doctors' went back to farming or retrained to become private village doctors.

2.3. The Post-Deng Era

In the 1990s market-oriented reforms intensified and China experienced remarkable growth rates, but also increasing individual and regional disparities. A number of studies conducted in the early 1990s identified three sets of problems: rapid cost escalation, inefficiency in provision, and growing inequity in access.[5]

In 1994 the central government launched a pilot reform in two selected cities, Zhengjiang and Jiujian, to experiment with medical insurance for urban workers. The pilot reform introduced mandatory contributions, individual medical savings accounts (MSAs), high individual copayments and innovative mechanisms for paying providers.[6] An early study in Zhengjiang showed evidence of success as patients became more likely to seek care, total health expenditure fell, and services appeared to be utilised more efficiently (Liu et al., 1999, p. 505). Meanwhile, a locally initiated reform in Shanghai saved costs by raising copayments and setting maximum growth targets for hospital budgets and drug revenues. The reform may have reduced the consumption of 'unnecessary' expensive diagnosis and treatments, but could have inadvertently caused under-provision of necessary services (Bitran and Yip, 1998, p. 5; Dong, 2001, p. 20).

After the 1996 NHC, the State Council (SC) announced new reform guidelines[7] and in 1998 the Basic Medical Insurance System was established for urban workers.[8] The system combines individual MSAs with 'social risk-pooling', and represents a major step towards 'socialisation'[9] by removing the direct link between employers' liabilities and workers' entitlements. Risk-pooling at the municipal level should spread the cost of ill health between healthy and sick individuals and between more and less profitable enterprises. While certain problems remained to be addressed, by the end of 2003 the system was under implementation throughout China's over 600 cities (Liu et al., 2002, pp. 9–10).

The idea of reviving rural cooperative healthcare resurfaced at regular intervals during the 1990s, as the central government encouraged local governments to establish and co-finance voluntary schemes resembling the CMS.[10] However, little progress was made since village governments lacked legitimacy and incentives to collect individual premiums and local tax revenues were frequently insufficient to cofinance the schemes. Mandatory local contributions or fees were illegal under the central government's tax relief policies (Liu et al., 2002, p. 41). In poor rural areas farmers simply could not afford even the lowest premiums, while in richer areas they preferred private insurance. At the 2001 NHC government officials admitted that rural medical resources, insurance systems, and income levels remained inadequate, and at the end of 2002 the central government reaffirmed its goal of establishing cooperative medical services in all rural counties, townships and villages by 2010. For the first time central budget resources were committed to central and western regions where economic preconditions might be insufficient for the schemes to be self-sustaining.[11]

3.   MAIN FEATURES OF PUBLIC HEALTHCARE TODAY

3.1.   Regulation and Administration

A number of different departments and government levels are involved in regulating and administering the healthcare sector. The Communist Party and the SC establish broad national policy guidelines and decisions, based on inputs from single ministries and commissions, which are adapted and translated into local regulations by lower government levels. The State Development and Reform Commission (SDRC)[12] is responsible for public investment in health infrastructure and for ensuring that yearly health expenditure complies with the five-year-plan. The Ministry of Health (MOH) formulates and drafts policies, administers and finances public health facilities, regulates private practitioners, and manages the insurance scheme for government employees (Bloom and Fang, 2003, p. 19). In 1999 the MOH's staff was reduced and responsibility for the new urban health insurance scheme was transferred to the Ministry of Labour and Social Security (MOLSS). Thus the urban system formally ensures a separation between purchaser (MOLSS) and provider (MOH) of healthcare services, a principle that is applied in most developed countries to improve efficiency and transparency. At the end of 2003 no single ministry or commission was responsible for implementing national policies on health protection in rural areas; the task was left to the discretion of local governments.

Administratively, China's government apparatus is divided into three levels: provinces, counties, and townships.[13] Each level approximately replicates the structure of the Central Government whereby the Ministry of Finance (MOF) is responsible for annual budgets and monitoring health expenditure, the Ministry of Civil Affairs (MOCA) for policies and projects targeting the poor and, together with the Ministry of Agriculture, for rural CMS. Consequently, there are numerous local departments and bureaux, including health and social security departments, involved in the organisation of healthcare at the provincial and county level.[14]

The evolution of a policy statement into a change in the behaviour of local governments and other economic actors is a lengthy and complicated process (Bloom and Fang, 2003, p. 11). The central government presents national guidelines at national conferences attended by provincial-level officials. National guidelines are then elaborated to suit regional circumstances, and presented to lower-level government officials at provincial conferences. Local governments at county, municipal and township levels are ultimately responsible for implementing health policies and administering public health institutions and insurance programmes.

The degree to which the centre can impose its policy objectives nationwide depends on the balance of power and the distribution of fiscal resources between the centre and the localities. China's government structure is at the same time hierarchical and decentralised, and the distribution of taxing and spending competences has been in constant evolution since the establishment of the PRC. The 1980's 'fiscal-responsibility' system decentralised the responsibility for developing and financing social infrastructure, together with the power to levy taxes and other administrative fees, and limited the centre's ability to redistribute resources and impose uniform standards on the provision of social services (Bogg, 2002, p. 53; Liu et al., 2002, pp. 43–7). In 1994 the new 'tax-sharing' system strengthened the centre's fiscal revenue, paving the way for a series of national social welfare reforms. Central policies may be resisted or delayed by lower government levels with different incentives. Effective implementation and enforcement relies on a complex hierarchical relationship[15] influenced by the aforementioned balance of power. Nevertheless, local governments also contribute to the reform process by carrying out and sharing experiences from pilot reform programmes. In several cases, provinces or municipalities have taken autonomous initiatives towards successful institutional innovation, which have subsequently been incorporated into national guidelines (Ding, 2003, p. 47).

3.2. Healthcare Providers: Hospitals and Clinics

China has a large and capillary healthcare infrastructure organised into three tiers according to a functional and territorial division of competences. The three tiers differ in size, ownership, and capacity to offer specialised care, and are interconnected by a hierarchical system of referral. At the end of 2002, 290 000 healthcare institutions provided 3.21 million beds, including 65 000 hospitals and healthcare stations with 2.20 million beds. The sector employed 4.44 million health workers, including 2.11 million doctors[16] and 1.30 million senior and junior nurses. Thereby, China has more medical personnel per capita than most developing countries with 3.5 medical technical personnel, 1.6 doctors, and 1.0 nurse per 1000 residents (NBS, 2002, 2003).

In urban areas street and workplace clinics offer preventive and primary care, district and enterprise clinics and hospitals offer secondary and limited inpatient care, while municipal (city) hospitals offer comprehensive and specialised care, including hospitalisation. Public clinics and hospitals are owned and operated by local governments as health-sector SOEs though their staffs are considered government employees.[17] In addition, SOEs active in other business areas often operate their own health facilities to provide services mainly, but not necessarily, for their workers.[18] Public clinics and hospitals enjoy a double competitive advantage over private- and SOE-operated providers; they receive subsidies to cover labour costs and capital investments, and the fees that they charge are usually reimbursed by the state insurance schemes. However, public providers have less control over their profitability since MOH departments decide the size and remuneration of their staff and the State Price Commission regulates the fee structure.

In rural areas, only a fraction of village health stations remain public, while the majority of the 1.29 million village doctors and health workers are private practitioners. Township governments manage and fund 48 000 public hospitals and health centres, employing 1.03 million full-time physicians and nurses and providing 750 000 beds. County hospitals offer specialised treatments and inpatient care, representing the third and highest tier of referral for rural residents since few can afford to visit provincial or big-city hospitals (NBS, 2003).

Private medical practice was re-legalised in the 1980s, individuals and collective enterprises were authorised to open clinics and drug stores or operate state-owned facilities on a contractual basis. Private practice has grown steadily, initially in rural villages and more recently in urban areas in response to public shortages and rising demand. Medical education continues to be largely state-funded though physicians, nurses, and technicians are increasingly free to set up private practices. The government has encouraged the development of the private sector and even promoted public/private joint ventures hoping that increased supply might reduce the pressure on public facilities (Meng et al., 2000, p. 349; WHO, 2000, p. 125). Critics of privatisation are concerned that private practitioners might be less qualified than their public counterparts and more driven to generate income regardless of the best interest of the patient. For example, private doctors might be less willing to provide preventive care and refer patients to higher tiers, and more inclined to over-prescribe expensive drugs and treatments. However, a study of clinics in the eastern Shandong province showed that the quality of care, the willingness to provide preventive care, and the likelihood of providing unnecessary treatment, did not vary significantly between private and public ownership, considering that public facilities receive subsidies to cover personnel costs and capital investments (Meng et al., 2000, pp. 354–5).

3.3. Demand for Healthcare: The Patients

China is simultaneously undergoing a demographic and epidemiological transition, a transition to a market economy, and a transition to an urban, industrial society (Hussain, 2000, p. 3). The demand for treatments of age-related chronic conditions is rising as the elderly live longer, and the burden of disease is shifting from childhood disorders and infectious diseases towards non-communicable diseases. Rural and western areas are lagging, showing slower rates of reduction in the incidence of communicable diseases, while urban areas are experiencing ever more diseases associated with socioeconomic development, such as occupational accidents and injuries, diet induced heart-conditions, and tobacco- and drug-related illnesses (Bloom et al., 2002, pp. 2–3; WHO, 2003).

The *need* for healthcare can be defined as 'the existence of ill health for which an effective treatment is available', while *demand* is influenced by additional factors such as society's expectations of what constitutes wellbeing and medical need, and individual perceptions of physical and financial access to healthcare (Bogg, 2002, p. 30).[19] The existence of extensive health infrastructure and public financing, or widespread medical insurance coverage, typically raises the demand for healthcare services irrespective of need. Low income is a major constraint on healthcare consumption in China; surveys describe how the poor, despite reporting a medical need, often choose not to seek assistance or are forced to interrupt treatments early. The primary reasons for forgoing treatment are excessive cost and financial difficulty (Yu et al., 1998, p. 4; Liu et al., 2002, pp. 21–4; Bogg, 2002, p. 41).

Poverty contributes to the persistence of ill health, but the causal relationship may also be inverted since ill health is itself a major cause of poverty in countries that lack well-developed social insurance or welfare institutions. In China rural families with a sick member are often forced to sell assets or borrow to pay for drugs and treatments. The high medical cost relative to income is a frequent determinant of household impoverishment. In 2000, 87.3 per cent of patients in rural areas paid out-of-pocket, with one-quarter forced to borrow money (WHO, 2002). Ill health also causes temporary or permanent loss of wage income, or forgone investments into family businesses, and can significantly worsen the long–term economic circumstances and prospects of entire families. While the occurrence of ill health can be limited but not avoided, the organisation of a healthcare system can lessen the adverse impact by spreading the economic burden and ensuring that access to healthcare is affordable (Bogg, 2002, p. 23).

3.4. Financing Alternatives

Healthcare systems generally rely on three sources of financing: government funding (from tax revenue), prepaid insurance schemes, and private out-of-pocket spending. The recent spread of market-oriented economic theories and growing concern over expanding public sectors has influenced the organisation of healthcare globally. Many government-funded systems have been replaced by a mixture of explicit insurance mechanisms, including private commercial insurance, and out-of-pocket spending (WHO, 2000, pp. 16–17). Prepayment through national insurance schemes is considered the best form of healthcare financing to provide fair and equal access to all social categories. Out-of-pocket spending[20] is considered the most regressive and inequitable form of financing, as the poor spend a larger proportion of their income on medical costs and the very poor may not be able to afford medical assistance at all.

China's national healthcare expenditure rose on average 16 per cent a year in the second half of the 1990s reaching 5.3 per cent of GDP in 2000, barely above the WHO's recommended 5 per cent minimum target for developing countries. Government spending[21] fell from 17 per cent of total health expenditure in 1995 to less than 15 per cent in 2000, while social health expenditure,[22] mainly from the state insurance schemes, fell from a third to a quarter of the total. By contrast, individual out-of-pocket spending accounted rose from 50 to 60 per cent of total health expenditure between 1995 and 2000 (NBS, 2002). Private spending was very high by international standards, considering that commercial health insurance was practically non-existent (see Table 7.1).

Table 7.1   Health Care Financing by Source

	1998	1999	2000	2001
GDP	7834.5	8206.8	8946.8	9731.5
Total government expenditure	1079.8	1318.8	1588.7	1890.3
Government health expenditure[a]	58.7	64.1	71.0	80.1
% total government expenditure	5.4	4.9	4.5	4.2
% total expenditure on for public health	15.5	15.3	14.9	15.5
Social health expenditure[b]	100.6	106.5	116.8	123.6
% total expenditure on public health	26.6	25.5	24.5	24.0
Individual health expenditure[c]	218.3	247.3	288.7	311.3
% total expenditure on public health	57.8	59.2	60.6	60.4
Total expenditure on public health	377.7	417.9	476.4	515.0
% GDP	4.8	5.1	5.3	5.3

Notes:
a. budgetary allocation by governments at all levels;
b. non-government budgetary capital input, including health insurance, expenditure of institutions run by enterprises and rural collectives, enterprises' health expenditure, extra expenditure for government employees;
c. paid by residents from disposable income.

Source: NBS, 2002 and 2003.

In urban areas, the Basic Medical Insurance System is gradually replacing the old occupational schemes. In 2000, 97 per cent of prefectures and cities had begun implementing the reform and rapid expansion brought the coverage to 94 million urban workers in 2002. The coverage rate was 73 per cent of the 128 million employees of enterprises with specified ownership, but only 40 per cent of total urban employment (248 million), self-employed and unspecified employment. And since the 490 million farmers and rural employees are excluded, the system covers less than 13 per cent of China's total employed (NBS, 2002; CPIRC, 2000).

Urban health insurance is financed from mandatory premiums: employers pay 6 per cent of the total wage bill, split between employees' individual MSAs and the social pool, and workers pay 2 per cent of wages, entirely accredited to their accounts. Local social insurance agencies (SIAs) collect premiums, administer and disburse funds to workers, and select and pay healthcare providers. The MSAs are used to pay for ordinary outpatient services, while the pooled funds should cover (a share of) major expenses, such as hospitalisation and the treatment of certain chronic diseases. To avoid continuously escalating expenses and ensuing deficits, coverage is restricted to medicines and services listed by the government and provided by approved health providers and pharmacies. Patients are not reimbursed for medical costs incurred in other facilities, which may disadvantage private and foreign-invested clinics and hospitals. On balance, when central subsidies are included, total revenues exceed expenses in all provinces, implying that funds were accumulated (see Table 7.2) (NBS, 2002; CPIRC, 2000).

Table 7.2   Basic Medical Insurance

	1999	2000	2001	2002
Total contributors (million):	20.65	37.87	72.86	94.01
Workers	15.09	28.63	54.71	69.26
Retirees	5.56	9.24	18.15	24.75
Revenue (billion yuan)	8.99	17	38.36	60.78
Expenditure	6.91	12.45	24.41	40.94
Accumulated surplus	5.76	10.98	25.30	45.07

Source: NBS, 2003.

4.   UNRESOLVED PROBLEMS

4.1.   Rising Expenditure

Though China's national healthcare expenditure is comparatively low at $45 per capita, common health indicators, such as the life expectancy of 71.2 years, compare favourably with more developed countries. Comparative studies show that health spending can be allocated more or less efficiently, and that high total expenditure is no guarantee of performance. Many factors exert an upward pressure on expenditure without improving population health, such as rising unit prices of drugs and treatments due to technological development, price deregulation and service liberalisation, and inefficiencies such as moral hazard and supplier-induced demand. However, in China's case, policy reforms may have aggravated the pace of cost escalation and the declining efficiency of resource allocation by raising the inequality in per capita healthcare spending and by distorting the economic incentives that determine the composition of healthcare consumption for any given level of spending (see Table 7.3) (WHO, 2000 and 2002).

4.2.   Inequity in Access and Cost

The problem of inequity in access to and the financing of healthcare has become a major social and political issue in China. The *World Health Report 2000* ranked China's health system 188th out of 191 countries (above Sierra Leone, Myanmar and Brazil) for its (lack of) fairness in distributing the financial burden across the population. Inequality in access is apparent in the imbalanced consumption of healthcare as measured by spending and

Table 7.3   Comparative Health Indicators (2000)

Country	Total expenditure	Per capita expenditure, $[a]		Government health expenditure	Out-of-pocket	Under-5 mortality	Life expectancy at birth
	% GDP	Total	Government	% Government expenditure	% total expenditure	per 1000	Years
USA	13	4499	1992	16.7	15.3	8.0	77.0
Japan	7.8	2908	2230	15.4	19.3	4.5	81.4
Germany	10.6	2422	1819	17.3	10.6	4.5	78.2
Sweden	8.4	2179	1685	11.3	22.7	3.5	80.0
France	9.5	2057	1563	13.5	10.2	4.5	79.3
UK	7.3	1747	1415	14.9	10.6	6.5	77.5
Italy	8.1	1498	1103	12.7	22.9	5.5	79.3
Singapore	3.5	814	290	6.7	63.7	4.0	78.8
Republic of Korea	6	584	258	11.2	41.0	8.0	74.9
Malaysia	2.5	101	60	5.8	41.2	12.0	71.7
Russia	5.3	92	66	14.5	23.4	19.5	65.2
Thailand	3.7	71	41	11.4	36.2	34.5	68.9
China	5.3	45	17	11.0[b]	60.4	37.0	71.2
India	4.9	23	4	5.3	82.2	93.5	60.8
Vietnam	5.2	21	5	6.5	68.7	39.5	69.3
Indonesia	2.7	19	5	3.1	70.1	45.0	65.9

Note:
a. nominal $ exchange rates.
b. the share differs from Chinese data. The WHO pools public and social expenditure.

Source: WHO, 2002.

utilisation of services. Inequality is correlated positively with the proportion of out-of-pocket spending and the inequality of the income distribution, both high in China (WHO, 2002, pp. 37–8).

The most significant inequality derives from the hitherto strict separation between rural and urban areas, whereby politically and legally enforced barriers including the 'household registration system' (*hukou*) purposefully controlled the mobility of rural labour towards the cities. Rural migrant workers were either offered temporary residence permits or none at all, which severely limited employment opportunities and excluded them from access to urban social services, including the old-age, medical, and unemployment insurance schemes. Since the collapse of the CMS, the majority of rural residents are not covered by any health insurance. Rural residents pay almost 90 per cent of their total medical costs out-of-pocket, compared to a national average of 60 per cent, and many avoid seeking medical assistance. According to a National Health Survey from 1993, 60 per cent of rural and 40 per cent of urban households avoided public health facilities due to economic difficulties

(Hossain, 1997, p. 7; Bloom et al., 2002, p. 1). Under the current system, demand and supply of health services is concentrated in urban areas, sustained by the state insurance schemes, dynamic income growth, and government capital investment.

As a consequence, rural areas have half as many hospital beds and physicians per thousand residents, approximately 1.5 beds and 1.1 physicians, compared to 3.5 beds and 2.3 physicians in urban areas (Davis and Chapman, 2002, pp. 4–5). Even the quality of medical services is unequal: fewer rural physicians are university-trained compared to their urban peers, and rural health workers have minimal training. In the countryside doctors' and nurses' salaries and social status are low (WHO, 2000, p. 138). Talented doctors prefer to work in cities, and those already in rural areas seek ways of getting away.[23] The rural–urban inequality is evident in health statistics; between 1993 and 1998 morbidity rates fell faster in urban areas, and infant-mortality remained higher in rural areas though the gap seemed to peak in 1993. Morbidity rates are affected by healthcare and also by economic development, through improved housing, nutrition, and sanitation (Gao et al., 2002, p. 22).

Inequality between rich and poor was stronger within urban areas, due to the distinction between insured and uninsured, and the unequally distributed albeit dynamic income growth.[24] In 2001, the richest 10 per cent of urban households spent 4.5 times more on medical services than the poorest 5 per cent (NBS, 2002). The effects of state-sector restructuring, which intensified after 1997, caused many laid-off workers to lose both their income and their health benefits, while economic migration caused a rise in informal and temporary employment. These developments accentuate the urban inequity in healthcare access beyond the evidence of government statistics. An estimated 100 million migrant workers, the 'floating population', live and work without official permission, with low social status, low income and education levels, and remain excluded from the benefits received by the legal workforce. More than 90 per cent of migrant workers in Shanghai, almost a third of the labour force, paid for healthcare completely out-of-pocket, forcing many to do without or consume less than needed (Zhan et al., 2002, p. 49).[25] In addition, patients who pay out-of-pocket may not get the best available treatments or obtain needed referrals. Chinese providers have admitted that the source of financing affects the choice of treatment offered, with insured patients more likely to receive newer and more expensive drugs and inpatient care than the uninsured (Liu et al., 2000, p. 23, Bogg, 2002, pp. 41-2).

4.3. Over–prescription

Health sector reforms, especially the unfortunate policy-mix of subsidy cuts, financial responsibility, and partial price-deregulation, are blamed for distorting economic incentives and causing a severe problem of over-prescription of unnecessary drugs and services. Before the 1980s reforms, prices of basic medical procedures, services and tests were generally set below actual cost, and the ensuing operating losses were covered by government subsidies. After the reforms, subsidies were meant to be used for capital investment only, and clinics and hospitals were instructed to raise their own revenue through fee-for-service charges and drug sales, and to adopt bonus systems to encourage the medical staff to generate revenue.[26] The government retained the right to control the prices of basic services and drugs, while new drugs and high-tech procedures could be priced more freely to allow for a profit margin.[27] Consequently, public providers were forced to over-sell remunerative drugs and services to compensate for the losses incurred providing under-priced services. Studies have shown that drug sales may account for two-thirds of hospital revenues, and more than 90 per cent of outpatient fees in rural villages (Yu et al., 1998, p. 5; Liu et al., 2000).

In addition to quantitative overselling, the economic incentives offered by pharmaceutical producers favour the choice of branded products, with higher profit margins, over generic drugs. Drugs spending rose from 50 to almost 70 per cent of national healthcare expenditure between 1993 and 1999, significantly above international averages of 15–40 per cent for developing countries, and 6–12 per cent in developed Western countries (HDR, 2003, p. 114; Liu et al., 2000; WHO, 2000). The high demand for drugs is partly sustained by the natural preference Chinese patients have for pharmacological solutions over invasive procedures, but patients are also subject to supplier-induced demand and excessive prescribing. Due to the rising costs farmers have been known to spend two to five times the average daily per capita income on a typical prescription, and poorer Chinese frequently resort to self-treatments, with Chinese traditional or modern drugs (HDR, 2003, p. 114).[28]

4.4. Persistence and Spread of Infectious Disease

In recent years China has experienced a worrying resurgence of infectious disease, epitomized by the SARS epidemic in the first half of 2003, while a number of communicable diseases remain major public health problems, notably hepatitis-B, tuberculosis (TB), and HIV/AIDS. Until the 1980s, the Epidemic Prevention Service (EPS) carried out nationwide immunisation and endemic disease control programmes, financed by the central and provincial governments, through a network of county level EPS stations. When the EPS was instructed to raise its own revenue by charging for the vaccinations, many local programmes were shut down due to lack of funding leading to a decline in national immunisation coverage (World Bank, 1997, pp. 28–9). The resurgence of infectious diseases is also attributed to the large-scale internal migration and problems typically associated with rapid urbanisation, such as underdeveloped public services, poor and crowded living conditions, and the emergence of a sex industry (Hussain, 2000; Human Rights Watch, 2003).

During the 1960–70s China made significant progress in controlling TB by providing standard antibiotic treatments essentially free of charge. However, when hospitals began raising their fees, many low-income patients could no longer afford to commence or continue treatments (WHO, 2000). In 2001 the World Bank completed a ten-year project which had provided free TB treatment in 13 provinces, managing to reduce the incidence of the disease by 36 per cent.[29] Though TB has been eliminated in developed countries, China has an estimated 5 million cases, and a further 1.5 million are infected every year. Despite their manifest success, the government has not pledged to reinstate free TB treatments, evidencing the reluctance to make large and uncertain budgetary commitments.

Ever since the first cases of HIV were diagnosed among foreigners and overseas Chinese, in the open coastal cities in the 1980s, AIDS has been perceived as a foreign disease that affects social groups whose behaviour is deviant from Chinese norms. During the 1990s the disease spread mainly through three channels; intravenous drug use, blood collection schemes,[30] and sexual transmission. Needle-sharing among drug users, quoted as the most frequent mode of transmission, spread the epidemic mainly in southern regions on the drug route from Laos, Myanmar, Thailand and Vietnam. However, recent trends show that HIV is increasingly spread sexually, as travelling or migrant workers spend more time away from their families. In June 2002 the Chinese government reported that 1 million people had contracted the disease, with a transmission rate of 30 per cent a year. International organisations estimate 1–2 million HIV infected, with transmission rates ranging from 70 per cent in drug using communities to 7 per cent among the heterosexual population (Human Rights Watch, 2003, pp. 14–19; Rosenberg and Merson, 2003, p. 8).

Chinese AIDS patients have little access to treatment. Anti-viral drugs are expensive and generally not reimbursable by insurance schemes.[31] Healthcare providers may refuse to treat patients diagnosed as HIV-positive, and instead report the illness to employers and families, a practice that frequently leads to dismissal and social marginalisation. A first national action plan on AIDS was issued in 2001, and the SC has gradually begun to acknowledge the disease nationally and internationally. An unprecedented, government-approved, amount of media coverage followed the World AIDS Day held in December 2002 with the aim of raising awareness of HIV among the public. In 2002 China's application to the 'Global Fund for AIDS, Tuberculosis and Malaria', for funding to treat AIDS patients in seven particularly affected regions, was refused because of insufficient community-level participation. However, following pledges to establish rural community health centres and considering the growing number of NGOs involved in AIDS projects, China re-applied successfully in 2003 (Human Rights Watch, 2003, pp. 61–5; Rosenberg and Merson, 2003, p. 19).

4.5. Possible Developments

Two shocks, the WTO accession in November 2001 and the SARS epidemic in 2003, have influenced the organisation of China's healthcare system. The WTO admission in 2001 may affect the healthcare system in several ways: on the supply side, by allowing foreign expertise in hospital administration through business consultancy services, and ensuring the formal recognition of foreign professionals and technicians. Import tariffs on pharmaceutical products and medical equipment have been reduced considerably, and competition should accelerate the restructuring of China's pharmaceutical industry. On the demand side, foreign insurers will be allowed to offer health insurance products, both to individuals and enterprises, to complement public health financing in line with the policy of promoting the individual's responsibility to share healthcare costs. However, by intensifying the pressure on economic restructuring, particularly in agriculture, the WTO accession is also accelerating the pace of rural-to-urban migration thereby contributing to the pressure on urban public services.

The SARS epidemic that erupted in the beginning of 2003 turned the international spotlight on China's healthcare system and its deficiencies, and also raised domestic demand for effective reforms. The rural healthcare system has suffered two decades of severe neglect leaving medical facilities, equipment and staffing severely under-resourced. The SARS epidemic could encourage several developments in the public health sector:

1. Re-centralise control over the regulation, administration and supervision of providers. The lack of coordination between local health programmes on the one hand, and between research institutes, providers and local governments on the other hand, has been blamed for the inefficiency of the system.
2. Raise the priority of public health spending in the central budget. When it emerged that penniless SARS patients were refused care, the government pledged to provide free treatment to all sufferers. The government set aside funds equal to one-fifth of yearly government health-expenditure to fight the disease and to construct new hospitals specialising in infectious disease and emergency treatment centres.[32] New hospitals were erected in weeks, including a 1000-bed emergency quarantine centre in Xiaotangshan in just eight days,[33] demonstrating a capacity to mobilise vast human and capital resources when required.
3. Elicit a new approach to communication and transparency, domestically and internationally, which might affect the response to other epidemics,

such as AIDS. When the initial concealment strategy failed as the seriousness of the epidemic became apparent, the government was forced to save face by apologising publicly and promising to resolve the deficiencies. The legitimacy of the Chinese government rests firmly on its ability to provide effective governance and to fulfil the expectations of the citizens. Both the hierarchical party structure and the potential threat of social unrest can provide effective pressure for accountability. The SARS epidemic highlighted how China's economic interdependence puts new demands on the way the government should treat domestic issues that have possible international repercussions. China's pledge to the WHO that future outbreaks of communicable diseases would not be hidden clearly demonstrates the leaders realise that they cannot ignore the requests of the international community when participating in agreements such as the WTO.

5.   CONCLUSION

In urban areas the framework for a modern healthcare system is under implementation. Nevertheless, the decentralised and uncoordinated nature of the system generates a problem of inclusiveness, exacerbated by large-scale informal labour migration. Any sustainable solution should satisfy the need to balance the claims and revenues of existing schemes, which implies balancing the trade-off between coverage and the size of the benefit (Bloom et al., 2002, p. 13). Providing universal coverage in urban areas under the current scheme would put an excessive burden on workers and employers. To guarantee the participation of hitherto excluded social groups, such as migrant workers and the unemployed, the government could either subsidise insurance contributions, or subsidise providers directly to offer free care to the indigent. While both methods would require raising revenue from taxation, the first alternative could prove more efficient to administer, and more likely to guarantee equal access irrespective of income status.

In rural areas, the establishment of community health services, which should be completed by 2010, could be accelerated by the need to control outbreaks of epidemics. However, the size of the rural population and the large socioeconomic development gap compared with urban areas limit the possibility, respectively, for central transfers and local revenues. Integrating the two systems seems unfeasible at present.

NOTES

1.   a. Medicine should serve workers, peasants and soldiers;
     b. Preventive medicine should take precedence over therapeutic medicine;
     c. Chinese traditional medicine should be integrated with Western scientific medicine;
     d. Health work should be combined with mass movements (Sidel and Sidel, 1982, p. 28).

2. SOE-workers' dependents were covered and partially reimbursed by the LIS. COE-workers' dependents were generally not covered.
3. 'Barefoot doctors' had little formal training and were not professionals. In 1985 new examinations were introduced and the title was replaced by 'village doctor' (*xiangcun yisheng*).
4. Private outlays on public and private services and pharmaceuticals.
5. Studies performed by China's SDPC, Department of Social Development, MOH, SC Research Office, ADB, World Bank, UNICEF, and Harvard University.
6. Copayments refer to the share of the medical bill that is not reimbursed but is paid for by the insured. The remuneration mechanism (fee-for-service, capitation, per diem, fixed budget, or other) influences the operational choices of healthcare providers.
7. 1997 SC, 'Decisions on health reform and development'.
8. 1998 SC, 'Decision on establishing the basic medical insurance system for urban employees'.
9. Refers to public provision of social security, including medical insurance, managed by government departments or agencies rather than by employers.
10. 1997 SC, 'Recommendation for the development and improvement of rural medical care' and 2001 SC, 'Guidelines for rural health sector reform and development'.
11. Media coverage of the seminar on Macroeconomics and Health, held by MOF, MOH, SDRC and WHO in Beijing, December 2002.
12. Replaced the State Development and Planning Commission (SDPC) in October 2002.
13. Autonomous regions and municipalities directly under the Central Government are considered provinces, while cities and special districts are considered counties (WHO, 2003).
14. In addition, the State Family Planning Commission has a network of delivery institutions at the different government levels. Towns vary enormously in size and location, and smaller township governments may have simpler structures with single officials instead of bureaux.
15. Lower-level cadres are evaluated against performance targets by higher-level cadres or party officials.
16. Over 80 per cent are doctors or paramedics of western medicine, while the rest are trained in traditional Chinese medicine or integrate the two disciplines (NBS, 2002).
17. Generally of the local MOH department.
18. Workplace facilities are subsidiaries of the main enterprise, and their staffs remain employees of the main SOE.
19. For example, the propensity to report illness rises with socioeconomic development (Gao et al., 2001, p. 304).
20. The Chinese indicator seemingly includes private commercial insurance, while the WHO's does not. The WHO counts enterprise-spending in excess of mandatory insurance as private expenditure, while the Chinese count this as social expenditure.
21. Government spending at all levels, including GIS and direct subsidies to public health facilities operated by MOH departments.
22. Includes spending by enterprises under the LIS and the new basic medical insurance, rural collective entities, and expenditure of government employees outside the GIS.
23. *The Lancet*, **358** (9281), 18 August 2001, p. 567.
24. Rich–poor inequality was less pronounced in rural areas where income-growth has been less dynamic and, since everyone pays out-of-pocket, there are fewer incentives for rural healthcare providers to differentiate prices according to spending capacity.
25. The situation of migrant workers has been addressed locally, mainly in relation to the risk of epidemics. Recently new residence permits were introduced (fully-registered, newly-registered, temporary, and unregistered) with different entitlements to social benefits. According to government guidelines, migrant workers with permanent jobs and urban residence-permit should join the urban social insurance schemes
26. Fee-for-services charges include outpatient visits, operations, and inpatient daily hospital rates. Prices set by the State Price Commission are raised sporadically after negotiations between local governments and the Commission.
27. Most hospitals own and operate pharmacies and sometimes manufacture their own drugs.
28. Many Chinese choose to '… buy some pills or try local and traditional medical methods, such as herbal tinctures or acupuncture' (*The Lancet*, **358** (9281), 18 August 2001, p. 567).

29. *Time Asia Magazine*, 'China's Failing Health System', 11 June 2003.
30. The most controversial transmission-mode was the blood-collecting scandal centred in the Henan province. Local government were involved in the commercialisation of blood plasma. Donors were tapped for blood and then reinjected with contaminated pooled blood-products (HRW, 2003).
31. In 2002 only two Chinese enterprises produced anti-AIDS drugs.
32. *The Lancet*, **362**, 27 September 2003, p. 1050.
33. *The Lancet*, **361** (9370), 17 May 2003, p. 1708.

BIBLIOGRAPHY

Bitran, R. and Yip, Winnie C. (1998), *A Review of Health Care Provider Payment Reform in Selected Countries in Asia and Latin America*, Working Paper (August), Maryland: Partnership for Health Reform.

Bloom, G. (2001), *China's Rural Health System in Transition: Towards Coherent Institutional Arrangements?*, paper presented at the Conference on Financial Sector Reform in China, 11–13 September, Boston: Harvard School of Public Health.

Bloom, G., Lu Yuelai and Chen Jiaying (2002), *Financing Health Care in China's Cities: Balancing Needs and Entitlements during Rapid Change*, IDS Working Paper 176, Brighton: Institute of Development Studies (IDS).

Bloom, G. and Fang Jing (2003), *China's Rural Health System in a Changing Institutional Contex*, IDS Working Paper 194, Brighton: IDS.

Bogg, L. (2002), *Health Care Financing in China: Equity in Transition*, PhD dissertation, Stockholm: Karolinska Insitutet, Department of Public Sciences, Division of International Health (IHCAR).

China Population Information and Research Center (CPIRC) (2000), *White Paper on Population*, http://www.cpirc.org.cn/en/eindex.htm.

Davis, D. and Chapman, N.E. (2002), 'Turning Points in Chinese Health Care: Crisis or Opportunity?', *The Yale–China Health Journal*, **1**, New Haven, CT: The Yale–China Association.

De Geyndt, W., Zhao Xiyan and Liu Shunli (1992), *From Barefoot Doctor to Village Doctor in Rural China*, Technical Paper No. 187, Asia Technical Department Series, Washington, DC: The World Bank.

Ding, Kaijie (2003), 'The Crucial Role of Local Governments in Setting up a Social Safety Net', *China Perspectives* (July–August), pp. 37–49.

Dong Weizhen (2001), *Health Care Reform in Urban China*, Working Paper 2001/2, Canada: Munk Centre for International Studies at the University of Toronto.

Fewsmith, J. (2003), 'China's Domestic Agenda: Social Pressures and Public Opinion', *China Leadership Monitor* (6).

Gao Jun, Tang Shenglan, Tolhurts, R. and Rao Keqing (2001), 'Changing Access to Health Services in Urban China: Implications for Equity', *Health Policy and Planning*, **16** (3), UK: Oxford University Press, pp. 302–12.

Gao Jun, Qian Juncheng, Tang Shenglan, Eriksson, B. and Blas, E. (2002), 'Health Equity in Transition from Planned to Market Economy in China', *Health Policy and Planning*, **17** (Suppl. 1), UK: Oxford University Press, pp. 20–29.

Hossain, Shaikh I. (1997), *Tackling Health Transition in China*, Working Paper 1813, Washington, DC: World Bank.

Hu Shanlian, Chen Wen, Cheng Xiaoming, Chen Keyong, Zhou Haiyang and Wang Longxing (2001), 'Pharmaceutical Cost–Containment Policy: Experiences in Shanghai, China', *Health Policy and Planning*, **16** (Suppl. 2), UK: Oxford University Press, pp. 4–9.

Huang Yanzhong (2002), *Reform as Pandora's Box: China's Public Health Crisis*, Presentation at the Conference 'China in Transition: A Look Behind the Scenes', 25 September, Washington, DC: Centre for Strategic and International Studies (CSIS).

Human Development Report (HDR) (2003), 'Public Policies to Improve People's Health and Education', New York: United Nations Development Program, Chapters 4 and 5.

Human Rights Watch (2003), *Locked Doors, The Human Rights of People Living with Aids in China*, New York: Human Rights Watch.

Hussain, A. (2000), *Social Welfare in China in the Context of Three Transitions*, China Working Paper No. 66, Stanford Centre for International Development.

Liu, Gordon G., Cai Renhua, Zhao Zhongyun, Yuen Peter, Xiong Xianjun, Chao Shumarry and Wang Boqing (1999), 'Urban Health Care Reform Initiative in China: Findings from its Pilot Experiment in Zhengjiang City (1)', *International Journal of Economic Development*, **1** (4), pp. 504–25.

Liu, Gordon G., Wu Xiandong, Peng Chaoyang and Fu Alex Z. (2002), 'Urbanization and Health Care in Rural China', *Contemporary Economic Policy*.

Liu Xingzhu, Liu Yuanli and Chen Ningshan (2000), 'The Chinese Experience of Hospital Price Regulation', *Health Policy and Planning*, **15** (2), UK: Oxford University Press, pp. 157–63.

Liu Yuanli and Hsiao William C. (2001), *China's Poor and Poor Policies: The Case of Rural Health Insurance*, presented at the Conference on Financial Sector Reform in China, 11–13 September, Boston: Harvard School of Public Health.

Liu Yuanli, Rao Keqin and Hu Shanlian (2002), *People's Republic of China Towards Establishing A Rural Health Protection System*, Manila: Asian Development Bank.

Liu Yunguo and Bloom, G. (2002), 'Designing a Rural Health Reform Project: The Negotiation of Change in China', Working Paper 150 (January), Brighton: IDS.

Lu Aiguo (2002), 'Economic Reforms and Welfare Changes in China', in Lu Aiguo and Montes, M. (eds), *Poverty, Income Distribution and Well-Being in Asia During the Transition*, Basingstoke, UK: Palgrave Macmillan, pp. 83–103.

Meng Qingyue, Liu Xingzhu and Shi Junshi (2000), 'Comparing the Services and Quality of Private and Public Clinics in Rural China', *Health Policy and Planning*, **15** (4), UK: Oxford University Press, pp. 349–56.

Meng Qingyue, Sun Qiang and Hearst, N. (2002) 'Hospital Charge Exemptions for the Poor in Shandong, China', *Health Policy and Planning*, **17** (Suppl. 1), UK: Oxford University Press, pp. 55–63.

National Bureau of Statistics (NBS) (2002), *China Statistical Yearbook* (CSY), Beijing: China Statistical Publishing House.

National Bureau of Statistics (NBS) (2003), *Statistical Communiqué 2002*, February 2003.

Rosenberg, A. and Merson, M. (2003), 'The Challenges of HIV/AIDS in China: An Overview', *The Yale–China Health Journal*, **2**, CT: The Yale–China Association, pp. 7–21.

Sidel, R. and Sidel, V.W (1982), *The Health of China*, London, UK: Zed Press; Boston, US: Beacon Press.

Strand, M.A. and Chen A.I. (2002), 'Rural Health Care in North China in an Era of Rapid Economic Change', *The Yale–China Health Journal*, **1**, New Haven, CT: The Yale–China Association, pp. 11–24.

World Bank, (1997), 'Financing Health Care, Issues and Options for China', *China 2020 Series*, Washington, DC: The World Bank.

World Health Organization (2000), *The World Health Report 2000 – Health Systems: Improving performance*, Geneva, Switzerland: World Health Organization (WHO).

World Health Organization (2002), *The World Health Report 2002 – Reducing Risks, Promoting Healthy Life*, Geneva, Switzerland: World Health Organization (WHO).

WHO (2003), *Website*: Country: China: 'key health indicators' and 'health expenditure indicators', http://www.who.int/country/chn/en/.

Yu Hao, Lucas, H., Gu Xing-Yuan and Su Bao-Gang (1998), *Financing Health in Poor Rural Counties in China: Experiences from a Township-Based Cooperative Medical Scheme*, Working Paper 66, Brighton: Institute for Development Studies (IDS).

Zhan Shaokang, Sun Zhenwei and Blas, E. (2002), 'Economic Transition and Maternal Health Care for Migrants in Shanghai, China', *Health Policy and Planning*, **17** (Suppl. 1), UK: Oxford University Press, pp. 47–55.

8. Liberalisation of Trade in Insurance Services: Widening Opportunities for Foreign Suppliers?

Benedetta Trivellato*

1. INTRODUCTION

Over the last decade, the Chinese authorities have increasingly been forced to face the need to restructure loss-making state-owned enterprises and gradually phase out the associated 'cradle-to-grave' welfare system. The government's partial withdrawal from its role as a pension and social welfare provider is therefore likely to provide opportunities for non-state services providers, particularly in the fast-growing insurance sector.

In a situation where the domestic insurance sector is still relatively under-developed, China's recent accession to the World Trade Organisation (WTO) provides a chance for foreign suppliers to enter a potentially vast market. Foreign investors' enthusiasm should, however, be balanced against the actual entry conditions of the Chinese market, and the effects of the changes that are taking place within the domestic insurance industry. Given the strategic nature of insurance services, the Chinese authorities have carefully regulated the speed and scope of foreign involvement in order to protect the country's still nascent domestic insurance industry and to match insurance industry growth with society's demand for insurance services.

This chapter explores China's opening commitments under the WTO and relevant related regulatory provisions, together with a number of important developments that are taking place within the domestic insurance market, in order to assess whether social security reform in conjunction with WTO-related opening will indeed provide widening opportunities for foreign investors.

2. CHINA'S OPENING COMMITMENTS UNDER THE WTO

2.1. The Importance of Direct Investment for the Supply of Insurance Services

Insurance services play a relevant role in a modern economy, protecting enterprises against risks such as business failure and natural disasters, and providing individuals with security in key areas such as health care, property, and pensions. Moreover, the insurance industry acts as a fundamental financial intermediary by transferring funds from the insured to capital investment, which is critical for China's continued economic expansion (Ji and Thomas, 2001).

As Wu and Strange (1998) point out, insurance is one of those service sectors where location still matters. Although recent developments in information technology have opened up the possibility of some direct transactions of insurance business across borders, insurance companies worldwide seem to believe that a local presence remains essential for the effective development of business. The authors note that a local presence is less critical when risks are generally accepted and may be written in a standardised form by licensing agreements with local agents. Such is the case, for instance, with risks that are 'personal lines' in relation to property and liability held by private individuals, where no detailed risk assessment is required because the liability on any one risk is small, and the number of homogeneous risks is large enough to ensure that the use of probability laws will allow secure underwriting. On the other hand, in the case of life insurance and some forms of health and personal accident cover, a local presence becomes key to success, because it allows close contacts and trust between the insurer and the insured. This is even more important in those contexts where there is an insufficient local supply of suitable agents and telecommunication facilities offering products at competitive prices. Moreover, a local presence is often needed in the case of complex insurance products, such as the property or liability risks generated by large institutions.

In China's case, the partial withdrawal of the state from its role as pension provider will provide the momentum for medium-to-long term growth in the insurance industry, opening a potentially vast market to foreign suppliers. Following the country's accession to the WTO, foreign life insurers will be allowed for the first time to provide health insurance to Chinese citizens. In order fully to exploit the potential offered by China's developing insurance market, foreign insurance companies will therefore need to prioritise mode 3 (commercial presence)[1] as their choice of entry, despite a number of restrictions which have indeed been introduced by the Chinese authorities.

2.2. China's Commitments with Regard to Insurance Services

A detailed analysis of China's WTO commitments[2] highlights the fact that market access for foreign direct investment in the insurance sector is subject to considerable restrictions, ranging from the form of an establishment, to its geographic and business scope, to its capitalisation requirements. While some of the restrictions for foreign players are due to be phased out over the next few years, other measures will remain, thereby limiting the actual degree of liberalisation.

According to China's Schedule of Commitments under the WTO, licences are to be awarded to foreign insurers solely on the basis of prudential criteria, without economic-needs tests or quantitative limits on the number of licences issued. This implies reliance on a transparent and objective process, rather than on criteria based on nationality. Three requirements need to be satisfied by foreign applicants: thirty years of experience as an insurer in a WTO member country; having maintained a representative office in China for at least two years; and total assets exceeding $5 bn at the end of the year prior to application, except for insurance brokers.[3] This marks a change relatively to the past, when decisions to grant licences to foreign insurers have been opaque and highly politicised.

China has agreed to gradually lift all geographic restrictions that were previously applied to foreign insurers and insurance brokers. In addition to Shanghai and Guangzhou, China has agreed to open Dalian, Foshan, and Shenzhen upon WTO accession, ten additional cities (Beijing, Chengdu, Chongqing, Fuzhou, Suzhou, Xiamen, Ningbo, Shenyang, Wuhan and Tianjin) within two years after accession, and to eliminate all geographic restrictions to the market within three years after accession.[4]

The WTO agreement provides for considerable expansion of foreign providers' business scope. In the past, products issued by foreign insurers were highly restricted: foreign non-life insurers could only underwrite the risks of foreign-invested enterprises, and foreign life insurers could only sell individual life policies and were prohibited from selling group life products or any types of health, pension, and annuity products. Upon China's accession to the WTO, foreign non-life insurers are allowed to provide master policy insurance, and to insure large scale commercial risks. They are also permitted to insure Chinese enterprises abroad, and to provide property insurance, related liability insurance, and credit insurance to foreign-invested enterprises in China. Within two years after accession, foreign non-life insurers will be permitted to provide the full range of non-life insurance services to both foreign and domestic clients. As far as life insurers are concerned, upon accession they have been permitted to provide individual (not group) insurance to foreigners and Chinese citizens; within three years after accession, they will be permitted to provide health insurance, group insurance and pension/annuities insurance to foreigners and Chinese citizens.

A number of restrictions have been included in the Agreement as regards the form of establishment in the Chinese market. Upon the country's accession to the WTO, foreign non-life insurers are permitted to establish as a branch or as a joint venture with 51 per cent foreign ownership; these restrictions are to be phased out within two years after accession, with non-life insurers thereby allowed to establish as a wholly-owned subsidiary. Foreign life insurers are permitted 50 per cent foreign ownership in a joint venture with the partner of their choice (not necessarily an insurance company). The joint venture partners can freely agree the terms of their engagement, provided they remain within the limits of the commitments contained in the schedule.

Provisions related to brokerage for insurance of large scale commercial risks, brokerage for reinsurance, and brokerage for international marine, aviation, and transport insurance and reinsurance, are as follows: upon accession, joint ventures with foreign equity not exceeding 50 per cent will be permitted; within three years after China's accession, foreign equity share can be increased to 51 per cent; within five years after accession, wholly foreign owned subsidiary will be permitted. Other types of brokerage services are not subject to restrictions. Internal branching for an insurance firm will be permitted consistent with the phase out of geographic restrictions.

The only restriction to the 'national treatment' principle includes the prohibition of foreign insurance institutions to engage in the statutory insurance business.

As for reinsurance, the WTO Agreement allows foreign insurers to provide upon accession reinsurance services for life and non-life insurance, and to establish as a branch, joint venture, or wholly foreign-owned subsidiary, without geographic or quantitative restrictions on the number of licences issued. There is, however, a limitation on the 'national treatment' principle, which requires a 20 per cent cession of all lines of the primary risks for non-life, personal accident and health insurance business with an appointed Chinese Reinsurance Company; the requirement is to be phased out within four years after accession.

3. THE REGULATORY FRAMEWORK[5] FOR FOREIGN PARTICIPATION IN CHINA'S INSURANCE INDUSTRY

The legislative framework for China's insurance industry is provided by the 1995 Insurance Law, which aimed at strengthening the supervision and regulation of the industry and protecting the interests of all the parties involved. The 1995 Insurance Law is still in force, although it has been modified through subsequent amendments so as to keep up with the rapidly changing insurance market. Provisions that may be of particular interest to foreign insurers are included in the Amendment which was approved on 28 October 2002 (Chen and Mei, 2003). The amendment partially liberalises the formulation and regulation of insurance premium rates and insurance policy clauses: under the new Insurance Law, apart from premium rates and policy clauses for public interest-related insurance, mandatory insurance and new types of life insurance products, which remain under control of the regulator, all other types are determined by insurance companies themselves and reported to the authorities only for filing purposes. This helps alleviate the situation of high uniformity between insurance products and improve industry response to diverse specialised market sectors. Moreover, the new Insurance Law removes the prohibition of a single insurer from simultaneously providing property and life insurance services, by allowing property insurers to provide short-term health and accidental injury insurance services, subject to regulatory approval.

Amendments to the Administrative Measures for Insurance Companies, which have been in force since 1 March 2000, and which apply to both domestic and foreign insurers, became effective on 15 September 2003 (Freshfields Bruckhaus Deringer, 2003). The Amendments propose a single minimum registered capital requirement of RMB 200 million applicable to all insurance companies, and RMB 20 million for each additional branch up to RMB 500 million. Previously, national and regional insurance companies were required to have a minimum registered capital of RMB 500 million and RMB 200 million respectively. Moreover, they were required to provide additional capital amounting to RMB 50 million for each additional provincial-level branch up to RMB 1.5 billion and RMB 500 million for national and regional insurance companies respectively. The amended Administrative Measures also identify the categories of persons and institutions that are allowed to invest in a domestic insurance institution, together with shareholding limits for each category: equity investment by foreign financial institutions is capped at 25 per cent.

The Administrative Regulations on Foreign-Funded Insurance Companies (effective 1 February 2002, with 'Implementing Rules' subsequently drafted and effective 15 August 2003) are applicable specifically to foreign companies, and allow three forms of foreign-funded insurance companies: an equity joint venture, a wholly foreign-owned company and a branch of a foreign insurance company. This rules out the possibility of establishing a foreign-funded insurance company limited by shares (Chen and Mei, 2003). The minimum registered capital for equity JVs and wholly foreign-owned companies, and the minimum working capital for foreign insurance branches are both 200 million RMB. Foreign insurance companies may apply to set up branches one year after the establishment of their China operations. The new 'Implementing Rules' require each new branch to have an additional RMB 20 million in paid-up capital; companies whose paid-up capital exceeds RMB 500 million do not have to provide additional funding for new branches (Freshfields Bruckhaus Deringer, 2003). The approval of an application to establish a foreign-invested insurance company involves a two-step process over a relatively long timeframe: an approval of the initial application and a second approval of the documentation for establishment are required. The regulatory authority, the China Insurance Regulatory Commission (CIRC), has up to six months to examine and approve the initial application. Applicants who have received the first approval are then required to submit complete establishment documentation within another year, and the CIRC may take up to 60 days to issue the final approval (Chen and Mei, 2003).

Although China had agreed to phase out upon WTO accession all restrictions on reinsurance services to be provided by foreign suppliers, the Provisions on Establishment of Reinsurance Companies were only enacted on 17 September 2002 (Chen and Mei, 2003). Before that time two foreign reinsurance companies, Swiss Re and Munich Re, had been allowed by the CIRC to establish branches in China, but could not commence business due to lack of guidance as regards business scope, funding, and branch operations. According to the Provisions, foreign insurers can provide life reinsurance, non-life reinsurance, or comprehensive reinsurance (a combination of the first two) upon approval by the CIRC. The minimum paid-up capital for life as well as non-life reinsurance is RMB 200 million, rising to 300 million for comprehensive reinsurance. These provisions also apply to domestic reinsurance companies and branches of foreign reinsurers.

4.   CHINA'S INSURANCE MARKET AND ITS OPENNESS TO FOREIGN INVESTMENT

China's insurance sector is still relatively underdeveloped and characterised by a limited variety of insurance products. Moreover, it suffers from relatively high costs and limited consumer knowledge about the role of insurance (Benfield Group, 2003). However, there is strong potential for growth, and opportunities for foreign companies to contribute to greater market maturity.

At the end of June 2003 the combined total premiums of domestic and foreign insurance companies in China reached $25.7 bn, an increase of 32 per cent year-on-year. In the first six months of 2003, life insurance premiums rose by 39.3 per cent year-on-year to reach $20 bn. Property insurance premiums rose by 11.8 per cent to $5.7 bn, while the combined assets of Chinese and foreign insurance companies stood at $94.3 bn at the end of June 2003 (Oxford Analytica, 2003). In terms of total premium volume, in 2002 China was the third largest insurance market (both for life and non–life business) in Asia, after Japan and South Korea, with a global ranking of eight for the life business and thirteenth for the non–life business (Swiss Re, 2003).

In terms of insurance penetration,[6] however, China ranked 48th among the world's insurance markets in 2002, with a penetration rate of only 2.98 per cent. The life insurance market is growing at a particularly high rate, and

Table 8.1   China's Life and Non-life Premium Volume in 2002

	Premium volume ($ million)		Change in %		Share of world market 2002 (in %)
	2002	2001	Nominal (in $)	Inflation-adjusted	
Life	25 054	15 556	61.1	62.2	1.63
Non-life	11 834	9 928	19.2	20.1	1.08

Source: Swiss Re (2003).

recent figures reveal that this trend is likely to continue. For instance, the market has grown by around 37 per cent a year since 1995, and was valued in 2002 at about $25 bn; penetration grew to 2.03 per cent in 2002, compared with 1.5 per cent in 2001, while life insurance density[7] rose to $28.7 per capita, compared with $13.5 per capita in 2001. The market is forecast to grow at around 20 per cent annually between 2002 and 2010, reaching $118 bn.

Similar growth and opportunities can be seen in the non-life insurance sector, where in 2002 automobile and fire insurance accounted for more than 80 per cent of the non-life insurance market. The sector has seen intense competition, while growing at an average annual rate of 10 per cent over the past ten years, and was worth around $11.8 bn in 2002, compared with $8 bn in 2001. Penetration rose to 0.96 per cent in 2002, from 0.70 per cent in 2001, while insurance density rose to $9.2 per capita in 2002, compared with $6.5 per capita in 2001. The market is expected to continue to grow at about its current rate (10 per cent) until 2010 (Oxford Analytica, 2003).

Table 8.2   Insurance Penetration (Premiums as percentage of GDP) in 2002

Country	Ranking	Total business	Life business	Non–life business
China	48	2.98	2.03	0.96
Hong Kong	21	6.65	5.20	1.45
Taiwan	6	10.16	7.35	2.81
Malaysia	30	4.91	2.94	1.97
Singapore	31	4.91	3.48	1.43
Indonesia	72	1.49	0.66	0.83
Philippines	73	1.48	0.87	0.61
Japan	5	10.86	8.64	2.22
South Korea	4	11.61	8.23	3.38
United States	7	9.58	4.60	4.98
World	–	8.14	4.76	3.38

Source: Swiss Re (2003).

The high growth of the life–insurance segment relatively to the non-life is partly explained by the reform of the state-owned enterprises and the associated reduction of welfare services provided by the state. Other factors supporting such growth include the high savings ratio and rising household income. Shrinking family size, prolonged average life expectancy, an ageing population and a diminishing dependence on the family as a support structure have resulted in increasing demand for pension insurance.[8] One element contributing to the growth of the life insurance market has also been the growth of sino-foreign joint ventures, given that the Chinese government does not provide life insurance, health insurance or other types of benefits to employees of joint ventures. Moreover, while in the past the life insurance business was almost only targeting corporate sales, today it is increasingly aiming to develop both group and personal business (D'Arcy and Xia, 2003).

Despite its relatively modest performance, the non-life insurance market shows a significant long-term growth potential. Current and future developments that are likely to prompt such growth include: an increasing number of infrastructure projects, the concentration of assets in areas subject to natural hazards, an increase in risk awareness among firms operating in China, the reform of the state-owned enterprises, and continued foreign investment (Benfield Group, 2003).

China's insurance market is currently dominated by a few domestic giants: at the end of 2002, PICC Property and Casualty Company (PICC),[9] China Pacific Insurance Company (China Pacific)[10] and Ping An Insurance (Ping An)[11] together controlled nearly 95 per cent of the non-life insurance market; as for the life segment, China Life Insurance Company (China Life), Ping An and China Pacific had a combined market share exceeding 90 per cent (Benfield Group, 2003). On a national basis, foreign companies' market share is very low in all sectors, ranging between 0.5 and 2.0 per cent, although it is higher in the geographical areas in which they operate.[12] As of December 2003, around 36 foreign insurance companies were running 57 branches and representative offices in China (Oxford Analytica, 2003).

4.1. Regulatory Barriers Faced by Foreign Insurers

As detailed above, China's accession to the WTO has been followed by the introduction of a number of regulations and legislative measures aimed at implementing the WTO commitments while gradually granting foreign investors access to the domestic market. While the need to adopt a prudent approach has been widely recognised as justifiable and reasonable by foreign investors, many have claimed that some of these implementing laws and regulations pose an excessive burden on prospective investors, thereby discouraging investment and acting as de facto regulatory barriers.

The most frequent cause of concern has been the high capitalisation requirements for the initial establishment of a foreign insurer and subsequent opening of new branches. As mentioned above, the insurance regulations issued by the CIRC initially imposed a minimum paid-up capital of RMB 500 million to obtain a nationwide licence, together with RMB 50 million for each additional branch. According to a report by the US Trade Representative published in December 2002 (United States Trade Representative, 2002), several US companies deemed those capitalisation requirements significantly more exacting than those of other populous countries with a similar interest in preserving a healthy insurance market. It was a widely shared belief that the effect of these requirements would have been to limit the ability of foreign insurers to make necessary joint venture arrangements, and thus to limit the viability of foreign participation in the Chinese insurance market. However, possibly also because of the pressures exerted by the international insurance business community (Smith, 2003), in 2003 China introduced an Amendment to the Administrative Measures for Insurance Companies lowering the relevant capitalization requirements (see above).[13]

Other prudential requirements also pose a considerable burden on potential investors. Successful international insurance companies may not have the required 30-year history. Moreover, new foreign insurers are required to maintain a representative office for two years before being allowed to apply for a licence. Given that during these two years their operations are strictly limited to offering consultations and market-study services, new entrants may be deterred by the long lead time required before reaching profitability.

An issue which continues to be of particular concern to foreign insurance companies relates to branching rights and their characteristics. As part of its WTO commitments, China allowed non-life firms to establish a branch in the country upon accession, and agreed to permit internal branching in accordance with the lifting of geographic restrictions. China further agreed that foreign insurers already established in the country which were seeking authorisation to establish branches or subbranches would not have to satisfy the requirements applicable to foreign insurers seeking a licence to enter the domestic market. Despite these commitments, the regulations are vague on foreign insurers' branching rights, and the CIRC has maintained that non-life insurers that are already in the market as a single branch and that wish to establish branches or subbranches cannot do so unless they first establish as a subsidiary, an option which is deemed costly and unnecessary by several US corporations (United States Trade Representative, 2002). Another issue raised by the American Council of Life Insurers relates to branch boundaries. Based on the assumption that it is more efficient to establish provincial-level branches rather than only municipal-level branches, Smith (2003) notes that Chinese companies are allowed to operate at the provincial level with access to all cities and localities that are part of the province. On the contrary, foreign companies that have obtained a licence are allowed to operate only at the city level, and not at the provincial level.

Some regulations appear to introduce additional requirements that were not included in the WTO schedule of commitments. A communication by the Government of Canada to the WTO Committee on Trade in Financial Services (WTO, 2002) refers, for instance, to the fact that under mode 4 China agreed to allow temporary entry for senior employees of a foreign financial institution. However, according to the Administrative Measures for Insurance Companies, an insurance company establishing a branch office should have senior management for such office who meet specific qualifications as specified by the CIRC. One of these qualifications is that senior management personnel must be able to speak Chinese, a requirement which was not included in China's Schedule of Specific Commitments.

Additional obstacles are perceived to be caused by a generalised lack of transparency. The regulations permit considerable bureaucratic discretion and offer limited certainty to foreign insurers seeking to operate in China's market. In a number of cases, this lack of transparency has manifested itself particularly in the licensing process. Even though China had agreed to award new licences to qualified foreign insurers based solely on prudential criteria, with no need for an invitation to apply and no quantitative limits on the number of licences or restrictions such as an economic-needs test, US companies noted that the CIRC has been slow to act on pending applications (United States Trade Representative, 2002). This may be due to the fact that the approval procedure as specified by the Administrative Regulations on Foreign Funded Insurance Companies requires a lengthy two-step process, which has been criticised as acting as a barrier to market access and being more trade restrictive than necessary.

More generally, licensing requirements for foreign participation have complex multi-stage approval processes for establishment, which appear to contradict the spirit of the Working Party Report, which states that 'China's licensing procedures and conditions would not act as trade barriers to market access and would not be more trade restrictive than necessary'. Moreover, opportunities for public comment on China's new insurance regulations are limited by the short periods of time given for such comments to be provided, whereas the WTO accession protocol requires '… a reasonable period for comment to the appropriate authorities before such measures are implemented …' (WTO, 2002).

4.2. Non–regulatory Barriers Faced by Foreign Insurers

Prospective foreign investors have also come across a number of non-regulatory barriers to market access. Several foreign firms, for instance, are encountering difficulties in joint venture negotiations, mostly over pricing and resistance encountered towards surrendering any management control for a minority stake. Lack of mutual trust and agreement on management practices may be related to cultural differences: there have been instances where managers with different cultural backgrounds had different points of view on issues such as marketing of insurance products and employee compensation (Ji and Thomas, 2001).

According to Headey et al. (2002), the alternative represented by equity investment may in some cases bring more fruitful results, despite the foreign firm having less management control relative to the joint venture option. The authors refer to the deal involving the Belgian financial group Fortis and the Chinese firm Tai Ping (where Fortis acquired a 24.9 per cent stake in Tai Ping) as an example where the foreign investor managed to obtain a certain degree of management control, such as veto powers and rights to appoint senior management, and to be in a position to provide strategic guidance, training and technical support. Moreover, equity investment allows the foreign insurer to gain immediate access to the national market with no limitations on business scope. This route could be particularly attractive to companies that do not meet the prudential criteria, for instance by having less than 30 years' life insurance experience, and therefore do not qualify for a joint venture licence. Alternatively it may be a preferred option for multinationals that have limited presence and resources in the Greater China region, in that it offers an opportunity to build up local market experience without the need to play an active management role. However, valuation and due diligence are significant challenges for foreign investors considering a minority equity stake. Whether the domestic company is a greenfield or relatively new start-up or an established company, the main component of value is likely to be future business value. In a rapidly developing market such as China, the valuation of future business is particularly difficult. Nevertheless, this has not prevented multinationals from undertaking considerable investments as shown in Table 8.3, which lists the acquired stake in a number of recent transactions.

Table 8.3   Selected Foreign Insurers' Minority Investment in Domestic Insurance Companies

Domestic Company	Foreign Insurer	Purchase Share
Taikang	Winterhur	10%
Xinhua (New China)	Zurich	10%
Xinhua (New China)	Meiji Life	4.5%
Tai Ping	Fortis	24.9%
Hua Tai	ACE	22%

Source: Headey et al. (2002).

D'Arcy and Xia (2003) mention a number of additional challenges that foreign insurers are likely to face: a limited supply of employees with expertise in insurance (finance, actuarial science, and marketing); imbalances in supply and demand based on the geographical distribution of competition; investment restrictions and relatively immature capital markets that limit the potential for investment returns and can expose insurers to substantial investment risk; low consumer awareness of the benefits of insurance. Moreover, the establishment of the CIRC in 1998, while being a welcome development from the viewpoint of insurance regulation and supervision, introduced a further element of rigidity into the system. All new products must be approved by the CIRC before they can be issued, all changes in the ownership structure of a company need to be authorised before they can be implemented, and any change of investment allocations must be approved. This implies that decisions that are normally considered the internal affairs of a company – such as developing new products, distributing policies in different geographic areas, and appointing senior managers – in China require the involvement of the regulatory authority.

4.3. The Changing Structure of the Domestic Insurance Market as a Result of WTO Accession

Although they do not necessarily represent a barrier to accessing the Chinese market, foreign investors should also take into consideration the changes that are currently shaping the domestic insurance sector and its main players. Since the late 1990s, the Chinese government has taken a number of steps and measures to prepare China's insurance market for the post-WTO accession competition. This includes improving the legal structure by having the CIRC issue new regulations for insurance firms in general and also for foreign-funded insurance firms.

The regulation allowing foreign investors to own up to 25 per cent of selected Chinese insurance companies was already in place before WTO accession. The CIRC has encouraged Chinese companies to increase their capital base through foreign participation in order to strengthen them for the coming WTO market competition (Ji and Thomas, 2001). For example, Xinhua (New China) Insurance, China's fourth largest national insurance company, has been developing rapidly since its establishment in 1996. In 2001 it sold 24.9 per cent of its equity for $116.9 million to five foreign investors including Zurich Insurance Company, the International Financial Corporation (a member of the World Bank), the Japan-based Meiji Life Insurance Company, Holland Financial Services Company, and a fifth unnamed company. The five foreign investors have also agreed to provide advanced technology and management know-how. Similarly, China's fifth largest life insurance company, Taikang Insurance, has been approved for foreign investment and has also successfully carried out a year-long international private placement. The company's new foreign shareholders include Winterthur Life and Pensions (WLP), The Government of Singapore Investment Corporation (GIC), and Japan's Softbank. Foreign shareholders have also agreed to provide comprehensive assistance to Taikang in terms of technology, staff training, and e-commerce, and send their experts to Taikang for diagnosis of company management and practices, leading to specific recommendations for improvement.

Other Chinese insurance companies have made alliances with banks and other financial institutions to strengthen their marketing and customer service capabilities. Pingan Insurance Company and Guangdong Development Bank, for instance, have teamed up to offer credit card service to their customers. The Industrial and Commercial Banks of China (ICBC) and PICC completed an agreement for long-term cooperation, where they will act as each other's agents, and where ICBC will collect insurance premiums and pay claims on behalf of PICC. Chinese companies have also been encouraged to develop new insurance products, such as Pingan and Xinhua Life's new 'unit-link' policies, tying insurance products more closely to financial investment.

In addition to a number of Chinese insurers ceding part of their equity to foreign investors, some of the biggest state-owned insurers had started preparing for partial listing on international financial markets. Already in 2000, PICC and China Life reorganised their operations and streamlined their workforces by 8 000 and 383 respectively. On 6 November 2003, PICC successfully made an initial public offering (IPO) raising HK$5.4 bn (approximately $693 million) through the sale of 28 per cent of its enlarged share capital on the Hong Kong Stock Exchange. A measure of the attractiveness of PICC's shares is given by the fact that retail investors in Hong Kong subscribed for about 130 times the number of shares in the public offer. It is also likely that PICC benefited from the announcement made before the IPO by American International Group (AIG), the world's largest insurer by market value, that it would buy a 9.9 per cent stake in the firm. On IPO completion, the new company had a market capitalisation of approximately $2.5 bn (CNN News, 'China insurer raises $693 million', 31 October 2003).

In a similar but larger IPO, the largest in the world in 2003, China Life shares debuted in New York on 17 December, and in Hong Kong on 18 December, rising 27 and 26 per cent respectively. The total value of the global offering was HK$23.23 bn ($3 bn); again, the retail part of the offering was 170 times oversubscribed (*The Economist*, 'Off with a bang', 18 December 2003). According to several analysts, such a high investor interest reflects the expectations for growth by the mainland Chinese largest life insurer – a growth that will be driven by demographic trends, social welfare reform, a solid economic outlook and an under-spenetrated market compared with either Europe or Asia. Moreover, China Life is widely considered China's most attractive life company because of its large distribution network and stronger brand recognition than its competitors.

Financial markets' interest in PICC and China Life is surely a positive sign, but a number of observers invite a more cautious approach, pointing out that a number of Chinese life insurers are saddled with millions of dollars in potential losses arising from policies with high guarantees sold in the early 1980s and late 1990s. As of December 2003, the ratings agency Standard and Poor's had assigned a 'developing' outlook to China's insurance sector facing a period of structural change and exceptional growth. While the growth is expected to help insurance companies to improve their financial strength through earnings, significant capital shortfalls are still expected at major companies, which will increasingly turn to external sources of capital to address the problem. Standard and Poor's estimated that China's life insurance sector must increase capital by $1.8 bn–$2.4 bn, and the non-life insurance sector by $845 million–$1.2 bn, to achieve adequate levels of capitalisation. Domestic companies are also hampered by relatively inaccurate data for risk calculations, such as credit ratings and morbidity tables (Oxford Analytica, 2003).

5. CONCLUDING REMARKS

China's accession to the WTO will bring profound changes to the domestic insurance market. The progressive loosening of restrictions will provide an expanded range of products for China's citizens and corporations, thereby fostering growth and development. Chinese insurance companies enjoy a competitive advantage relative to their foreign counterparts, based on factors such as a better understanding of domestic consumers' needs and culture, long-term relationships with their clients, and extensive networks of agencies throughout the country. However, several Chinese firms are to a great extent inefficient because of the monopolistic market situation which they were allowed to enjoy, causing a high degree of uniformity in product, market, distribution, and pricing strategies among companies in the insurance sector. Insurance awareness among the Chinese population needs to be improved: in the not-so-distant future, insurance products could become an alternative to bank deposits as a way to invest people's savings.

Despite the concern voiced by some sources, foreign competition is likely to bring more advantages than damage to the Chinese insurance sector. As Wu and Strange (1998) point out, foreign multinational companies benefit from ownership advantages allowing them to provide better quality and a more extensive range of insurance policies at more competitive prices than domestic insurers. This is partly due to economies of scale and scope, which not only reduce costs but are positively correlated with financial institutions' propensity to enter foreign markets, as large companies with diversified assets are better able to absorb risks and are often the only companies able to meet the high capitalisation requirements imposed by several governments. Moreover, insurance activities require a substantial degree of financial and marketing expertise. Operating internationally helps to create a prestigious corporate reputation for foreign insurers, and this advantage is in turn conducive to business development. Multinationals are not only able to offer new products, but also to package existing ones in new ways to provide contracts which give wider coverage at lower cost. Lastly, the authors note that because of easier access to capital markets and world-wide reinsurance agreements, international insurance companies often have larger underwriting capability for high risks, and have the technical competence to estimate possible loss frequency and severity from underwriting similar risks elsewhere in the world, thereby providing better services to multinational corporations operating in the local economy.

China's accession to the WTO provides a significant widening of opportunities available to foreign investors to access the domestic insurance market – including the life segment, which is widely believed to have a substantial growth potential following the reform of the Chinese welfare system. However, prospective investors should pay attention to two elements in particular: the details of the evolving regulatory framework, and the changing characteristics of the domestic market structure.

As highlighted by D'Arcy and Xia (2003), the WTO opening measures and the related regulatory developments mark a significant change from the recent past, where market access was permitted but subject to a much wider range of restrictions. Foreign insurers' efforts to tap the Chinese market were hindered by the demanding criteria required by the People's Bank of China (the relevant regulatory authority before the establishment of the CIRC) for approval to operate within China, the special requirements for a business licence from local governments, the slow development of comprehensive insurance legislation, and the relatively high incidence of protectionism. Most of these restrictions have been lifted, and many more will be gradually phased out in the near future. The need to protect a still developing insurance industry implies that the Chinese authorities have been introducing – and will probably continue to do so – a number of regulatory measures which may pose an unforeseen burden to prospective investors. Such investors should therefore continue to monitor these regulatory developments closely, and to cooperate with the Chinese authorities[14] to reduce their impact where possible. On the other hand, as Cavalieri (2003) points out, China's accession to the WTO will not only affect the trade and investment regime, but the entire legal system. Key principles such as normative uniformity, transparency, equal treatment, and jurisdictional control over the acts of the public administration will need to be included in the Chinese legal system. Over the longer term, this trend is likely to have a positive impact on the uncertain legal environment which appears to be of major concern to several foreign insurance companies.[15]

A second important factor to be closely watched by foreign insurance companies interested in accessing the Chinese market is the changing structure of the country's insurance industry. Such changes are being prompted by the progressive entrance of foreign insurers, either through joint venture agreements – many of which involve a Chinese non-insurance partner[16] – or through equity shares acquisitions. As noted above, most of the latter involve partnership agreements where the foreign investors may provide training and contribute management and marketing skills. The success of PICC's and China Life's IPOs is likely to encourage other Chinese insurers to tap overseas markets in the short to medium term, and limited but significant increases in foreign involvement will help introduce best practices in areas such as risk calculation as the market matures. International insurance companies will need to take into account the increasingly important role that Chinese companies will play domestically and possibly, over the longer term, within the international insurance market.

NOTES

* The author would like to thank Renzo Cavalieri and Maria Weber for their insightful comments on earlier drafts of this manuscript.
1. The Editor's Introduction to this volume outlines the four modes through which foreign services can be supplied under WTO rules.
2. See WTO (2001).
3. Insurance brokers are allowed lower requirements, which are also bound to diminish over time after China's accession to the WTO: upon accession, total assets had to exceed $500 million; within one year after accession, the requirement amounted to 400 million, to become 300 within two years after accession, and 200 within four years after accession (WTO, 2001).
4. Early in 2002, the Chinese regulatory authority decided to lift certain geographic restrictions applicable to foreign life insurers ahead of schedule. It approved life insurance operations in Beijing, Suzhou and Tianjin two years before China had committed to do so in its services schedule (USTR, 2002).
5. Considerations of space and relevance do not allow an exhaustive description of all the laws and regulations that apply to China's insurance industry. Therefore, only new regulations and amendments to existing laws (as of December 2003) that aim to implement WTO commitments, and are therefore of major concern to foreign investors, will be considered here. For a review of the laws and regulations relevant to foreign investors which were introduced before China's WTO accession see Wu and Strange (1998).
6. Insurance penetration is defined as total premiums as a percentage of Gross Domestic Product (GDP).
7. Insurance density is defined as premiums per capita.
8. See chapters by Boati, and Weber and Stenbeck in this volume.
9. PICC and China Life originate from the only insurance company (also called PICC – People's Insurance Company of China) which was established in 1949 to replace all domestic insurance operations at the time. After a first restructuring in 1996 (where PICC was renamed PICC Group), in 1999 the company was divided into four independent state-owned insurance companies: the new PICC, China Life, China Reinsurance Company (the country's only reinsurance company) and China Insurance Company (established in Hong Kong and consisting of all 83 official overseas representative offices and branches of the former PICC

Group). Both PICC and China Life performed a successful IPO at the Hong Kong Stock Exchange (and at the New York Stock Exchange in the case of China Life) in the fourth quarter of 2003.

10. Established in 1991 as a joint stock company, China Pacific was previously owned by the Bank of Communications; its current shareholders comprise state-related entities.
11. Ping An was established in 1988 as a joint venture between China Merchants Group, Industrial and Commercial Bank of China, and China Ocean Shipping Company. It was the first to use international auditors and have foreign shareholders who jointly own 24.9%.
12. As of January 2004, antitrust legislation had not yet been included into the Chinese regulatory framework.
13. It should be noted, however, that given that branches are supported by the entire capital of the parent company, in most countries they are exempt from minimum capital requirements (Wu and Strange, 1998).
14. Smith (2003) provides some examples of instances where the dialogue between US and Chinese industry representatives, aided by their respective governments, has led to positive results.
15. It should be noted, however, that the central government is expected to experience several difficulties in the implementation of the news norms, due to a lack of the technical and political capabilities that would allow the central and local administrations to fully adapt to them (Cavalieri, 2003).
16. Examples of such JVs include: Aegon–CNOCC Life Insurance, where the foreign and domestic partners are represented by Aegon NV and China National Offshore Oil Corporation (CNOOC) respectively; and Haier New York Life Insurance Company, where the relevant partners are NY Life International Inc. and Haier Group (Benfield Group, 2003).

BIBLIOGRAPHY

Benfield Group (2003), *China Insurance Market Review*, December.

Cavalieri, R. (2003), *Implicazioni giuridiche dell'adesione della Cina alla WTO*, Lecce: Argo.

Chao, H. (2002), 'The WTO and Foreign Financial Institutions in China', *Topics in Chinese Law*, An O'Melveny & Myers LLP Research Report, May.

Chen, L. and J. Mei (2003), 'Recent Developments in the Chinese Financial Industry', *Topics in Chinese Law*, An O'Melveny & Myers LLP Research Report, June.

D'Arcy, S.P. and H. Xia (2003), 'Insurance and China's Entry into the WTO', *Risk Management and Insurance Review*, **6** (1), 7–25.

Freshfields Bruckhaus Deringer (2003), 'Formation, Registration, Licensing, Conduct and Operation of Insurance Companies', *Insurance* (11), August.

Headey, P., J. Law and C. Zhang (2002), 'China Life insurance Market: Opportunities for Foreign Entrants', *Milliman Global Insurance*, August.

Ji, C. and S. Thomas (2001), *The Role of Foreign Insurance Companies in China's Emerging Insurance Industry: An FDI Case Study*, Paper to be presented at the Conference on Financial Sector Reform in China, 11–13 September.

Mattoo, A. (2002), *China's Accession to the World Trade Organization – The Services Dimension*, Policy Research Working Paper No. 2932, The World Bank, December.

Monti, A. (2001), *The Law of Insurance Contracts in the People's Republic of China. A Comparative Analysis of Policyholders' Rights*, ICER Working Paper No. 28.

Oxford Analytica (2003), 'Spectacular Debut for China Life', www.oxweb.com, 19 December.

Smith, B. (2003), *Is China Playing by the Rules? Free Trade, Fair Trade, and WTO Compliance*, Statement of the Managing Director for International Relations, American Council of Life Insurers, at the Congressional–Executive Commission on China, 24 September.

Swiss Re (2003), 'World Insurance in 2002', *Sigma* (8).

United States Trade Representative (USTR) (2002), *2002 Report to Congress on China's WTO Compliance*, 11 December.

Wang, X. (2001), *China's Pension System Reform and Capital Market Development*, Paper presented at the International Conference on China and the WTO: The Financial Challenge, Kennedy School of Government, Harvard University, 12 September.

World Trade Organization (2001), 'Schedule of Specific Commitments on Services', in *Report of the Working Party on the Accession of China*, 10 November.

World Trade Organization, Committee on Trade in Financial Services (2002), *Communication from Canada*, 1 October.

Wu, X., and R. Strange (1998), 'The Insurance Industry in China: The Experience of Europe, US, and Japanese Firms', in R. Strange, J. Slater, and L. Wang (eds), *Trade and Investment in China: the European Experience*, London: Routledge, pp. 228–65.

Wu, X., and R. Strange (2000), 'The Location of Foreign Insurance Companies in China', *International Business Review*, **9**, 383–98.

9. Conclusions

Maria Weber

---

1. THE GROWTH OF CHINESE HIGH-TECH EXPORTS

China's participation in international trade increases year after year: the volume of business transactions was approximately $851.2 billion in 2003 and the value of China's trade balance surplus was $25.54 billion for the same year. Export composition highlights a significant increase in technological products from the IT, electronic, and telecommunication sectors. In 1995, technological products only accounted for 8 per cent of Chinese exports, compared to 23 per cent in 2002 (Walsh, 2003). As Vice-Premier Wu Yi pointed out: 'China exported $110 bn of high-technology products in 2003, accounting for 25 per cent of overall exports in the year' (Xinhua News Agency, 7 January 2004).

Figure 9.1   China's High Technology Exports in billions US$

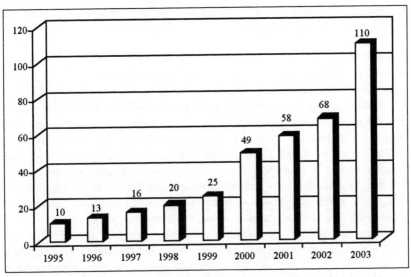

Source: *China Statistical Yearbook*, 2002; Xinhua News Agency, 7 January 2004; Saxenian 2003, p. 12.

China ranks third in the world today in terms of information technology (IT) production, including computers, hardware, software, and telecommunication equipment. In the computer sector, China is the world's fourth manufacturer. Seventy per cent of the domestic PC market is controlled by Chinese companies and the country is the second world exporter of hardware and the first foreign supplier of the United States. The semiconductor sector is also widely expanding: 11 per cent of the semiconductors manufactured in the world come from China. Moreover, in high-tech sectors like electronics in 1995, 80 per cent of China's exports came from foreign-invested companies, compared to only half of such exports today. The other half is directly manufactured by fully Chinese-owned companies. Success cases in high-tech sectors are the result of strategic alliances with foreign companies, of highly skilled and relatively cheap human capital, and of strong government support.

The expansion of the high-tech sector in China is the result of targeted policies aimed at promoting progress in research and technology. Through their cooperation with Western enterprises, Chinese companies learned effective organisational and management models, as well as multinational business strategies. The Chinese company that drew the greatest benefit from this process is Legend Computer Systems, established in the 1980s as a spin-off of the Academy of Sciences and today a leader in Asia in the production of personal computers. Legend recently opened an R&D laboratory in California, which it intends to use as a listening post in order to learn about novelties in the Silicon Valley environment. Other Chinese companies opened R&D laboratories abroad, including Huawei, Zhongxing Telecom, Huge Dragon, Konka, and yet others are now following their example. The decision to open listening posts abroad could be an expression of the wish to pursue a global strategy: a prerequisite for survival in the challenging high-tech market.

The overseas Chinese have contributed significantly to the development of technology in China. Besides investing heavily in their country of origin, they have chosen international centres of excellence in order to provide the best education to their children. In 2000, more than 11 million people in the United States had a college degree in scientific or engineering subjects and/or were involved in scientific or engineering activities. Of these, 102 000 were resident in the US, but were born in China. The Chinese government, in turn, adopted policies aimed at promoting the return of such valuable human capital, offering benefits and high salaries to anyone going back to the motherland. The crisis of the new economy forced many, especially in the information technology and electronic sectors, to accept such enticements.

While research and development expenses more than doubled between 1995 and 2000, they are actually not very high. In 2000 they accounted for 1 per cent of GDP, in line with the average of developing countries, but much less than in industrialised countries, where they normally reach 2–2.5 per cent of GDP. According to government plans, however, R&D expenses should reach 1.5 per cent by 2005. Sixty per cent of R&D is funded by private or public companies, 28 per cent by government-controlled research institutes, and 10 per cent by universities. However, despite the significant increase, China is still far from equalling technologically advanced countries. The US manufacturing system, in particular, has innovative skills that China still does not enjoy. China's high-tech imports, in fact, exceeded exports by $1.9 bn. China still has a long way to go before it reaches the same technological level as America or Japan.

2. THE WORLD DREADS THE CHINESE GIANT

The steady growth of China's economy is seen by many as a huge risk to well-established economies. Thanks to the size of its population, China may become richer than Japan, and even than the United States, within a few years. In Mearsheimer's words: 'If China's per-capita GDP only equalled just half of the current per-capita GDP of Japan, it would total $20 400 bn, which would make China almost five times richer than Japan ... In short, China has all the qualities needed to become much more powerful than even the US' (Mearsheimer, 2001, p. 361). And a rich China is seen by the Americans as a very dangerous competitor, both at strategic and economic levels: 'While it is clear that China's interest is to become the leader of North-East Asia, it is equally clear that it is not America's interest that this may happen' (Mearsheimer, 2001, p. 365). On the other hand Terril (2003), in his recent book with the provocative title *The New Chinese Empire*, emphasises the fear of a possible cultural hegemony of China, which may extend to the whole of Eastern Asia.

This is not the first time the world has dreaded China,[1] but today's strong growth in exports emphasises again the perceived Chinese danger. In particular, the USA has been recording a growing current account deficit with respect to China for some years. Its concern is that China's exports may have increased so sharply because of a depreciated Chinese currency. The depreciation of the RMB is then seen as a source of unfair competition, which keeps the prices of Chinese products artificially low. Indeed, since 1994 the RMB has been set by Beijing at a fixed rate vs. the dollar ($1:RMB8.28). A hint to the depreciation of the RMB comes from the foreign currency reserves of the People's Bank of China (PBOC), now exceptionally totalling $403.3 bn (without considering the Hong Kong and Macau reserves).[2]

International pressures on Beijing for the RMB to be re-evaluated have multiplied. However, it should not be taken for granted that the USA prefers a very strong RMB on the exchange market. The USA needs to finance a large balance deficit fuelled by the fiscal policy and the costs of the Iraq war.

Funding occurs mostly through the issuing of treasury bonds, and the PBOC is a significant bond buyer: in fact, it holds more than $126 bn worth of American Treasury bonds. China is then the second holder of US financial papers, following Japan. By supporting their demand, it prevents any rises of the interest rate paid by the US to attract investors. Thus indebtedness costs the US significantly less than it would cost if China adopted a different currency policy.

Moreover, a weak RMB should not be seen as negative by the US (or even by Europe), not least because it implies that it costs less to invest in China. Manufacturing in China is even more profitable (especially due to low labour costs), and multinational companies that manufacture there and export their products throughout the world actually earn from the depreciation of the RMB.

3. ASYMMETRICAL COMPETITION

According to some observers, China exploits its domestic conditions (low-cost labour, poor social protection, low environmental standards, high political discretionary power, and currency dumping) to support a legal but asymmetric competition, capable of upsetting international markets and earning a clear advantage over other international competitors (Fortis and Quadrio Curzio, 2003). In other words, China's exports would be legally but asymmetrically competitive, not only because the RMB is devaluated, but also because Chinese export products are manufactured at much lower costs. Protectionist spurs come from several parties: the USA has already introduced customs duties on Chinese imports in the textile sector, and protective measures for some European products will also certainly be introduced in the next few months. Europe is suffering from the competitiveness of Chinese exports. The impact of the RMB exchange rate is, for Euro-area countries, even worse: the RMB is linked to the dollar, which has generally depreciated vs the Euro. The European economy is stagnating, in some countries in a downswing, and this further increases public awareness of the Chinese threat.

In order to cope with this legal but asymmetrical competition, the European Union provides for a protection tool to be applied to certain industrial sectors, affected by strong price disturbance. Each member state may apply for the adoption of such measures for one or more products affected by Chinese competition, and the adoption of duties or quotas on about 30 products imported from China is also expected. The protocol for accession to the WTO provides for a 12–year period during which the WTO members may, during the liberalisation process in favour of Chinese products, adopt temporary protection measures for certain economic sectors that may suffer a serious crisis following the sudden opening-up to Chinese competition. This is why on 28 January 2003 the EU Council approved the system for protection against China, known as TPSSM (Transitional Product-Specific Safeguard Mechanism), which allows protection to EU companies through the introduction of safeguard duties and quotas or other kinds of solutions negotiated with Beijing, such as voluntary export restrictions. The TPSSM is available to all EU manufacturers, except companies manufacturing textiles and other products that are already regulated with quota systems with respect to China. Companies may apply for the adoption of safeguard measures (import quotas or customs duties) if the imports of certain products increase to such an extent as to cause or threaten material damage to the EU industry, or if the EU market is disturbed or at risk of disturbance due to diversions in the trade of a given product following the trade protection measures adopted by a third-party WTO member state or voluntary export restrictions adopted by China itself.

Textiles (excluded from the TPSSM) are dealt with by a specific safeguard clause contained in the Protocol for China's accession to the WTO, in force until 31 December 2008. This clause states that, if these products' exports increase to such an extent as to jeopardise the smooth course of trade, the Commission may, on request of a member state or by its own decision, start consultations with Beijing.

The TPSSM also allows the adoption of temporary measures to be implemented only when any further hesitation would cause irreparable damage to the EU industry. These may be in force for a maximum of 200 days and take the form of duties, quotas, or tariff restrictions. Final safeguard measures are adopted when a review of the collected information highlights the prerequisites for their enforcement (if no satisfactory solution is found within 60 days of consultation with the Chinese counterparts). Their enforcement should be notified to the Council, which shall decide by qualified majority whether to confirm, amend, or revoke the decision. These measures may only be in force strictly as long as necessary and anyway not longer than four years. This Council regulation will be in force until 2013.

4. THE FORGERY ISSUE

The perceived overgrowth of Chinese exports goes hand in hand with the high risk of imitation on the Chinese market. The forgery issue is very serious. Despite the existence of a patent protection law (Cavalieri, 2003), copying brands or patents was a well-developed practice in the past, often when European companies sold equipment or technology in China without registering their patent in Beijing. According to OECD data quoted by the EU's webpages dealing with the issue, forgery accounts for 5 to 7 per cent of world trade and was responsible for the loss of 200000 jobs in Europe (Fortis and Quadrio Curzio, 2003). The European Union voiced its concern by issuing a new regulation against forgery on 22 July 2003 (1383/2003, in force as of 1

July 2004). Forgery should be understood widely, in that it includes counterfeited goods with unauthorised brand display on the product, case, or packaging; unauthorised goods, which are or contain copies without the approval of the copyright or design-right holder; or goods that, based on the legislation of individual member states, infringe certificates of geographic indication or controlled origin.

The EU expressed its intention to fight against forgery and piracy through mechanisms of cooperation between the customs authorities in charge in the individual member states. An application sent to the competent national authorities allows EU customs to adopt special measures to check and identify products that do not comply with intellectual property rights. The regulation also provides for the customs authorities to stop the trade of suspected forged products, retain them, and inform the injured manufacturers, providing detailed information, such as the volume and the nature and description of the goods seized, and the names and addresses of the parties involved in the trade of the forged goods, in order to allow the injured parties to start lawsuits against them at their discretion. The regulation further provides for the shipping of samples of the seized goods in order to simplify their analysis and provide information to the customs in case of doubt.

However, the most important issue is the possibility, pursuant to the national legislation of member states and subject to the approval of the applicants, to provide for the disposal of the goods that do not comply with the intellectual property rights (even if the regulation expressly specifies that the consensus of the injured manufacturer is not required for disposal). The request for disposal by the customs authorities is valid for one year and may be renewed at the request of the interested party. This provision is a first step forward, but it will take years before it may actually be implemented.

5.   IS THERE A RISK OF MILITARY CONFRONTATION WITH THE UNITED STATES?

The US Department of State has explicitly and repeatedly expressed the need to implement a policy of containment towards China. The supporters of containment consider that China's economic growth and the resurgence of nationalism will generate an attempt by the Chinese to build up hegemony in Asia, hence the need for an international effort to contain China. However, the growing importance of China's business and the huge potential of its market has increasingly attracted the interest of the Americans because of its potential benefits. Clinton's trip to China in July 1998 marked the normalisation of relations between the two countries, as well as the acknowledgement by the Americans of the need to 'involve' Beijing in a constructive way in the management of the international system.

The Bush Administration's policy towards China rapidly transformed the relationship from a strategic partnership to strategic competition. Much more than the previous US government, the Bush Administration actively attempted to construct and consolidate an East-Asian security system with the USA as the sole superpower (see Maria Weber's chapter in this volume). However, the tragedy of September 11 transformed US–China relations once again. The Chinese government expressed its strong disapproval of international terrorism and its strong support for the American people (Weber, 2002). Since then, the overall relationship between China and the USA has been developing soundly.

The economic convergence between China and Taiwan on one hand and the war in Iraq on the other helped mitigate the Pentagon's anti-China attitude, but did not divert America's focus from China as an important player in the region. Since the end of the Korean war, the USA has kept a very large military contingent in Asia: 84 500 personnel and 575 aircraft, including 47 000 personnel and 350 aircrafts in Japan and 37 500 personnel and 225 aircraft in South Korea. In fact, the USA is considering moving most units further south in the peninsula, creating hubs there with material ready to be used in action and to be reinforced in case of crisis. After September 11, the USA increased their military aid and deployed troops in the Philippines, with anti-terrorist purposes.

But terrorism is not the only reason for America's interest in eastern Asia. According to the Quadrennial Defense Review Report (US Defence Department, 2003):

> Even if the US will not confront an equal competitor in the near future, Asia is gradually emerging as a region where military competition could develop on a large scale. A military competitor with a formidable resource base may emerge in the region [the reference to China is implicit]. The coast of Eastern Asia is a particularly demanding area. Distances are vast in Asia. The density of US bases in the area and the availability of infrastructures to reach them are lower than in other critical regions. The US is also less confident about the possibility to access facilities in the region.

The pillar of President Bush's military policy is still the Theatre Missile Defence System (TMD).

In the past few years Beijing has been increasing its military expenditure on modernising its armed forces.[3] In 2002, military expenses recorded a 17 per cent increase, up to approximately $20 bn (Karniol, 2003, 5). The modernisation of the Chinese armed forces does not only include the acquisition and direct development of better technologies and more advanced weapons, but also the reorganisation of the army's structure and the updating of military principles, operational strategies, and officer training and selection. Reorganising the army implies reducing regular units. Beijing has already decided to cut 200 000 units by 2005, from 2 500 000 to 2 300 000 in the People's Liberation Army (PLA). In the past few years, China has been acquiring technologically advanced weapons from Russia, its first trade partner in the sector. Russia is building for China two torpedo-boat destroyers, eight diesel submarines, one nuclear submarine to substitute the Xia, now on duty, one nuclear submarine of the Han class, 40 Su-30MKK fighter-bombers, a number of anti-aircraft missiles and other items, to a total value of approximately $4 bn.

In the nuclear sector, China has about 20 intercontinental ballistic missiles (ICBM) capable of striking the USA. In addition to the Navy's missiles and the strategic bombers (IISS, 2002), the US Air Force Space Command avails itself of about 550 ICBM (500 *Minuteman III* and 50 *Peacekeeper*). Beijing committed some time ago not to be the first to resort to nuclear weapons, but the Pentagon believes that China will raise the number of its ICBM to 30 by 2005, and maybe to 50 by 2010, even if the USA does not go ahead with its projects for missile defence. The implementation of the national missile defence (NMD) and of the theatre missile defence (TMD) in Eastern Asia by the USA would limit the strategic value of China's existing nuclear arsenal even further, almost fully depriving it of its deterrent and coercive power. Therefore China is expected to significantly increase the number of its nuclear weapons if the USA implements the NMD and the TMD.

The quality of China's weapons is not comparable to America's. The main limits of China's armed forces include a less developed technology and a poor projection capacity. In an article published in *Foreign Affairs* in 1997, Robert Ross claimed that China, deprived of cruisers and aircraft-carriers, and with poor amphibious assault vehicles, entrusts its projection capacity to the air force, which lacks ground bases. According to Ross (1997, p. 37), China may operate in the northern part of the Southern Chinese Sea, including the coast of Vietnam and the Paracel islands, disputed between Vietnam, China, and Taiwan. It may even reach Taiwan but it cannot operate in the southern part of the Southern Chinese Sea, i.e. in the waters of Malaysia, Singapore, Indonesia, the Philippines, representing the most strategic area of the Chinese Sea, being crossed through by trade routes. Moreover, even if the number of fourth-generation fighters on duty is increasing, the Chinese air force is relatively backward. China will need aircraft-carriers to become a big power in the remote waters of the Southern Chinese Sea, capable of challenging America's influence on the maritime countries in south-east Asia and its access to the strategic routes in the region.

Even if China achieved the logistic and organisational skills required to keep one aircraft-carrier out of three constantly on duty, it could not have the fleet at its disposal before 2020, while the USA have 12 aircraft-carriers on duty.

On the other hand, China's recent approach has been far from confrontational. Since September 11, Beijing has been trying to act as a mediator in all regional conflicts: first by encouraging Pakistan to mitigate the tone of its nuclear escalation against India, then mediating between North Korea and the USA during the North Korean nuclear crisis, which made many dread the opening of a new war front in Asia in 2003.

The North Korean crisis offered China the opportunity to demonstrate its capacity to be a responsible player in the international political scenario. While being the power closest to Pyongyang, China clearly stated it does not share the preferences of Kim Jong-il. Beijing sent several top-level emissaries to Pyongyang to convince the North Koreans to pursue the way of negotiations. Even President Hu Jintao, as soon as he was appointed in March 2003, asked the Pyongyang government to dismantle its nuclear programme, suggesting that, otherwise, China may stop granting economic aid to North Korea.

China is pursuing two strategic objectives with respect to the Korean peninsula. First, to prevent Korea from turning into a direct threat. To this end, since 1992 China has been implementing a policy of reconciliation with Seoul. The closer economic relations and diplomatic initiatives, such as the intention jointly expressed by both countries in 1998 to build a 'co-operative partnership' in view of the 21st century, seem highly promising. Second, to prevent Korea from turning into a 'catwalk' for a third-party power, capable of invading China. This makes it clear why it would be strategically useful for Beijing to see South Korea's political and military links with America loosened, something that should be achieved, however, without openly challenging the United States, but rather by creating a peaceful and stable environment, where a guarantee of security by America would no longer appear to be necessary.

China opposed the adoption by the UN Safety Council of a resolution on North Korea, but voted within the International Atomic Energy Agency in favour of the idea of reporting North Korea's breach of the Non-Proliferation Treaty to the same UN Safety Council. It is clear that China has an interest in a prompt and peaceful settlement of the matter, possibly also achieving Pyongyang's nuclear disarmament. This would mitigate the impact that the current situation is having on a strategic level. The opportunities for Washington to strengthen its alliance with Japan and South Korea and, on the other hand, the unrest that North Korea is causing, which could lead new regional players – including Tokyo, Seoul, and even Taiwan – to equip themselves in turn with atomic weapons, certainly do not represent positive developments from China's point of view, since they all limit its influence. Moreover, Beijing has a more general interest in avoiding severe tensions in East Asia, simply because these could negatively influence the economic dynamics of the region and, thus, China's economic relations with the rest of the world.

6. CONCLUDING REMARKS

6.1. Considerable Challenges Remain, but Optimism Prevails

China's labour market dynamics seem to pose one of the main challenges to future social stability. Our overview of Chinese unemployment highlights a labour market in transition from an SOE-centred social welfare unit, to an independent system with a comprehensive social safety net. Moreover, the reforms of the public sector entail a need to re-absorb millions of SOE redundant workers. Estimates of future entrants in the labour market based on IMF studies indicate that the working-age population will grow by 10–13 million annually until 2010 and that today there is still surplus labour in SOEs. The negative effects of unemployment will probably spread throughout society, jeopardising social stability. However, as Giacomo Boati highlights in his contribution to this volume, the recent increase in the number of protests by discontented workers may not necessarily be a threatening sign, as a number of factors weaken the workers' bargaining power and position vis-à-vis the authorities. Examples of such elements include: the atomisation of the labour market, which hinders the identification of the unemployed as a single class; the fact that workers or laid-off individuals from various enterprises have different goals and are reluctant to share information; and the lack of freedom of association together with the authorities' explicit effort to contain the protests. If the social impact of unemployment is to depend on the ability of the working class to unite in a single body, Boati is confident that social stability will be preserved over the next few years, and the peak of instabilities created by redundant workers will be overcome.

A second important challenge is provided by China becoming an ageing society: between 1978 and 2002, China's share of elderly grew by half, more rapidly than in most developed countries, with the exception of Japan. China's exceptionally rapid ageing is attributed to a combination of longer life expectancy – which increased from 61.7 years in 1970 to 71.4 years in 2000 – and the government's population-control policy. This demographic development raised the issue of security in old age, particularly in rural areas where pensions have traditionally been absent. The urban reforms of the 1990s entailed a shift from 'welfare by enterprises' to 'welfare by society'. The Chinese government adopted a social insurance model to provide the social security mechanisms that are required in a market economy. Compared to China's old policy of lifetime employment and social security benefits in urban areas, and land- and family-based support in rural areas, the new social order has created a new set of uncertainties.

Social insurance assumes a risk (like old age or poor health) which may affect all members of a social group, and whose likelihood can be calculated. The key characteristics of social insurance include compulsory participation, social redistribution, and an independent agency that administers contributory funds and entitlements. As highlighted by Anna Stenbeck and Maria Weber, China adopted similar schemes for pensions, healthcare, and unemployment, based on a combination of social pooling and individual accounts. This design may be less optimal for health and unemployment insurance, which needs mainly intra-generational risk sharing, than for old-age insurance, which requires intra-generational as well as inter-generational risk-sharing. Considering China's vast population and its hitherto underdeveloped administrative and financial capacities, a social insurance model may be less risky than the national welfare system models characterising many Western countries.

As far as health policy is concerned, China's approach has always reflected the dominant political ideology of the period: egalitarianism and central planning under Mao Zedong, pragmatism and liberalisation under Deng Xiaoping, and a rationalisation of socioeconomic transformations under Jiang Zemin. It is widely recognised that the health status of China's population improved quickly during the 1960s and 1970s, a result which has often been attributed to the country's well-developed healthcare system. The economic liberalisation introduced under Deng created the prerequisites for two decades of impressive economic growth that rescued millions of Chinese from utter poverty. However, partial liberalisation in the healthcare sector left the system with three main problems: inefficiency, poor funding, and a glaring inequality in access to health care.

Two external shocks – the WTO accession in 2001 and the SARS epidemic in the first half of 2003 – highlighted the shortcomings of China's healthcare system and put additional pressure on its reorganisation. The rapid changes in the economic structure, especially the consequences of large population transfers to the cities, required a set of reforms in the healthcare system in an ongoing effort to maintain equitable access to medical services and control of infectious diseases. In urban areas, the framework for a modern healthcare system is in place, although it will take time to implement and fine-tune the parameters of its financing. Providing universal coverage in the urban areas under the current scheme would put an excessive burden on workers and employers. To guarantee the participation of vulnerable social groups, the government could either subsidise contributions to the scheme, or subsidise providers directly to offer free care to the indigent. In rural areas, the establishment of community health services, which should be completed by 2010, could be accelerated by the need to control outbreaks of epidemics. However, the size of the rural population and the wide socioeconomic development gap compared to urban areas limit the scope, respectively, for central transfers and local revenues.

While not substituting for a much needed social security system, commercial insurance products and other savings-related products represent a valid complement. Both China's life and non-life insurance markets are indeed growing rapidly, providing opportunities for foreign companies to enter a still relatively underdeveloped market. WTO-related loosening of restrictions will provide an expanded range of products for China's citizens and corporations, thereby fostering growth and development. Chinese insurance companies enjoy a competitive advantage over their foreign counterparts, but several of them are to a great extent inefficient because of the monopolistic market situation which they were allowed to enjoy, causing a high degree of uniformity in product, market, distribution, and pricing strategies among companies in the insurance sector. Moreover, insurance awareness among the Chinese population is still relatively low and needs to be improved. Despite the concern voiced by some sources, foreign competition is likely to bring more advantages than damage to the Chinese insurance sector. As Benedetta Trivellato points out, foreign multinational companies can offer a higher degree of security to policyholders due to their size, their large capital bases, their ability to spread risk internationally, their easier access to international capital and reinsurance markets, and a better knowledge of foreign markets, which reduces the risk involved in the investment environment.

China's accession to the WTO undoubtedly provides greater opportunities for foreign insurers to enter the domestic market. However, prospective investors should pay attention to two elements in particular: the details of the evolving regulatory framework and the changing characteristics of the domestic market structure. On the one hand, the need to protect a still developing insurance industry implied the introduction by the Chinese authorities of a number of regulatory measures, which may pose an unexpected burden on prospective investors. Such investors should therefore continue to monitor these regulatory developments closely. On the other hand, the structure of the country's insurance industry is undergoing significant changes. Such changes are being prompted by the progressive entrance of foreign insurers – either through joint venture agreements or through equity share acquisitions – as well as by domestic companies efforts' to get ready for post-WTO increased competition. International insurance companies will need to take into account the increasingly important role that Chinese companies will play domestically and possibly, over the longer term, within the international insurance market.

A third challenge that the Chinese authorities are increasingly required to face is that provided by growing spatial inequalities. In his contribution to this volume, Vasco Molini broke down Theil's index into subgroups in order to understand the contributions of different types of inequality to total inequality. The index was first broken down into urban and rural; then into macroregions; and finally, into rural and urban areas within each macroregion. The main contributor to inequality turns out to be the rural–urban divide. Local and central governments progressively abandoned redistribution policies, and the economic growth in urban areas attracted most of the investments, both private and public. This led to an even greater divide and to increasing concerns about the social sustainability of this development. The breakdown residual – the inequality within rural areas and the inequality within urban areas – shows an increasing divide in the urban areas and a declining divide in the rural areas.

The breakdown into macroregions shed light on another important aspect of unbalanced growth in China. Starting from the late 1980s, the three macroregions grew at different paces, and there is no evidence of convergence to a common steady state. While the Eastern provinces, favoured by their geographic location and infrastructure endowments, managed to integrate into the world market, the Central and Western provinces, where about 60 per cent of the total population is located, seem to lag behind. Central and local government policies accentuated, rather than corrected, this imbalance. Nonetheless, in 2000 there were positive signs of a changing attitude towards inland areas. To encourage the development of the Western provinces, the government launched the 'Great Western Development Strategy' or 'Go West Strategy', a campaign of public investment in infrastructures and creation of special economic zones aimed at fostering the competitiveness of Western regions and create opportunities for foreign investors.

A review of the current challenges that China is now facing would not be complete without reference to the environmental situation. Nicoletta Marigo suggests that not only are environmental improvements possible, even at low income levels, but also that the associated costs would not be prohibitive. China is certainly aware that the 'pollute first, clean up later' approach is no longer viable and is indeed taking major corrective steps to shift the emphasis from quantitative development to a more qualitative one. However, putting China on the path towards sustainability is not only an opportunity to be grasped, but also a serious challenge for the Chinese to be faced with. A major problem lies not so much in the lack of regulations on environmental protection, as on their enforcement. Despite the complex system of legislative and policy tools in place and the extensive network of environmental officials, compliance with environmental regulations remains low. Major problems arise from municipal and local authorities, who are struggling to keep pace with rapid economic growth and who are generally reluctant to enforce environmental regulations that are perceived as adverse to the economic growth indexes representing the yardsticks of their achievements. Further challenges come from tight budget constraints, institutional inadequacy, and poor diversification of the instruments implemented to achieve environmental objectives; and the government should diversify the environmental tools it uses to ensure that the solutions developed better match the problems experienced in different parts of the country. In this respect a more significant role should be entrusted to market forces and to public participation in the decision-making framework of social affairs.

Yet despite all these significant challenges, Boltho's contribution to this volume supports an optimistic view of China's prospects to maintain high rates of growth. International experience shows that economic 'miracles' similar to that of China have not been unique and have at times lasted for several decades. Moreover, Chinese income per capita (measured in PPP) is still a fraction of that of the USA, implying that there is still wide scope for further catch-up. Surely, for such catch-up potential to be fulfilled, resources will need to be mobilised and put to work efficiently. There is vast scope for shifting underemployed labour from agriculture, and capital formation can count on an extremely high domestic saving ratio. As for the debates surrounding the efficiency issue, recent estimates show that total factor productivity (TFP) has grown at a sustained pace in the 1990s, and several trends suggest that this is likely to continue over the near future:

1. WTO membership will put pressure on most industries to improve productivity;
2. the private sector is expected to go on increasing its share in the economy at the expense of inefficient SOEs;
3. there is still a huge technology gap between China and the West;
4. the appetite of foreign firms to invest in China remains unabated, and it is foreign firms that are most likely to stimulate technological progress;
5. the banking system is under strong pressure to diversify its loans towards private firms and a better allocation of credit should raise efficiency.

Boltho believes that further rapid economic growth is possible, despite the many problems the country faces. Indeed, rapid growth would by itself solve several of these problems. A difficult public finance situation would benefit from growing incomes and so would employment levels. And even if regional differentials remained large, absolute living standards would presumably rise fairly rapidly throughout most of the country as they have done in the past, thereby lowering potential tensions. Hence the emphasis put by the authorities on the pursuit of further economic success. With it, many of the problems that have been highlighted could be defused. Without it, they might all reinforce each other and degenerate into crisis.

6.2. An Evolving Authoritarian System?

In his report to the Fourteenth CCP Congress of October 1992, the then-president Jiang Zemin thus summarised the reasons for the political stability preserved after the shock of June 1989: economic growth and political control. The strategic mix of economic modernisation and political authoritarianism was allowed by the country's sustained economic growth, which resulted in the effective distribution of resources and the hope of future economic wealth for the whole population, thus promoting support of the political leadership by most Chinese. More than ten years after this statement, what is new within the Communist Party?

The Sixteenth CCP Congress, held in Beijing in November 2002, confirmed the will to continue along the path of reform. The 2 000 delegates elected the 356 members of the new CCP Central Committee (CC). This was an unprecedented generational turnover: half of the CC members were newly appointed, 20 per cent were younger than 50 years old, and 27 were women. Hu Jintao was acclaimed as Secretary General of the CCP in place of Jiang Zemin, and the new permanent Committee of the CC also decided on other major political appointments – then ratified by the national Assembly in the spring of 2003 – including Hu Jintao himself as President of the PRC, Wen Jiabao as prime minister, Wu Bangguo as president of the People's National Assembly in place of Li Peng, and Jia Qinglin as president of the Political and Consulting Conference; finally, Jiang Zemin was confirmed as president of the Political and Military Commission. The People's National Assembly (Parliament) convened in Beijing in March 2003 to formally elect the fourth-generation leaders, appointed by the party's Sixteenth Congress.

The Sixteenth Congress also entered the theory of the 'three representations', suggested by Jiang Zemin, into the Statute of the CCP. According to this theory, the party should represent the advanced manufacturing forces, the advanced culture, and the country's wider interests. From 1921, when the CCP was established, until November 2002, the party's statute stated that 'the CCP represents the vanguard of the working class'. Now the statute still contains this expression, specifying at the same time that the CCP is also the vanguard of the Chinese people and nation, and allows all the members of the different social classes to apply for membership. This points to a possible diversification of the interests represented at the top of the Chinese political system, with greater influence given to the more market economy-oriented members of society.

Are these the signs of the evolution of an authoritarian system? Most scholars agree that China will continue to pursue its economic reform policy preserving the typical properties of authoritarian political systems, namely strong control by the single party over civil society. There are, however, moderate signs that China's authoritarianism is developing from the typical vertical form to a new horizontal form (Weber, 2001). Horizontal authoritarianism is still an authoritarian system, however less linked to individual personalities and more institutionalised, i.e. more capable of responding to the challenges posed by the social environment in a country heading towards fast economic modernisation. In other words, horizontal authoritarianism has some opportunities to develop, in turn, into a potentially more pluralist system.

This is how the new village-election trials should be interpreted. Village elections are employed to elect both an assembly representing the village, made up of 25–30 elected members plus a few directly appointed by the Communist Party, and an executive board, usually made up of about 12 members. The village assembly decides on the resolutions passed by the executive board.

The new village elections were implemented pursuant to the Organic Law on Village Committees, which came into force in 1992. This law introduced the secret ballot and multiple appointments, ensuring a minimum of two candidates for each seat. The power of representation of village assemblies largely depends on the will of the local government. In particular, in the Fujian province, the local government emphasised the importance of current democratisation and encouraged all village dwellers to fulfil their voting duty: a very high attendance was then recorded (more than 97 per cent of eligible people), and most of the elected assemblies returned were effectively pluralist. In addition major differences were then observed between provinces. In May 1994, an American commission of the International Republican Institute was invited for the first time to ensure regular elections in a number of villages in the Fujian province, and in March 1997 a delegation from the Carter Center reviewed the voting process in other villages in the Fujian and Hebei provinces. The Carter Center Commission noted that the electoral committee often did not include a single member of the Communist Party.

Despite these important novelties, it should be noted that the party's political control over civil society is still very strong and that respect for human rights is still far from Western standards. China, then, is not becoming democratic, except in its recognition of the need for some formal representation facilities that are crucial to managing a complex society, where capitalist and socialist elements coexist under the single concept of free market socialism, with the subsequent appearance of new social groups.

NOTES

1. The birth of the PRC in 1949 was seen in America as the 'loss of China'. Since then, China's communist threat was strongly perceived by the Pentagon and its allies.
2. China's reserves rank second in the world after Japan's, which exceed $500 bn.
3. The USA spends much more than China on defence: in 2004 defence will be allocated a budget of approximately $401 bn (IISS, 2002).

BIBLIOGRAPHY

Cavalieri, R. (2003), *Implicazioni giuridiche dell'adesione della Cina alla WTO*, Lecce: Argo.
Fortis, M. and Quadrio Curzio, A. (2003), 'Concorrenza asiatica: quali rimedi per un sano mercato internazionale?', *Il Mulino* (6).
Holbig, H. and Ash, R. (eds) (2002), *China's Accession to the World Trade Organization*, London and New York: Routledge Curzon.
IISS (International Institute for Strategic Studies) (2002), *The Military Balance 2002–2003*, Oxford: Oxford University Press.
Karniol, R. (2003), 'US Report on Beijing Defence Spending', *Jane's Defence Weekly*, **40** (5).

Ko, I. (2003), *The Export, the Foreign Reserve and the Currency*, Hong Kong Policy Research Institute, 9 September.

Mearsheimer, J.J. (2001), *The Tragedy of Great Power Politics*, Norton, Italian Edition (2003), *La logica di potenza*, Milan: New York and London, Università Bocconi Editore.

Medeiros, S.S.and Fravel, M.T. (2003), 'China's New Diplomacy', *Foreign Affairs*, **82** (6), November–December, pp. 22–35.

OECD (2001), *Thematic Review of the First Years of Tertiary Education. Country Note: Peoples Republic of China*, December.

Ross, R. (1997), 'Beijing as a Conservative Power', *Foreign Affairs*, **76** (2), March–April.

Saxenian, A.L. (2003), *Government and Guanxi: The Chinese Software Industry in Transition*, University of California at Berkeley, DCR Working Papers.

Terril, R. (2003), *The New Chinese Empire and What it Means for the United States*, New York: Basic Books.

US Defence Department (2003), *Annual Report on the Military Power of the People's Republic of China*, Washington, DC.

Walsh, R. (2003), *Foreign High Tech R&D in China*, Washington, DC: The Henry L. Stimson Center.

Weber, M. (ed.) (2001), *Reforming Economic Systems in Asia*, Cheltenham, UK: Edward Elgar.

Weber, M. (2002), 'China's 21st Century Challenge: a Balance of Power between Japan and US', *The European Union Review*, **7** (1).

Xinhua News Agency (2004), 7 January.

Xia Liping (2002), 'South Korea's Northern Policy and Development of Sino South Korean Relations', in *SIIS Journal*, **9** (2), May, pp. 40–53.

Index